The Bible Speaks Today

Series Editors: J. A. Motyer (OT)

John R. W. Stott (NT)

Derek Tidball (Bible Themes)

The Message of Evil and Suffering

Light into Darkness

The Message of Evil and Suffering

Light into Darkness

Peter Hicks

InterVarsity Press

InterVarsity Press, USA
P.O. Box 1400, Downers Grove, IL 60515-1426, USA
World Wide Web: www.ivpress.com
Email: email@ivpress.com

Inter-Varsity Press, England
Norton Street, Nottingham NG7 3HR, England
Website: www.ivpbooks.com
Email: ivp@ivpbooks.com

InterVarsity Press®, USA, is the book-publishing division of InterVarsity Christian Fellowship/USA®, a student movement active on campus at hundreds of universities, colleges and schools of nursing in the United States of America, and a member movement of the International Fellowship of Evangelical Students. For information about local and regional activities, write Public Relations Dept., InterVarsity Christian Fellowship/USA, 6400 Schroeder Rd., P.O. Box 7895, Madison, WI 53707-7895, or visit the IVCF website at <www.intervarsity.org>.

Inter-Varsity Press, England, is closely linked with the Universities and Colleges Christian Fellowship, a student movement connecting Christian Unions in universities and colleges throughout Great Britain, and a member movement of the International Fellowship of Evangelical Students. Website: www.uccf.org.uk.

All Scripture quotations, unless otherwise indicated, are taken from the Holy Bible, New International Version®. NIV®. *Copyright © 1973, 1978, 1984 by International Bible Society. Used by permission of Zondervan Publishing House. Distributed in the U.K. by permission of Hodder and Stoughton Ltd. All rights reserved. "NIV" is a registered trademark of International Bible Society. UK trademark number 1448790.*

USA ISBN-10: 0-8308-2410-3
    ISBN-13: 978-0-8308-2410-6
UK ISBN-10: 1-84474-148-6
    ISBN-13: 978-1-84474-148-9

Printed in the United States of America ∞

Library of Congress Cataloging-in-Publication Data has been requested.

British Library Cataloguing in Publication Data

A catalogue record for this book is available from the British Library.

P	19	18	17	16	15	14	13	12	11	10	9	8	7	6	5	4	3	2	1
Y	23	22	21	20	19	18	17	16	15	14	13	12	11	10	09	08	07		

Contents

| BST | The Bible Speaks Today

GENERAL PREFACE

THE BIBLE SPEAKS TODAY describes three series of expositions, based on the books of the Old and New Testaments, and on Bible themes that run through the whole of Scripture. Each series is characterized by a threefold ideal:

- to expound the biblical text with accuracy
- to relate it to contemporary life, and
- to be readable.

These books are, therefore, not 'commentaries', for the commentary seeks rather to elucidate the text than to apply it, and tends to be a work rather of reference than of literature. Nor, on the other hand, do they contain the kinds of 'sermons' that attempt to be contemporary and readable without taking Scripture seriously enough.

The contributors to *The Bible Speaks Today* series are all united in their convictions that God still speaks through what he has spoken, and that nothing is more necessary for the life, health and growth of Christians than that they should hear what the Spirit is saying to them through his ancient – yet ever modern – Word.

ALEC MOTYER
JOHN STOTT
DEREK TIDBALL
Series editors

Author's preface

I started writing this book and soon gave up. A publisher urgently wanted a book on God, and I decided that God was a much more attractive theme than evil and suffering.

But I am very grateful that, once I had spent two or three months focusing on God, I returned to evil and suffering. Starting with a long hard look at God is a tremendous help when we have to face any problem issue. And the fact is that I personally have been greatly helped and encouraged by studying what the Bible says about evil and suffering. For a quarter of a century I have worked with students at undergraduate and postgraduate level on the philosophical problem of evil. Wise though the insights of many thinkers through the ages may be, it has been so refreshing and exciting to turn from human theodicies to God's own answer outlined for us in the Bible.

Yes, the problem is big. But God is bigger.

PETER HICKS
May 2006

Chief abbreviations

AV   The Authorized (King James) Version of the Bible,
           1611
Goodspeed *An American Translation* by E. J. Goodspeed;
           New Testament 1923; complete Bible (with J. M.
           Powis-Smith) 1939
GNB   The Good News Bible (Today's English Version);
           New Testament 1971, 1976; Old Testament 1976
NEB   The New English Bible, 1970
NIV   The New International Version of the Bible; New
           Testament 1973; Old Testament 1978; complete Bible
           revised 1984
NLT   The New Living Translation of the Bible, 1996
Phillips   *The New Testament in Modern English*, translated
           by J. B. Phillips, 1947–57, revised 1972
RV   The Revised Version of the Bible, 1881
RSV   The Revised Standard Version of the Bible; Old
           Testament 1952; New Testament 1946, 1971
TNIV   Today's New International Version of the Bible,
           2002

Bibliography

Atkinson, D., *The Message of Job*, The Bible Speaks Today (IVP, 1991)

Barth, K., *The Epistle to the Philippians* (SCM, 1962)

Bauckham, R., ' "Only the suffering God can help": Divine passibility in modern theology', *Themelios* 9/3 (1984)

Beale, G. K., *The Book of Revelation* (Eerdmans, 1999)

Beare, F. W., *The First Epistle of Peter* (Blackwell, 1970)

———, *The Gospel according to Matthew* (Blackwell, 1981)

Beasley-Murray, G. R., *The Book of Revelation* (Oliphants, 1974)

———, *Highlights of the Book of Revelation* (Lakeland, 1972)

———, *Jesus and the Kingdom of God* (Eerdmans, 1986)

Bruce, F. F., *The Book of Acts* (Marshall, Morgan and Scott, 1965)

———, *1 and 2 Corinthians* (Oliphants, 1971)

———, *The Epistles to the Colossians, to Philemon, and to the Ephesians* (Eerdmans, 1984)

———, *The Letter of Paul to the Romans* (IVP, 1985)

Brueggemann, W., *Genesis* (John Knox Press, 1982)

———, *Theology of the Old Testament* (Fortress, 1997)

Caird, G. B., *Paul's Letters from Prison* (Oxford University Press, 1976)

Calvin, *The Second Epistle of Paul the Apostle to the Corinthians and the Epistles to Timothy, Titus and Philemon*, trans. T. A. Smail (Oliver and Boyd, 1964)

Chambers, O., *Studies in the Sermon on the Mount* (Simpkin Marshall, n.d.)

Clines, D. J. A., *Job 1 – 20* (Word, 1989)

Craigie, P. C., *Psalms 1 – 50* (Word, 1983)

Crenshaw, J. L., *Defending God: Biblical Responses to the Problem of Evil* (Oxford University Press, 2005)

Davis, S. T. (ed.), *Encountering Evil*, 2nd edn (Westminster John Knox Press, 2001)

Dray, S., *Exodus: Free to Serve* (Crossway, 1993)

Dunn, J. D. G., *Romans 1 – 8* (Word, 1988)
Durham, J. I., *Exodus* (Word, 1987)
Eaton, J. H., *Kingship and the Psalms* (JSOT Press, 1986)
Ellison, H. L., *Exodus* (Saint Andrew Press, 1982)
Evans, E., *The Welsh Revival of 1904* (Evangelical Press, 1969)
Fee, G. D., *Paul's Letter to the Philippians* (Eerdmans, 1995)
Forsyth, P. T., *The Justification of God* (Duckworth, 1916)
France, R. T., *The Gospel according to Matthew* (IVP, 1985)
———, *The Gospel of Mark* (Eerdmans, 2002)
Fretheim, T. E., *Exodus* (John Knox Press, 1991)
Green, J. B., *The Gospel of Luke* (Eerdmans, 1997)
Gundry, R. H., *Matthew* (Eerdmans, 1982)
Guthrie, D., *The Pastoral Epistles* (Tyndale Press, 1957)
Harris, M. J., 'Prepositions and Theology in the Greek New Testament', in C. Brown (ed.), *New International Dictionary of New Testament Theology* 3 (Zondervan, 1975–8)
Hick, J., *Evil and the God of Love* (Collins, 1968)
Hicks, P. A., *Discovering Revelation* (Crossway, 2004)
Hillyer, N., 'Salt', in C. Brown (ed.), *New International Dictionary of New Testament Theology* 3 (Zondervan, 1975–8)
Hodge, C., *1 and 2 Corinthians* (Banner of Truth Trust, 1974)
———, *Systematic Theology* (Charles Scribner, 1871–3)
Hughes, P. E., *Paul's Second Epistle to the Corinthians* (Marshall, Morgan and Scott, 1962)
Jackman, D., *The Message of John's Letters*, The Bible Speaks Today (IVP, 1988)
Kitchen, K. A., 'Plagues of Egypt', in J. D. Douglas and N. Hillyer (eds.), *The Illustrated Bible Dictionary* (IVP, 1980)
Kirk, A. (ed.), *Handling Problems of Peace and War* (Marshall Pickering, 1988)
Kuschner, H., *When Bad Things Happen to Good People* (Pan, 1982)
Lewis, C. S., 'Meditation on the Third Commandment' (reprinted from *The Guardian*, 10 January 1941), in *Undeceptions* (Geoffrey Bles, 1971)
———, *The Problem of Pain* (Geoffrey Bles, 1940)
———, *Voyage to Venus* (Pan Books, 1960)
Lewis, P., *The Message of the Living God*, The Bible Speaks Today (IVP, 2000)
Lloyd-Jones, D. M., *Studies in the Sermon on the Mount*, 2 (IVP, 1960)
Manson, T. W., *The Sayings of Jesus* (SCM, 1949)
Marshall, I. H., *The Gospel of Luke* (Paternoster, 1978)
———, *Kept by the Power of God*, 3rd edn (Paternoster, 1995)

Martin, H., *The Lord's Prayer* (SCM, 1951)

Martin, R. P., *Philippians* (Oliphants, 1976)

Michael, J. H., *The Epistle of Paul to the Philippians* (Hodder and Stoughton, 1928)

Milne, B., *The Message of Heaven and Hell*, The Bible Speaks Today (IVP, 2002)

Mitton, C. L., *Ephesians* (Oliphants, 1976)

Moltmann, J., *The Crucified God*, trans. R. A. Wilson and J. Bowden (SCM, 1974)

Moo, D. J., *The Epistle to the Romans* (Eerdmans, 1996)

Morris, L., *The Gospel according to John* (Marshall, Morgan and Scott, 1971)

Motyer, A., *The Message of Philippians*, The Bible Speaks Today (IVP, 1984)

Peels, E., *Shadow Sides* (Paternoster, 2003)

Plantinga, A., *God, Freedom and Evil* (Harper and Row, 1974)

Rad, G. von, *Genesis*, 2nd edn (SCM, 1963)

Robinson, J. A., *St Paul's Epistle to the Ephesians* (Macmillan, 1914)

Sanday, W., and Headlam, A. C., *The Epistle to the Romans*, 5th edn (T. and T. Clark, 1902)

Sartre, J.-P., *What is Literature?*, trans. B. Frechtman (Methuen, 1950)

Seebas, H., 'Adam, Eve', in C. Brown (ed.), *New International Dictionary of New Testament Theology* (Zondervan, 1975–8)

Selwyn, E. G., *The First Epistle of St Peter* (Macmillan, 1955)

Silva, M., *Philippians* (Moody Press, 1988)

Simundson, D., *Faith under Fire* (Augsburg, 1980)

Skinner, J., *A Critical and Exegetical Commentary of Genesis* (T. and T. Clark, 1910)

Spurgeon, C. H., *The Gospel of the Kingdom* (Passmore and Alabaster, 1893)

———, Sermon 61, 'The Beatific Vision', *New Park Street Pulpit*, 20 January 1856

———, *The Treasury of David* (Passmore and Alabaster, 1882)

Stauffer, E., *Jesus and His Story* (SCM, 1960)

Stott, J., *The Message of Acts*, The Bible Speaks Today (IVP, 1990)

———, *The Message of Romans*, The Bible Speaks Today (IVP, 1994)

Strachan, R. H., *The Second Epistle of Paul to the Corinthians* (Hodder and Stoughton, 1935)

Tasker, R. V. G., *The Gospel according to St Matthew* (Tyndale Press, 1961)

———, *The Second Epistle of Paul to the Corinthians* (Tyndale Press, 1958)

Thomas, J. C., *The Devil, Disease and Deliverance: Origins of Illness in New Testament Thought* (Sheffield Academic Press, 1998)

Weiser, A., *The Psalms* (SCM, 1962)

Wenham, G. J., *Genesis 1 – 15* (Word, 1987)

Westcott, B. F., *The Gospel according to St John* (James Clarke, 1958)

———, *Saint Paul's Epistle to the Ephesians* (Macmillan, 1906)

Wink, W., *Engaging the Powers* (Fortress Press, 1992)

Wright, C. J. H., *Old Testament Ethics* (IVP, 2004)

Wurmbrand, R., *Tortured for Christ* (Hodder and Stoughton, 1967)

Part 1
Evil and suffering – and God

Revelation 15:3–4
1. The end of the story

1. Future focus

I got hooked on Sherlock Holmes early in life. I loved the descriptions of Victorian and Edwardian London with its fogs and cabs and three postal deliveries each day. I shuddered at the grotesque and the horrific. I puzzled over the mysteries and shared the obtuseness of Watson. Most of all, I was deeply impressed at Holmes's ability to solve a problem even when it appeared impossible to everyone else, including me.

Since Holmes was Conan Doyle's creation, I decided that the credit for this amazing ability to solve impossible mysteries should go to him. I remember suggesting this to my father, who wisely replied, 'Maybe so. But you've got to remember that Conan Doyle knew the end of each story before he started to write it.'

We are going to start our study of evil and suffering in the Bible at the end of the story. That is because, although for us humans suffering and evil are a mystery, they are not a mystery to God, who stands behind the whole story of planet Earth. He knows the answer. He writes the end of the story. What is more, in the Bible he has revealed to us enough of that answer to enable us to cope with the tough chapters that make up the main part of the story. By being aware of the future we can live through the present.

The Bible's attitude to evil and suffering, unlike ours, is not dominated by the current evil and suffering that are around us in the world. Rather, it is dominated by what is going to happen at the end of the world. Both the Old Testament and the New Testament, in essence, look forward. Both see the present in the light of the future. Right at the start, the book of Genesis announces God's ultimate purpose as nothing less than blessing for 'all peoples on earth'.[1] The whole of the Old Testament pointed forward to the coming Day of

[1] Gen. 12:3.

the Lord, when God would break into the story of planet Earth to save and redeem, and to judge and purge his creation of all evil. The law was 'a shadow of the good things that are coming',[2] and the prophets looked forward to the day when 'the earth will be full of the knowledge of the LORD as the waters cover the sea'.[3] The New Testament proclaims that this Day has already dawned in the coming of God in Christ, and that his kingdom is already in process of being established.[4] But the process is not yet complete, so the New Testament also rings with the 'living hope' of the final coming of the King and the full establishing of his kingdom.[5] This looking forward is vital to our understanding of the Bible's teaching on evil and suffering. If we fail to grasp it we will end up with only a limited answer to all the questions evil and suffering raise.

This future focus, says the writer to the Hebrews, was key to Christ's suffering and work on the cross. It was 'for the joy that was set before him' that he 'endured the cross, scorning its shame'.[6] Paul stated, 'I consider that our present sufferings are not worth comparing with the glory that will be revealed in us',[7] and 'our light and momentary troubles are achieving for us an eternal glory that far outweighs them all'.[8] Peter encouraged his readers to put up with all the suffering they were facing because God 'has given us new birth into a living hope ... an inheritance that can never perish, spoil or fade – kept in heaven for you, who through faith are shielded by God's power until the coming of the salvation that is ready to be revealed in the last time. In this you greatly rejoice, though now for a little while you may have to suffer grief in all kinds of trials.'[9] The book of Revelation constantly encourages the persecuted and struggling Christians of the churches in Asia to refocus on the certainties of the future in order to keep going through the uncertainties of the present.

Such focusing on 'future fact' is very out of fashion today. It is condemned as 'unscientific' and mocked as wishful thinking by those who reject the Christian message. Even among Christians there is a certain amount of reticence that dulls its impact. But there was no such reticence in New Testament times. To declare the good news, the story of God's mighty acts in Jesus, without its final

[2] Heb. 10:1.
[3] Isa. 11:9.
[4] For example Matt. 4:17.
[5] For example 1 Pet. 1:3–7.
[6] Heb. 12:2.
[7] Rom. 8:18.
[8] 2 Cor. 4:17.
[9] 1 Pet. 1:3–6.

chapter would have been unthinkable. All the purposes of God in the Old Testament, all the work and ministry of Jesus, all the witness and ministry of the church, lead up to and find their fulfilment in this great event. Here is the climax of the Bible story; here is the fulfilment of all God's purposes; here is the crowning moment of the work of Christ; and here is the final revealing of what it is the amazing love and wisdom of our God has been preparing for those who love him.

2. Four foundational facts

Whatever approach we may take to the interpretation of the book of Revelation,[10] there can be little dispute over the following four statements of its teaching on evil and suffering.

a. The world is overwhelmed with evils

The book of Revelation mentions falsehood, exploitation, injustice, sexual immorality, abuse of power, war, economic exploitation, death, earthquakes and natural disasters, Satanic and demonic forces, worship of demons and idols, murder, magic arts, theft, false religion, blasphemy, destruction of the earth, plagues, crime, mourning, famine, cowardice and unbelief.

b. Suffering is the lot of all humankind

Forms of suffering mentioned include grief and mourning, affliction, poverty, persecution and martyrdom, death, sorrow, tears and crying, 'ugly and painful sores', fear, pain, sickness, demonic attack and oppression.

c. Suffering is especially the lot of the people of God

The book is written against the backdrop of John's exile on Patmos, 'because of the word of God and the testimony of Jesus'.[11] It was addressed to churches for whom persecution was a fact of life, whether in the form of exclusion from family or trade guild, or of the confiscation of property, imprisonment and martyrdom. In a graphic passage in the central interlude of the book, we see Satan, thwarted in his attempts to destroy Jesus, in rage turning 'to make war against ... those who obey God's commandments and hold to

---

[10] For the approach that I prefer see my *Discovering Revelation* (Crossway, 2004).
[11] Rev. 1:9.

the testimony of Jesus'.[12] If you are a Christian you can expect a particularly tough time!

d. Evils will continue to the end of the age

The book of Revelation makes it very clear that evil and suffering will continue until the Lord returns. The three series of God's sevenfold judgments[13] picture with graphic symbolism[14] the chaos of a world that refuses to turn away from its sin, and of the suffering that inevitably follows. Many commentators understand the book as teaching that evils will get worse towards the end of the age, a view supported perhaps by verses like 2 Timothy 3:13. But even if this is not so, it is very hard to square the teaching of Revelation with the optimistic view, common for much of the last century, that the world would steadily become a better and better place, where evils would gradually be eliminated by education or science or whatever. Even in the twenty-first century, despite our disillusionment at the failures of human efforts to deal with evil, there still seems to be a residual hope among some that we are capable of making effective progress. But, as Beasley-Murray points out:

> There are some things which only God can do. One of them is to provide an atonement for evil, and another is to put a stop to the progress of evil, and they are not the same thing. In both respects God works through Christ. We may be grateful that he will achieve the second so sure as he has done the first through his Son. Part of the importance of the book of Revelation is its teaching on God's intention to do this very thing.[15]

---

[12] Rev. 12:17.

[13] Rev. 6:1–17; 8:6–21; 16:1–21.

[14] Most of the things the book of Revelation seeks to describe – the glory of God and of the risen Christ, the wonders of heaven, the awfulness of hell, and the events at the end of the age – are in fact beyond description. So John's vision, like Jesus in his parables, uses pictures. Some have tried to understand the pictures literally, and have raised all sorts of problems for themselves as a result. But, as with the parables, the true meaning of the pictures lies in the underlying message, not in the literal details of the pictures. Almost all the imagery in the book of Revelation has its roots in the Old Testament; the part of the Old Testament that is used most of all is the story of the exodus. Many of the awesome events pictured in the threefold series of the seven seals, the seven trumpets and the seven bowls are based on the plagues that God sent on the Egyptians. God's final response to evil, his final deliverance of his people from suffering, is pictured in terms of what he did when he rescued his people from the evils of Egypt.

[15] G. R. Beasley-Murray, *Highlights of the Book of Revelation* (Lakeland, 1972), p. 60.

Only God can put a stop to the progress of evil. He has pledged himself to do so, but we have to wait for the coming of his Day.

3. Revelation 15:3–4: Six sure statements

The book of Revelation gives us many glimpses of the end of the story. One of them is *the song of Moses the servant of God and the song of the Lamb* (Rev. 15:3–4), a title which effectively sums up the whole story of God's mighty purposes in the Old Testament and the New Testament.

> '*Great and marvellous are your deeds,*
> *Lord God Almighty.*
> *Just and true are your ways,*
> *King of the ages.*
> ⁴*Who will not fear you, O Lord,*
> *and bring glory to your name?*
> *For you alone are holy.*
> *All nations will come*
> *and worship before you,*
> *for your righteous acts have been revealed.*'

This great hymn of worship is preceded by a graphic and horrible description of the judgment-day 'harvest' of the earth, and the terrifying trampling of its 'grapes' in 'the great winepress of God's wrath'.[16] It is followed by one of the most horrific passages of the whole of the Bible. Within a few verses John is describing ugly and painful sores on a large part of humankind, the sea and rivers and springs turned to blood, the sun scorching and searing, darkness and agony, demonic powers let loose upon the earth, a mighty earthquake, the disruption of the whole earth, and terrible hailstones from the sky[17] – all this as the outpouring of the wrath of God.[18]

Yet in the middle of all this come the six great assertions of this song, which shine out all the stronger and all the more brilliant against so dark a setting.

a. God is totally good (15:3–4)

Living in an evil world continually raises issues that challenge the goodness of God. 'How can a good God allow wars, and cancer,

---

[16] Rev. 14:18–20.
[17] Rev. 16:2, 3–4, 8–14, 18–21.
[18] Rev. 15:7.

and tsunamis, and innocent deaths from terrorist bombs?' we cry. 'Could it be that in fact he is not good; he is cruel and vindictive, a savage God taking a sadistic delight in hurting his creatures?' Even though surrounded by horrific accounts of God's judgments, these two verses state unequivocally that when we see the whole picture there will be no doubt whatever that God is totally good. We shall declare emphatically that he *alone* is *holy*, uniquely morally pure, that his *acts* are manifestly *righteous*, legally and ethically right, and that his *ways* are *just and true*, with no trace of unfairness or deceit. If he judges he judges rightly; if he condemns he condemns fairly; if he forgives he is justified in doing so. When we see the whole picture we shall see how absolutely right all his actions have been. In all his ways he will be seen to be nothing other than totally good. Faced with such total goodness and perfect holiness, objections and complaints will die on our lips; we can only bow in submission and awe and holy *fear* (15:3–4).

b. God is sovereign (15:3)

The song of triumph of God's people at the end of the age is modelled on the song that Moses and the people sang in Exodus 15 after God had rescued them and destroyed their enemies at the Red Sea. There on the shore of the sea they celebrated God's power both over nature, in the dividing of the sea, and over Pharaoh and his army. Only hours before, they had been in an impossible situation, trapped by Pharaoh's army, between the desert and the sea, with no hope of escape. What is more, it was God who had got them into that situation, by sending Moses to bring them out of Egypt. Little wonder that they were terrified and turned on Moses, and so on God, bitterly attacking them for getting them into such a mess.[19] But God knew what he was doing: 'I will gain glory for myself through Pharaoh and all his army, and the Egyptians will know that I am the LORD.'[20] And so he did, and the people celebrated his mighty power and sovereign purposes:

> 'I will sing to the LORD,
>   for he is highly exalted.
> The horse and its rider
>   he has hurled into the sea.
> The LORD is my strength and my song;
>   he has become my salvation.

[19] Exod. 14:10–12.
[20] Exod. 14:4.

He is my God and I will praise him,
    my father's God, and I will exalt him.
The LORD is a warrior;
    the LORD is his name ...
Who among the gods is like you, O LORD?
    Who is like you –
        majestic in holiness,
        awesome in glory,
        working wonders?'[21]

The story is repeated again and again throughout Scripture and down through history: impossible problems and apparent disasters are gloriously turned to good by a God who is sovereign, who knows what he is doing, and who allows a hopeless situation to develop only because he can use it for his great purposes of wisdom and grace. God's people defeated by their enemies and taken into exile, Daniel cast to the lions, Jesus nailed to a cross, Stephen stoned, Paul shipwrecked, the church persecuted – all taken up and turned to good by our amazing God. On a smaller scale there are the setbacks and hurts and problems he allows into our lives, which, if we let him, he can use in his sovereign wisdom, to work out his purposes of goodness and grace for us and those around us. One of the key themes of Revelation is that though the powers of evil seem to be doing their own thing and wreaking havoc in the world, nothing that they do is outside of the power of God. God permits them to do their awful deeds only because through them in wisdom and power he can show his glory.[22]

So the people of God in heaven worship him as *Lord God Almighty* and *King of the ages* (Rev. 15:3). Both titles go back to the language of the Old Testament. 'Lord God Almighty' embraces the I AM WHO I AM[23] and the God, or LORD, of hosts;[24] he is the great incomprehensible, eternal, self-existing God, who rules over all other powers and sovereignly directs his people's history. There is a textual variant in the next phrase and commentators and translators are divided between *King of the ages* and 'King of the nations'.[25] The meaning of both titles is similar. *King of the ages* emphasizes God's sovereignty over time and history and over the powers that were

---

[21] Exod. 15:1–3, 11.
[22] See the amazing statement in Rev. 17:16–17 that even the antics of the powers of evil are in some sense put into their hearts by God in order to accomplish his purpose.
[23] Exod. 3:14.
[24] *Ṣĕbā'ôt* is generally translated in the NIV as 'Almighty', e.g. Ps. 24:10.
[25] 'King of the ages': RSV, NEB, NIV; 'King of the nations': GNB, NLT, Beale, Swete, TNIV.

thought to dominate the various epochs.[26] 'King of the nations'[27] stresses God's sovereignty over each specific worldly power, from Pharaoh's Egypt and Nebuchadnezzar's Babylon and Caesar's Rome to Hitler's Germany and Stalin's Russia and Blair's Britain and Bush's America.

c. God will deliver his people from evil (15:3)

'Deliver us from evil,' we pray. But evil doesn't go away; often it gets worse. Things had been tough enough for God's people when they were in Egypt; they were slaves; their lives were 'bitter with hard labour'.[28] But then the immediate result of Moses' intervention was that life got even tougher; they were given the virtually impossible task of making bricks without being given straw.[29] Then when God had shown his mighty power and the people had escaped from Egypt they found themselves trapped between Pharaoh's pursuing army and the sea. It looked as though everything was lost; but then God stepped in with the greatest miracle of all, parting the sea and saving his people and destroying the enemy army for ever. So the people sang the Song of Moses, the song of deliverance. This is the song God's people will sing at the end of the age; it is *the song of Moses the servant of God*, but it is also *the song of the Lamb* (3), celebrating an even greater deliverance than that brought about by Moses. It is not a song celebrating a problem-free existence, or a song that declares that God never allowed any evil to darken our lives on earth. Rather it is a song that declares that God has brought us through the darkness out into his glorious light; he has taken the hurts and the problems that he has allowed us to go through and has broken their power to harm us and turned them to glory and blessing.

d. God is dealing with evil (15:3)

In no way is he standing idly or helplessly by. He is at work in every part of his creation, not least in those places where evil seems most active. In the presence of our enemies he is busy laying out a table.[30] When we see the whole picture we will declare, *Great and*

---

[26] The phrase appears at 1 Tim. 1:17, where it is inadequately translated by the NIV as 'the King eternal'.

[27] A common Old Testament concept (e.g. Jer. 10:7; Ps. 22:28), which is reflected in the title given to Christ in Rev. 1:5, 'the ruler of the kings of the earth'.

[28] Exod. 1:14.

[29] Exod. 5:6–23.

[30] Ps. 23:5.

marvellous are your deeds, whether they are deeds of deliverance out of evil, or of sustaining his people through times of evil, or of using the powers of evil to fulfil his purposes, or of turning evil to good, or of finally destroying all that is evil.

e. All history, and so all suffering, is purposeful

Our generation is indoctrinated with the humanistic concept of meaninglessness and chance. Such a concept has been able to take root in our culture because people either do not believe in God or view God as uninvolved in his world. In contrast, the Bible sees God as sovereign and the events in the world as his *deeds* and *acts*. Pharaoh undoubtedly hardened his own heart and chose to pursue his escaping slaves. But the Bible is able to say that God hardened Pharaoh's heart and caused him to pursue them.[31] Herod and Pilate freely chose to kill Jesus, but they were doing what God's 'power and will had decided beforehand should happen'.[32] There is no such thing as a meaningless event or meaningless suffering in the Bible; in all things God is working out his sovereign purposes, to be revealed at the end of the age.

f. At the end of the age everyone will acknowledge the justice and glory of all that God has done (15:4)

Today, when there is a war or a disaster, many are quick to lay the blame at God's door and use it as grounds for rejecting him. But at the end of the story, when the whole picture is revealed, everyone, *all nations*, will fall in worship and acknowledge that all his acts have been *righteous*. Paul has a parallel concept in Philippians 2:9–10, where he pictures every knee bowing at the name of Jesus, and every tongue confessing that he is Lord. Even those who, right to the end, reject his truth and his salvation and so come under his judgment will at the last concede that every one of his sovereign acts is righteous.

Here in the song of Moses and the song of the Lamb is the key that enables us to begin to unlock the mystery of evil and suffering. Viewed in themselves they present an insoluble problem. But viewed in the context of the end of the story we can begin to make sense of them. The future focus enables us to live in the present, however tough it may be.

[31] Exod. 14:4.
[32] Acts 4:28.

Though they come at the end of the story of the Bible, these verses, based as they are on the Song of Moses in Exodus, are full of concepts and terms taken from the Old Testament. It is to the Old Testament we now turn in order to trace the story from its beginning.

Genesis 6:5–8
2. The beginning of the story

The first chapter of Genesis tells us that God made a world that was good.[1] In this world he placed human beings, to fill the earth and subdue it and to rule over its creatures. That made everything 'very good'.[2] The world was very good because it had been made by a good God; it was his creation and it was in a harmonious and beautiful relationship with its Creator.

But sin, and so evil, entered this 'very good' world.[3] The essence of sin and evil was the refusal to accept that God is God. The fact is, of course, that God can never be anything other than God. That is, he can never stop being the creator; he can never cease to be holy and good and true; what he says must always be right; his ways are always perfect. But though we can never stop God being God, we can choose to behave as though he is not God. We can ignore the fact that he is the Creator, and pretend that our world and our bodies and our possessions are ours, for us to do as we like with. We can claim that we know better than he does, that his standards and commands are unsatisfactory; we can decide for ourselves what is right or wrong, good or bad, true or false; we can make up our own rules and reject his. We can, in effect, set ourselves up as gods, and push him off his throne.

To refuse to accept God as God means, of course, that we live a lie. It makes not the slightest difference to the reality – God remains God. But it means that we turn away from what is right and good and true and beautiful to what is false and wrong and perverted and ugly. We turn from light to darkness, from wholeness to brokenness, from meaning to absurdity. No longer is the creation in a wholesome and beautiful relationship with its creator.

[1] Gen. 1:10, 12, 18, 21, 25.
[2] Gen. 1:31.
[3] Gen. 3:1–6.

God has been thrust aside; we have chosen to live as though we have cast him off his throne. From a broken relationship with God came broken relationships between humans;[4] from one act of disobedience came a deluge of sin and evil: 'From the first Fall sin had grown like an avalanche.'[5] So we find that by Genesis chapter 6:

> *The* LORD *saw how great man's wickedness on the earth had become, and that every inclination of the thoughts of his heart was only evil all the time.* [6]*The* LORD *was grieved that he had made man on the earth, and his heart was filled with pain.* [7]*So the* LORD *said, 'I will wipe mankind, whom I have created, from the face of the earth – men and animals, and creatures that move along the ground, and birds of the air – for I am grieved that I have made them.'* [8]*But Noah found favour in the eyes of the* LORD.[6]

1. The human heart (6:5)

The heart is the key, said Jesus; out of it come 'evil thoughts, sexual immorality, theft, murder, adultery, greed, malice, deceit, lewdness, envy, slander, arrogance and folly'.[7] You may look on the outside appearance, said God, but I look on the heart.[8] And when, in Genesis 6, he saw the human heart, God saw something horrific. We tend to imagine that the human race has enough goodness in itself to be able to produce reasonably good behaviour even if it has turned its back completely on God. Underlying this, perhaps, is our experience of residual goodness in our own culture even though the majority have no time for God, or our awareness that those who follow religions other than Christianity, or, indeed have no religion at all, can live lives that express at least some goodness and love. Such goodness is recognized by Paul in Romans 2:14–15, but it should not be allowed to blind us to the fact that if individuals or cultures do cut themselves totally off from God, eventually all that is of God in them will die; they will reach the point where *every inclination of the thoughts* of their hearts are *only evil all the time* (5). It could be that this point, the condition of total rejection of all that is of God, is something parallel to what Jesus was referring to when he spoke of blasphemy against the

[4] Gen. 4:5–8, 23.
[5] G. von Rad, *Genesis* (SCM, 1963), p. 113.
[6] Gen. 6:5–8.
[7] Mark 7:21–22.
[8] 1 Sam. 16:7.

Holy Spirit as the unforgivable sin.[9] Here was a condition of hopelessness, of hearts completely closed to anything good or true, totally closed to God.

Genesis 6 uses several words to describe human sin and evil. 'Wickedness' (*ra'*) and 'evil' (*rā'â*) (verse 5) are words from the same Hebrew root and are general words for evil, with a basic meaning that suggests spoiling or harming. Verses 11–12 use the word 'corrupt' (*šāḥat*) three times; here too the basic meaning is 'spoilt' or 'ruined and destroyed'. Verses 11 and 13 state another result of human sin: that the earth, besides being corrupt, is 'filled with violence'. Here the word used is *ḥāmas*, which has an all too familiar ring to us today;[10] underlying its meaning of 'violence' is the concept of harming and destroying. So all the words used for evil in Genesis 6 suggest that evil is what spoils and destroys that which is good. It is the perversion and corruption of the world that God made 'very good'. There is a feel of finality about it; the human heart, and so every area of God's creation where humans claim lordship, has been hopelessly corrupted; the beautiful creation has been smashed to fragments, irreparably broken.

2. The heart of God (6:6)

If we were asked to guess what words the early chapters of the Old Testament would use to describe God's reaction to the mess sin and evil have made of his 'very good' creation, we might well think of 'anger', 'wrath', 'judgment' and the like. But, though these words have their place later in the Scriptures, they are not used here. Instead, before they are introduced, we have an amazing description of the heart of God when confronted with evil. The first of the two verbs used in verse 6 (*nāḥam*), though legitimately translated in the NIV *was grieved*, could carry the meaning of 'was sorry' or 'regretted', and could be taken as an anthropomorphism for 'God decided that creating the human race had been a mistake'. But the second verb (*'āṣab*), linked as it is with *his heart* (*lēb*), that is, his innermost personal being, makes it quite clear that we are confronted here with a God who is

---

[9] Mark 3:28. R. T. France comments that the allegation of blasphemy against the Holy Spirit 'involves a total perversion of the truth and a repudiation of the rule of God'; R. T. France, *The Gospel of Mark* (Eerdmans, 2002), p. 177. For further discussion of 'the unforgivable sin' see pp. 103–104.

[10] The origin of the name Hamas as used today in the Middle East is, however, an Arabic acronym for 'The Islamic Resistance Movement' (Harakat al-Muqawamah al-Islamiyya).

hurting.[11] Graphically, and correctly, the NLT translates it, 'It broke his heart.' God's first reaction to the sin and evil of the world is pain. A broken world means a broken-hearted God.

Down through the centuries, philosophers and theologians, especially those influenced by the main Greek tradition of philosophy, have followed a simple piece of logic which has led them seriously astray. It is this:

> Pain and suffering are evil.
> God is good and contains nothing that is evil.
> Therefore God cannot feel pain or suffer.

The logic of this argument is impeccable. But Genesis 6 and much else in Scripture tell us clearly that its conclusion is false. So we have to conclude that one of its premises is false, or that both are. We shall need other Bible passages, which we shall be looking at later in this study, to unpack just what this might entail; for the moment we have to take on board the clear teaching of Genesis 6 that our God suffers; the evil and brokenness of our world cause him pain and break his heart.

3. The act of God (6:7)

Faced with the hopeless sinfulness of the human race, with all its attendant evils, God states that he will wipe out the vast majority of humankind, along with many others of his creatures: *The LORD said, 'I will wipe mankind, whom I have created, from the face of the earth – men and animals, and creatures that move along the ground, and birds of the air'* (7). To us, such a step seems to stand in stark contrast to the broken heart of our God revealed in the previous verse. If the evil of the world causes such pain and suffering to God, why inflict further evil on it and on himself by destroying it? But that is to misunderstand the Scriptures; verse 7 needs to be understood in the light of verses 5 and 6: the pronouncement of destruction is inseparable from the wickedness and evil that are in the world and from the pain that is in the heart of God. Evil is destruction. For God to speak destruction over a totally evil world is to speak the truth, to say what is right. In no way could he see the wickedness of the earth and say, 'OK; all is well. Peace and goodness, joy and beauty.' When God spoke destruction he was

---

[11] 'The root *'āsab* is used to express the most intense form of human emotion, a mixture of rage and bitter anguish. Only here is the verb supplemented by the phrase 'in his heart' ... underlining the strength of God's reaction to human sinfulness'; G. J. Wenham, *Genesis 1 – 15* (Word, 1987), pp. 144–145.

being truthful and right and just. The evil of the world inevitably called down the judgment of a righteous God; a holy God and a sin-ridden world cannot coexist. But such a judgment was costly; as much as the evil that caused it, it gave God pain; it broke his heart.

There is a telling parallel in Luke's account of the triumphal entry of Jesus into Jerusalem, the coming of the holy King into his unholy city.

> As he approached Jerusalem and saw the city, he wept over it and said, 'If you, even you, had only known on this day what would bring you peace – but now it is hidden from your eyes. The days will come upon you when your enemies will build an embankment against you and encircle you and hem you in on every side. They will dash you to the ground, you and the children within your walls. They will not leave one stone on another, because you did not recognise the time of God's coming to you.'[12]

It was through his tears, with a broken heart, that Jesus spoke of God's judgment on his city and its inescapable destruction. Were his tears caused by the city's rejection of its God? Or did he weep at the horrors of AD 70? We cannot be dogmatic, but I suggest he wept at both. Here is the same God as in Genesis 6, deeply hurt by the sin and evil of his world, and broken-hearted at its results and inevitable outcome.

4. The grace of God (6:8)

But Noah found favour in the eyes of the LORD (Gen. 6:8). In stark contrast to the total wickedness of those around him, 'Noah was a righteous man, blameless among the people of his time, and he walked with God'.[13] We are not to take this as implying that Noah was completely sinless. Rather, he was in a right relationship with God. In graphic contrast to those who had thrust God right out of their lives, Noah walked with God. He 'did everything just as God commanded him';[14] three times in chapter 7 his obedience is specifically stressed.[15] Here was a man who, though fallen, was still ready to let God be God in his life. This was a man with whom God could do business.

God looked on Noah with *favour*. This is the first occurrence in the Bible of *ḥēn*, one of the Old Testament words for grace. Its

[12] Luke 19:41–44.
[13] Gen. 6:9.
[14] Gen. 6:22.
[15] Gen. 7:5, 9, 16.

special emphasis is undeserved favour from a superior to an inferior; God was under no obligation to Noah; but out of a heart of love and mercy he looked favourably on him.

And not just upon him. Genesis 6:7 has pronounced the righteous verdict of a just God on a sinful world: destruction. But into the inexorable darkness comes a shaft of light. Humankind must be wiped from the earth, but one man and his family will be preserved. And through that man humankind will be restored upon the earth: a new beginning, a new chance, a new hope. To humankind and to the world through Noah God gave a new promise and a new covenant. As long as the earth endured he would hold back from total judgment: 'Never again will I destroy all living creatures, as I have done.'[16] And in glorious Technicolor symbolism, God took from his shoulder his weapon of war and destruction, his bow,[17] and set it in the clouds as a symbol of hope, so that we should be constantly reminded that even when darkness and disaster look as though they are about to overwhelm us, the grace of God will hold them back.

So the stage is set for a new beginning, a new chapter in the story of the human race. Here is a new world, one washed clean of the wickedness and evil of its earliest human inhabitants. Here is a new humanity, miraculously preserved by God from destruction, given a new beginning, with the blessing of the Creator upon it. Here is a God who promises grace and commits himself to enduring whatever evil humankind may bring about on planet Earth, however much pain it may bring him.

And how does the story go? You know it; it is there in the Bible, and you and I are part of it. At times it has gone well; there have been those who have let God be God in their lives, whom God has blessed and used for his glory. At other times it has gone badly, very badly. Perhaps it has never since reached the depths of Genesis 6:5, though assuredly at times it has not been far off. Perhaps by God's grace those who are 'the salt of the earth'[18] have preserved it from utter corruption. But God's grace has remained constant; he has remained faithful to his promise: while the earth remains he will not destroy.

While the earth remains. But one day the heavens and the earth will pass away. On that day, judgment and destruction, so long held back, will finally fall. But in the meantime we live in a world in which God has allowed evil to continue, at the cost of suffering in the world and untold pain to his own heart.

[16] Gen. 8:21–22; cf. 9:8–27.
[17] The NIV translation 'rainbow' obscures the fact that the Hebrew word (qešet) here is the standard one for an archer's weapon.
[18] Matt. 5:13.

Exodus 34:5–7
3. The God of love and punishment

We have all encountered people who welcome the love and grace and goodness of God, but who find it very hard to accept that he is also a God who judges and punishes evil and sin. Surely, they argue, if he is gracious and compassionate, he will always forgive everyone's sin; not only would he never judge and destroy the earth, he would never inflict any suffering on any of his individual creatures, or, indeed, let any of his creatures suffer in any way. But, however reasonable this may sound, it is not what the Bible actually teaches. As we have seen in the previous chapter, God does judge and punish; it is this aspect of his nature and dealings with his world that we shall focus on in this chapter as we look at God's own self-description in Exodus 34:6–7.

1. One God

God is one, and all the elements of his nature, however disparate they may seem to us, make up one integrated whole. For this reason we should resist the suggestion that some elements of his nature are to be set over against others, that they exist 'in tension'. There is no tension in God; none of his attributes sits uneasily with any other. We may feel there is a tension between justice and mercy, or between the God who loves and the God who punishes.[1] But that is because our understanding of these things is warped and

---

[1] Brueggemann, commenting on Exod. 34:6–7, states that 'the tension or contradiction here voiced is present in the very life and character of Yahweh'; W. Brueggemann, *Theology of the Old Testament* (Fortress, 1997), p. 227. But there is no tension in the life and character of God, just as there is no tension between the persons of the Godhead in the Trinity. Any 'tension', whether regarding the character of God or the nature of the Trinity, is in us, in our capability to hold the various elements together.

inadequate. In God they fit perfectly together. Indeed, though for our convenience we categorize God's attributes into neat separate compartments, such as holiness, power and love, in him these things are in no way separated; God is not made up of lots of attributes; he is one integrated nature. So when, for instance, we think of God's love, we should not think of it in isolation. We need to see it as holy love and powerful love. His holiness, similarly, is loving and powerful holiness. His power can only ever be holy power and loving power. A significant application of this principle requires us to see that even when God is punishing he is still loving. We saw an example of that in the previous chapter, and the same point is made by the passage to which we now turn.[2]

2. Show me your glory

When Moses met God at the burning bush, one of the first things he asked was what was the name of God. This was much more than simply asking for a title, a label that would distinguish him from all the other gods that were on offer. Rather, it was a request to see right into the character of God, to know what he was really like, to know him as he was. God's reply was both glorious and mysterious, both an amazing revelation of his nature and a statement that the inner nature of this God was far greater than could be put into a neat package to satisfy the curiosity of Moses and his people. 'I AM WHO I AM,' said God.[3] I AM. Reality. Life. Being. Source of all that is. That which holds everything else in being. Being, such that all else that exists is but a shadow compared with his burning and dynamic reality. Eternal, before time existed and after time will be no more. Complete, whole, sufficient, one. And yet at the same time mysterious, unfathomable, incomprehensible, other, different in essence from anything else. This is our God.

When they had been miraculously rescued from Egypt, Moses and the Israelites came back to Sinai, where God had spoken to him his name. There God revealed himself to his people in cloud and thunder and lightning, in smoke and in fire.[4] On the mountain he met with Moses and gave him his commands. But despite all that

---

[2] For a fuller exposition of Exod. 32 – 34 see Peter Lewis, *The Message of the Living God* (IVP, 2000), pp. 174–187. Brueggemann refers to Exod. 34:6–7 as a 'quite self-conscious characterization of Yahweh, a formulation so studied that it may be reckoned to be something of a classic, normative statement to which Israel regularly returned, meriting the label "credo".' It 'appears to be a rich convergence of Israel's preferred adjectives for Yahweh'; Brueggemann, *Theology of the Old Testament*, pp. 216, 215.

[3] Exod. 3:13–14.

[4] Exod. 19:16–25.

God had revealed and done, while Moses was on the mountain Aaron and the people made and worshipped a golden calf; rejecting the living God, they committed themselves to worshipping and following an idol.[5]

The holy anger of God burned against his people. Though, in answer to Moses' prayer, he did not destroy them completely, he sent a plague among them and three thousand were killed at Moses' command. 'Go up to the land flowing with milk and honey,' said God to Moses. 'But I will not go with you, because you are a stiff-necked people and I might destroy you on the way.'[6] Such an arrangement might well have been safer for the people, but Moses would have none of it. 'If your Presence does not go with us,' he said, 'do not send us up from here.' However fearsome it might be to have the living holy God among them, Moses could be content with nothing less. 'I will do the very thing you have asked,' replied God, 'because I am pleased with you and I know you by name.'[7] Then Moses made an awesome request: 'Now show me your glory.' In reply God did two things; he promised to proclaim his name, the LORD, in the presence of Moses, and he let his glory pass by while Moses was hidden in a cleft in the rock.[8]

3. Proclaiming the name

The promise to proclaim his name was kept when God met Moses again on the mountain.

> Then the LORD came down in the cloud and stood there with him and proclaimed his name, the LORD. [6] And he passed in front of Moses, proclaiming, 'The LORD, the LORD, the compassionate and gracious God, slow to anger, abounding in love and faithfulness, [7] maintaining love to thousands, and forgiving wickedness, rebellion and sin. Yet he does not leave the guilty unpunished; he punishes the children and their children for the sin of the fathers to the third and fourth generation'.[9]

Here is a magnificent self-portrait of God, the God of Israel and of the Old Testament, and also the God and Father of our Lord Jesus Christ, and our Lord and God. He is the God of the covenant, who commits himself to doing wonderful and awesome things for his

[5] Exod. 32:1–6.
[6] Exod. 32:9 – 33:3.
[7] Exod. 33:15–17.
[8] Exod. 33:19–23.
[9] Exod. 34:5–7.

people, despite their stiff necks and wickedness and sin, provided they obey what he commands.[10]

Eight things God says about himself in this self-portrait. Seven we find wonderfully attractive; the eighth, which speaks of punishing the guilty, many find hard. But in keeping with the principle we have seen above, this element of God's nature is not something to be set over against the other seven. This is no dark or shadow side, contrasting strongly with the more attractive aspects of who he is. Instead, the seven and the one are to be taken together; they are facets of the one nature of our God. Each belongs to the other; to understand one apart from the other would give us a distorted understanding of God.

a. Compassionate (34:6)

The God who punishes is the *compassionate* God; when he punishes he does it with compassion. The word God uses of himself here (*raḥûm*) is a deeply personal and emotional one; its root meaning is the 'womb', and it thus parallels the close identification and deep concern God feels for us with the feelings of a mother for the child of her womb.[11] The English word 'compassion' in its root meaning pictures God suffering with those he punishes, a concept we saw in the previous chapter; the old saying of the headmaster, cane in hand, to the wayward schoolboy, 'This is going to hurt me more than it hurts you', however insincere it may be in its human context, is definitely true in its divine context. God hears the cry of the child, the groaning of the sufferer, and they pierce his heart, even if the suffering is the result of his judgment upon human sin.

b. Gracious (34:6)

The God who punishes is the *gracious* God. Again, I suggest we are being unfair to the essential unity of the nature of God if we assume that to some people God is gracious, showing unmerited favour, and to others he is ungracious, turning an angry, punitive face. Picking

[10] Verses 8–11. 'He is willing to give himself to them, but they must take him as he is, exactly as he is. He will not compromise, and therefore *they* must not. Such a confession not only makes all the more clear what a rebellion the disobedience with the calf was, it also anticipates what the next step simply *must* be: the people must renew their commitment ... the covenant relationship ... Once more the people must hear what they are to obey; once more Yahweh, favorably disposed and full of unchanging love, is opening himself to them'; J. I. Durham, *Exodus* (Word, 1987), pp. 454–455.

[11] 'Feeling of pity which a mother has for her helpless baby'; S. Dray, *Exodus: Free to Serve* (Crossway, 1993), p. 198.

up God's description of himself in these verses, the Psalmist declares:

> The LORD is gracious and compassionate,
>   slow to anger and rich in love.
> The LORD is good to all;
>   he has compassion on all he has made ...
> The LORD is righteous in all his ways
>   and loving towards all he has made.[12]

This is not to say that the grace that God shows to all results in the salvation of all;[13] but it is to say that there is no-one to whom God fails to show goodness and love, that everyone is the object of his unmerited favour and grace, even those whom he punishes.

c. Slow to anger (34:6)

The third element of his character that God declares to Moses is that he is *slow to anger*. As we have seen, our holy God is deeply affected by evil and sin and all that comes from them. He cannot see these things and remain unmoved; and while part of his reaction is pain, another part is what the Bible unashamedly calls anger or wrath. In Paul's familiar words, 'The wrath of God is being revealed from heaven against all the godlessness and wickedness of men who suppress the truth by their wickedness.'[14] Those who object to the concept of God's anger generally do so because they feel that anger is an unworthy emotion for God to feel. But that is because they pattern God's anger on human anger, which is often, if not always, tainted with our sinfulness. But God's anger is not patterned on our anger; it is uniquely his, and because it is his it is holy and good and righteous and all that God is. It is absolutely right that our holy God of compassion and grace and love should feel anger when he sees the

---

[12] Ps. 145:8–9, 17.

[13] Paul wrestles with the specific issue of saving grace in Rom. 9 – 11, using Exod. 33:19 in his argument that God is perfectly righteous to save some and not others. F. F. Bruce, referring to Romans 11:32, comments that though saving grace is not universal 'God's grace is far wider than anyone could have dared to hope ... God delights to show mercy, and he has lavished it upon men and women beyond counting from Gentiles and Jews alike'; F. F. Bruce, *The Letter of Paul to the Romans* (IVP, 1985), pp. 180–181. I. Howard Marshall, in his discussion of Rom. 9 – 11 and election, concludes, 'Grace was shown to a number of Israelites and they accepted it and so joined the company of the elect, but it is never said that their response was predetermined by God, or that the offer of God's grace was limited to the number of those who actually responded to it'; I. H. Marshall, *Kept by the Power of God*, 3rd edn (Paternoster, 1995), p. 104.

[14] Rom. 1:18.

devastation caused by war, or the damage done to a child by a paedophile or by the break-up of a marriage. But it is worth noting that in this passage God does not list anger as a foundational aspect of his nature; he does not say, 'I am compassionate, gracious and angry.' As Calvin has put it, anger is not a disposition of God[15] as is, say, holiness; it is not an essential part of his nature. What, according to this passage, is essential to his nature is 'slowness to anger', that is, slowness to give legitimate expression to his anger. He does not immediately condemn; he does not immediately destroy. He gives a second chance, and a third, and a fourth . . . He waits to see if we will turn from our sin and cry to him for mercy.

The phrase 'slow to anger' is used all through the Old Testament, and is illustrated again and again in God's dealings with his people. In the New Testament it is picked up in the great word *makrothymia* (literally 'long temper' as opposed to short temper) which the AV translated 'longsuffering' and the NIV renders 'patience'. The Lord 'is patient with you,' wrote Peter, 'not wanting anyone to perish, but everyone to come to repentance.'[16] Longsuffering, then, or patience, is the third element of his nature that God reveals to us, and which we need to set alongside the truth that he is a God who punishes.

d. Abounding in love – maintaining love to thousands (34:6–7)

The God who punishes is also the God who loves; indeed, he is *abounding in love* and *maintaining love to thousands*. The emphasis on love is very marked; not only is it mentioned twice, it is described as 'abounding' (*rab*, the standard Hebrew word for 'great, many, numerous, abundant'), and as being kept or preserved 'for thousands'. In the light of Deuteronomy 7:9 ('The LORD your God is God; he is the faithful God, keeping his covenant of love to a thousand generations of those who love him and keep his commands'),[17] this is to be understood as thousands of generations; this is love that 'endures for ever', as we are told twenty-six times in Psalm 136. This is *ḥesed*, unfailing, committed, loyal, covenant love. This is the amazing love of our God, abounding and unfailing, even when punishing.

e. Abounding in faithfulness (34:4)

Equally *abounding* is God's *faithfulness*. The word here is the great Old Testament word for truth (*'ĕmet*). It picks up the consistency

---

[15] Cited in E. Peels, *Shadow Sides* (Paternoster, 2003), p. 112.
[16] 2 Pet. 3:9.
[17] See also Exod. 20:6.

of our God we were stressing above; he is dependable, reliable, not capriciously changing his nature from one occasion to another, not abandoning his compassion and grace and love in order to punish, 'the same yesterday and today and for ever'.[18] Equally it stresses his justice. He is 'Faithful and True. With justice he judges and makes war.'[19] The God of the covenant, who promises blessing to those who love him and punishment on those who hate him, will be true to his word. He is trustworthy; we can trust him to be just, to keep his promise; we know exactly where we are with him.

But there is a further nuance to the phrase *abounding in faithfulness*, one that is unpacked further in the next phrase, *forgiving wickedness, rebellion and sin*. For the fact is that the covenant people of God were notorious for their unfaithfulness. Only days after meeting their Saviour God at Sinai they were worshipping a golden calf; their whole story was to be littered with failure to keep God's word and unfaithfulness to the covenant. But over against his people's fickleness and unfaithfulness, God is 'abounding in faithfulness'. As Paul put it in 2 Timothy 2:13, probably quoting an early Christian hymn, 'If we are faithless, he will remain faithful, for he cannot disown himself.'

g. Forgiving wickedness, rebellion and sin (34:7)

So we come to the final phrase: the God who punishes is the God who forgives *wickedness, rebellion and sin*. The three terms ('*āwōn*, *pešaʿ*, *ḥattā'â*) between them are all-embracing; there is no sin he will not 'forgive', carrying it, bearing it away (*nāśā'*).[20] How he could do this and remain consistent to his justice and truth may well have been a mystery to the people of God in the Old Testament; those of us who know Christ have a clearer idea of how he can be 'just and the one who justifies'.[21]

Here, then, is the climax of God's list of attributes in his self-description. His compassion, grace, longsuffering, love and faithfulness come together in the element of his nature that carries away our sin, that forgives and cleanses and justifies. This is our God; it is in this context that he calls himself the God who punishes.

---

[18] Heb. 13:8.
[19] Rev. 19:11.
[20] Ellison favours the translation 'bearing' in order to 'bring out the cost to God himself'; H. L. Ellison, *Exodus* (Saint Andrew Press, 1982), p. 180.
[21] Rom. 3:26.

4. The God who punishes (34:7)

God's commitment to punish is very clear, but, given the context, punishment with him is something very different from the capricious and vindictive thing that some have imagined. Indeed, the word used here (*pāqad*) means 'attend to' or 'care for' as well as 'punish'; the feel of the words is that God cannot ignore those who persist in 'wickedness, rebellion and sin'; he has to 'attend to' them, and he will do so in the appropriate and just way, by judging and punishing them. We can conclude our study of this passage by listing seven things about the God who punishes.

a. God calls himself the God who punishes in order to save us from punishment

The threat to punish is real, but its purpose is positive, to deter us from sin or from taking advantage of God's grace and compassion. After all, the context of Exodus 34 is Exodus 32, the people's ready rebellion against God to worship the golden calf.[22] Even those in our culture who reject the concept of retributive punishment are willing to advocate the value of punishment as a deterrent, and to concede that it will be a deterrent only if it is actually practised. God's basic desire is that he will have to punish no-one, that all will turn to him and be saved, that all will know the fullness of his blessing.[23] To help fulfil that desire he starkly paints the consequences of not receiving his compassion and grace for those who choose to hang on to their sin.

b. Punishment is a last resort

This is implicit in the phrase *slow to anger*. God waits in grace for repentance, so that he can show mercy and forgive.

c. When God punishes he does so in love

Not for one moment does he withdraw his compassion and grace and love. They are as strong at the moment of punishing as at the moment of forgiving. When David sinned over Uriah and Bathsheba, Nathan the prophet pronounced both the forgiveness of God

---

[22] Fretheim suggests that the declaration of 'the unconditionality of the divine love' makes reference to punishment essential, since God has to be seen as the upholder of 'the moral order'; T. E. Fretheim, *Exodus* (John Knox Press, 1991), p. 302.

[23] Isa. 45:22; Gen. 12:3.

and the punishment of God upon his sin.[24] 'The LORD has taken away your sin,' he said; but the repercussions of his sin would mean that his child by Bathsheba would die, that 'the sword would never depart' from his house, and that one of his own household would lie with his wives as David had lain with Bathsheba. Yet in no way did David see this punishment as anything other than just and gracious. 'As for God,' he wrote, 'his way is perfect ... He shows unfailing kindness (*ḥesed*, love) to his anointed.'[25]

d. There is no contradiction between sin being punished and the sinner being forgiven

In Exodus 34:7 God speaks of forgiveness and punishment virtually in the same breath. The example of David illustrates this; in response to David's repentance and prayer[26] God forgave his sin, but he did not spare David the punitive results of his sin. For us in New Testament times the situation is parallel, with one great difference: gloriously and graciously he forgives us our sin, but only by himself carrying the penalty and punishment for it in our place on the cross of Calvary.

As the Psalmist, traditionally David himself, puts it:

> The LORD is compassionate and gracious,
>   slow to anger, abounding in love.
> He will not always accuse,
>   nor will he harbour his anger for ever;
> he does not treat us as our sins deserve
>   or repay us according to our iniquities.
> For as high as the heavens are above the earth,
>   so great is his love for those who fear him;
> as far as the east is from the west,
>   so far has he removed our transgressions from us.[27]

e. God's punishment is purposive

His purposes are always larger than we can immediately see. In the case of David he needed to show his justice, not just to the nation David was leading, but to those whom he described as 'the LORD's enemies', who were showing 'utter contempt' as a result of David's

---

[24] 2 Sam. 12:7–14.
[25] 2 Sam. 22:31, 51.
[26] 2 Sam. 12:13; Ps. 51.
[27] Ps. 103:8–12.

sin.[28] Moses emphasized that God's punishment of his people's sin was in order to turn them back to him in repentance,[29] and in his great prayer at the dedication of the Temple Solomon several times pictured God's people turning back to him in repentance and obedience as a result of God's punishment on their sin.[30] Whenever he punishes, in some way or another God is seeking to bring out of the punishment and its repercussions something that is good and that will further his purposes of grace and love.

f. Both sin and punishment hurt innocent people

A father molests his daughter. In just punishment he is separated from his daughter and sent to prison. His daughter suffers from the sin and, in that she loses her father, suffers from the punishment. When one generation sins against God the next generation suffers. Some commentators try to lessen the apparent harshness of the last part of Exodus 34:7 by suggesting that it means that the second, third and fourth generation of 'children' suffer only if, once they are grown up, they follow the sin of their 'fathers'.[31] This may well be a right reading of the text, but even if we are to take it that innocent children suffer for the sins of their parents (as happened to David's child in 2 Sam. 12:14) we need to remember two things. First, God is totally committed to righting all injustices in the end. The Bible is full of innocent people suffering, not least Christians who suffer for following Jesus, but it is absolutely clear that on the Day of Judgment complete justice will be done and be seen to be done.[32] Second, there is a strong and deliberate contrast here between the extent of God's faithful love and the extent of his punishment. His love extends to thousands of generations; his punishment is consciously limited to a maximum of three or four generations.

[28] 2 Sam. 12:14.

[29] For example, Lev. 26:14–45.

[30] 1 Kgs 8:22–61.

[31] 'No doubt the 'children' in mind are the grown-up offspring who perpetuate their elders' wickedness'; Lewis, *The Message of the Living God*, p. 184. 'The force of "the third and fourth generation" has been very widely missed. In early Israelite society the sons, when they married, settled in the immediate vicinity of the parental home. Given the usual age of marriage, the aged head of the family would normally have four generations living in close proximity and being influenced by him. This would be bound to be harmful, if he had an inadequate concept of God as shown by his use of images'; Ellison, *Exodus*, p. 108.

[32] See, for example, Rev. 6:9–11.

g. The God who punishes is the God who has chosen himself to bear our punishment

Though only hinted at in Exodus 34 (the word translated 'forgiving' (*nāśā'*) in verse 7 is the standard Hebrew word for' 'bear' or 'carry'), this is the profound truth that underlies all the Bible's teaching on punishment. Never can we accuse God of heartlessly punishing the creatures he has made, for there is no punishment that he himself is not willing to undergo in his love for us.

In the eighth century BC Amos declared:

Hear this word the LORD has spoken against you, O people of Israel – against the whole family I brought up out of Egypt:

'You only I have chosen
of all the families of the earth;
therefore I will punish you
for all your sins'.[33]

Many among his hearers had assumed that the profound truth that God had specially loved and chosen Israel[34] would mean that he would turn a blind eye to their failure and sin. The opposite, said Amos, was the case. A nation that has a special relationship with a holy God must be holy; if it is not holy, its unholiness must be purged. A God who specially loves a people who then turn from him to evil and darkness cannot expect his love to remain idle. His presence among them may continue, but his coming will no longer be a matter for rejoicing, for it will inevitably bring judgment and punishment.[35]

Over eight hundred years after Amos, the writer to the Hebrews quoted from Proverbs:

'My son, do not make light of the Lord's discipline,
and do not lose heart when he rebukes you,
because the Lord disciplines those he loves,
and he punishes everyone he accepts as a son.'[36]

However uncongenial it may be to the mindset of those in our culture whose relativism means that they have effectively lost the

[33] Amos 3:1–2.
[34] Deut. 7:6–8.
[35] Amos 5:18–20.
[36] Heb. 12:5–6, quoting Prov. 3:11–12.

distinction between right and wrong, good and bad, sin and holiness, or whose moral theory has no room for punishment, the biblical teaching on God makes it clear that in him there is no tension between love and punishment, just as there is no contradiction between holiness and judgment. A special relationship entails special responsibilities; failure to live as God's special people must result in God's special action.

Psalm 2
4. Chaos and the King

There is an old story, magnificently set to music by Paul Dukas, of the sorcerer's apprentice. Left alone one day in his master's house, and weary of his routine task of fetching water, this bright young man decided that life would be much pleasanter if he used one of the sorcerer's spells to get his broom to do the work for him. The spell, and the broom, worked fine, and soon all the needed water had been brought. Unfortunately, the spell did not include instructions on how to stop the broom, so it continued bringing more and more water, with disastrous results. Only the return of the master, who knew how to stop the chaos, saved the day.

The book of Psalms is prefaced with a pair of contrasting introductory psalms. Psalm 1 is personal and individual, describing the blessedness of the person who, unlike 'the wicked', makes 'the law of the LORD his "delight"'. Psalm 2 moves from the individual to the cosmic. It pictures the chaos of the world, the raging of the nations, and it tells us how the Master saves the day. Old Testament scholars suggest that the origin of the psalm may have been in a specific historical situation when vassal kings seized their chance and rose in rebellion after the death of their overlord; its theme was then taken up into the Jewish liturgy and used at all enthronement ceremonies. In fact, in the form in which we have it, the psalm's vision is much too broad for any individual earthly king, and its use by New Testament writers to refer to God's kingdom through Christ[1] is sufficient justification for us to use it today as a picture of God's dealings with the world's rebellious powers throughout history.

[1] E.g. Acts 13:33; Heb. 1:5; Rev. 2:27; 12:5.

1. The question (2:1)

> *Why do the nations conspire*
> *and the peoples plot in vain?*

Psalm 2 is not the only psalm to ask the question, 'Why?' The psalmists covered the whole range of human experiences and emotions, and were not afraid to give expression to their frustrations and doubts and problems, confident that their God was big enough to cope with them. 'Why, O LORD, do you stand far off? Why do you hide yourself in times of trouble? ... Why does the wicked man revile God? Why does he say to himself, "He won't call me to account"?' 'My God, my God, why have you forsaken me? Why are you so far from saving me, so far from the words of my groaning?' 'Why are you downcast, O my soul? Why so disturbed within me?' 'I say to God my Rock, "Why have you forgotten me? Why must I go about mourning, oppressed by the enemy?"' 'You are God my stronghold. Why have you rejected me?' 'Awake, O LORD! Why do you sleep? Rouse yourself! Do not reject us for ever. Why do you hide your face and forget our misery and oppression?' 'Why have you rejected us for ever, O God? Why does your anger smoulder against the sheep of your pasture? ... How long will the enemy mock you, O God? Will the foe revile your name for ever? Why do you hold back your hand, your right hand?' 'Why should the nations say, "Where is their God?"' 'Why, O LORD, do you reject me and hide your face from me?'[2]

Only rarely do the psalms provide an explanatory answer to the question, 'Why?' Much more often they provide a different sort of answer, one that goes deeper than an intellectual explanation, that goes right to the heart, to the frustration and the pain that gave rise to the question. This is the case in Psalm 2. It starts with the question, 'Why is our world so rebellious against God?', but instead of answering that directly it goes on to put the rebellion and chaos of our world into their divine context. Once it has done that we can view the original question in its right perspective; in fact, the need to have a detailed answer becomes much less pressing: we do not need to understand in detail why the world is in such a mess once we have been assured that our God is still sovereign over it. The psalmist who cries, 'My God, my God, why have you forsaken me?' does not need a detailed explanation of why God is letting him go through hell at that time, once he has grasped the

---

[2] Pss. 10:1, 13; 22:1; 42:5, 9; 43:2; 44:23–24; 74:1, 10–11; 79:10; 88:14.

wider truth of the Lord's ultimate dominion and righteousness.[3] The real answer to 'Why?', as to the chaos that gives rise to it, is often, 'Be still, and know that I am God.'[4]

2. The powers (2:2)

What is happening in the world? Where is it all heading? Who is in control? Will evil come out on top? If God is in control, why does everything seem so chaotic?

The first two verses of Psalm 2 use two pairs of words to picture the powers at work in our world. They are set in the context of the ancient world, but we can easily update them and locate their contemporary equivalents. The first pair is *the nations* and *the peoples*. These are national or people groups of any size, and include the great nations and empires of the ancient world, such as Egypt, Assyria and Rome, and cover the great and small groupings of our own day, from the United States and China to persecuted minorities living under oppressive regimes. The second pair is *the kings* and *the rulers*, those who hold and exercise power. In our days these could be state presidents and heads of governments; but they could also be controlling commercial or ideological groupings whose policies dominate the lives of so many.

It is significant that, though the powers described here, as in the book of Revelation, are pictured in fierce opposition to God, the Bible makes it clear that they are not necessarily evil in themselves. Each nation is as much a creation of God as is Israel.[5] To each has been given the promises of God's covenant with Noah.[6] For each God's purpose is one of blessing.[7] To each is revealed enough of God for them to walk in his truth.[8] What is more, the great vision of Revelation 21:24, 26, of the nations and their rulers taking their place in the City of God, walking by its light, and bringing their splendour and glory and honour into it, is prefigured many times in the book of Psalms. 'All the nations you have made will come and worship before you, O LORD; they will bring glory to your name.'[9] Though the Old Testament naturally focuses on God's special relationship with Israel, it also makes it clear that God watches over and has purposes for every nation, including those that were specifically

[3] Ps. 22:1, 27–31. See also the discussion of Job in chapter 19, below.
[4] Ps. 46:9–10.
[5] Acts 17:24–28.
[6] Gen. 8:21–22; 9:12–17.
[7] Gen. 12:3.
[8] Rom. 1:18–21.
[9] Ps. 86:9; see also Pss. 22:27–28; 67:3–7.

Israel's' enemies.[10] So Isaiah speaks of the Egyptians crying out to the Lord and the Lord hearing and rescuing them:

> They will turn to the LORD, and he will respond to their pleas. In that day there will be a highway from Egypt to Assyria. The Assyrians will go to Egypt and the Egyptians to Assyria. The Egyptians and Assyrians will worship together. In that day Israel will be the third, along with Egypt and Assyria, a blessing on the earth. The LORD Almighty will bless them, saying, 'Blessed be Egypt my people, Assyria my handiwork, and Israel my inheritance.'[11]

Nevertheless, as the Psalmist looked at his world, and as we look at the world in the twenty-first century, the overwhelming picture is one of powers that are in rebellion against God.

3. The rebellion (2:3)

In chapter 2 we saw that the essence of sin and evil is the refusal to accept that God is God. This is graphically expressed in the cry of the powers in verse 3:

> *'Let us break their chains,' they say,*
> *'and throw off their fetters.'*

'If there were gods,' declared the atheist Nietzsche, 'how could I endure not to be a god? Therefore there are no gods.' Though ignored in his own day (1844–1900), Nietzsche, with his violent antipathy to Christianity, has become a favourite guru of popular postmodernity. Our generation will not accept the true God because to do so would mean submission, being willing to take second place, to accept the authority of another, to cease to be gods ourselves. Each wants to be his or her own authority, to make up the rules, to write the metanarrative, to shape the morals, to be in control, to break the chains and throw off the fetters. Some gods, of course, are no threat to the divinization of the human individual. New Age gods make no demands; they are a power we can choose to plug into if it suits us and if it is to our advantage. But the real God can only be God; he alone can make the rules, determine what is true, shape the universe; if we accept him we have to abdicate our own thrones. This the powers will not do, so they gather all their

[10] For an illuminating discussion of God's relationship with the nations see W. Brueggemann, *Theology of the Old Testament* (Fortress, 1997), pp. 492–527.
[11] Isa. 19:23–25.

energies to cast God off his throne. The climax of their rebellion is seen in the non-battles of Revelation 16:13–16 and 20:7–9:

> Then I saw three evil spirits that looked like frogs; they came out of the mouth of the dragon, out of the mouth of the beast and out of the mouth of the false prophet. They are the spirits of demons performing miraculous signs, and they go out to the kings of the whole world, to gather them for the battle on the great day of God Almighty ... Then they gathered the kings together to the place that in Hebrew is called Armageddon...

> When the thousand years are over, Satan will be released from his prison and will go out to deceive the nations in the four corners of the earth – God and Magog – to gather them for battle. In number they are like the sand on the seashore. They marched across the breadth of the earth and surrounded the camp of God's people, the city he loves. But fire came down from heaven and devoured them.

4. God's response, 1: sovereignty (2:4)

> *The One enthroned in heaven laughs;*
> *the Lord scoffs at them.*

We have seen two responses of God to the sin and evil of the world, that of a broken heart and that of compassion and grace. The response described here does not contradict these; we need to view God's laughter and scoffing as directed against the plots and machinations of the powers rather than against the people and their rulers. The stress in the verse is on *The One enthroned in heaven* rather than on the laughter; the nations and rulers may seem to be in charge of the events on planet Earth; but in no way is that so. God is God, and he is seated firmly on the throne. The laughter is that of the ocean tide at the commands of King Canute to stop. As the passages in Revelation make clear, so far from trembling at the great onslaught of the powers of evil, God can smile at their paltriness and scatter them by a flick of his fingers.[12] When, as often happens, we lose sight of the power of God, the powers of evil soon terrify us with their threats and their assaults, but they never terrify God.[13]

[12] Rev. 20:9.

[13] 'It is only when we know the overwhelming power of God, which surpasses all works of man, that we achieve that inward superiority, fearlessness and serene confidence which is so graphically expressed in the magnificent picture of God who from his exalted throne smiles at the manikins and mocks at them'; A. Weiser, *The Psalms* (SCM, 1962), p. 112.

5. God's response, 2: anger (2:5–6)

Again, the *anger* and *wrath* of verse 5 are no uncontrolled emotion; they are the holy and beautiful opposition of God to all that is evil. Though he may smile at the paltriness of the powers' rebellion, in no way can he condone the evil and suffering that come from it; everything in him cries out against it and is determined to judge it and destroy it. There are two significant aspects of God's anger, according to this passage. The first is that it has a definite purpose, to rebuke and terrify the powers so that they will stop short in their tracks and will turn from their rebellion (5, 10–11). The second is that it is expressed by the statement, *'I have installed my King on Zion, my holy hill'* (6).

To us God's declaration that 'Jesus Christ is Lord' may sound in no way terrifying; but to those who have given their total energies to rejecting the lordship of God and of his Christ the words are the pronouncement of their doom.

6. God's response, 3: Christ (2:6–9)

So we come to God's greatest response to the rebellion of the powers and to the evil that is in the world:

> [6] *I have installed my King*
> *on Zion, my holy hill.*

With divine authority, this King states his sovereignty:

> [7] *I will proclaim the decree of the LORD:*
> *He said to me, 'You are my Son;*
> *today I have become your Father.*
> [8] *Ask of me,*
> *and I will make the nations your inheritance,*
> *the ends of the earth your possession.*
> [9] *You will rule them with an iron sceptre;*
> *you will dash them to pieces like pottery.'* [14]

---

[14] Scholars differ over just who is speaking in the different parts of the psalm. Craigie, for example, lists four speakers, the nations, the Lord, the King, and the psalmist; P. C. Craigie, *Psalms 1 – 50* (Word, 1983), p. 65. Eaton states that there is no need to assume changes of speaker; the King is speaking throughout in the third and first person; J. H. Eaton, *Kingship and the Psalms* (JSOT Press, 1986), p. 111. Whichever position is adopted, the meaning remains the same.

These verses make four claims about the King, which are fulfilled in the Christ, the Lord Jesus.

a. His kingship and lordship are authenticated by God (2:7)

The powers claim kingship and lordship; they seek to set themselves up as gods; but their claim is empty; they are not gods, and their kingship and lordship are at most fleeting. But Christ's kingship and lordship are by divine decree.[15] The burning questions for those who watched Jesus during his ministry were, 'By what authority are you doing these things? ... Who gave you this authority?'[16] For those with ears to hear, the answer was plain. 'This is my Son, whom I love; with him I am well pleased'; 'This is my Son, whom I love. Listen to him!'[17]

b. His kingship and lordship arise from who he is, the Son of God (2:7)

Earthly kings may have authority given to them for a time and then lose it; their kingship is a function rather than part of their essence. But Christ's authority is rooted in who he is. The New Testament writers do not seem to have felt the need to tie the word *today* (7) down to a specific historic occasion, with the implication that before that occasion Christ's sonship was in some way deficient. They were confident that Christ was eternally the Son,[18] and so were able to apply verse 7 to a number of occasions when God chose to manifest and express Christ's sonship: echoes of this verse thus appear in connection with the incarnation,[19] Christ's baptism,[20] the transfiguration,[21] the resurrection[22] and the ascension.[23] We can safely conclude that, in one way or another, on every occasion that Christ is revealed, he is declared by God to be his Son, and so to be the King and the Lord.

---

[15] 'The "decree" is a document, renewing God's covenant commitment to the dynasty of David. The content of the decree establishes the nature and authority of the newly crowned king'; Craigie, *Psalms 1 – 50*, p. 67. Weiser describes it as 'probably the legitimation by prophets and priests of the so-called "royal protocol"'; Weiser, *The Psalms*, p. 113.

[16] Matt. 21:23.
[17] Matt. 3:17; Mark 9:7.
[18] See, for example, the argument of Heb. 1.
[19] Luke 1:32.
[20] Matt. 3:17.
[21] Matt. 17:5.
[22] Acts 13:33; Rom. 1:4.
[23] Heb. 1:5.

c. His kingship and lordship guarantee the destruction of evil and the coming of the kingdom of God (2:8–9)

God is committed to destroying all that is evil and establishing his kingdom of righteousness and truth. The way he will do this is through the King, the Son. In the book of Revelation it is the Lamb who is able to open the scroll of God's purposes of power and grace and put them into operation.[24] Because Jesus is Lord, God's kingdom will come, and his will will be done on earth as in heaven. The nations and peoples to the ends of the earth will bow the knee; every tongue will confess that Jesus Christ is Lord, to the glory of God the Father.[25] Every evil power that persists in its rebellion against God will be broken; again, the contrast between the power and authority of Christ and the weakness and fragility of earthly powers is graphically expressed; earthly powers, for all their flaunting and vaunting, are as flimsy as a clay pot when confronted by the irresistible strength of Christ's *iron sceptre* (9).

d. His kingship and lordship call for submission (2:10–12)

The issue is not in doubt. Jesus Christ is Lord; his kingdom will come; the rebellion of the powers will be shattered; evil will be destroyed, and 'he will reign for ever and ever'.[26] So the psalm ends with a gospel invitation: turn from your rebellion and sin and evil; turn to Christ; be reconciled to God (10–12). The threats of destruction are not prophecies set in concrete; they are 'warnings' to motivate us to change our ways, to let God be God (10). The parallelism in verse 11 pictures the rebellious kings coming to *the* LORD (the name of God is used almost interchangeably with *the Son* [12]), both in fear and trembling at the greatness of his holiness and the awfulness of their sin, and also at the same time in worship and submission that are joyous.[27] Once willing to repent and *take refuge in him* (12), though expecting judgment and destruction, they find grace and joy and blessing in the presence of the great Lord and King.

---

[24] Rev. 5:1–5.
[25] Phil. 2:10–11.
[26] Rev. 11:15.
[27] 'Serve' (11), *'ābad*, covers both worship and service.

Interlude
Evil and suffering – and God

Psalm 2 has made it clear that the key element in God's response to evil is Christ. In Part 2 of this study we shall take up this point and explore it further as we look at the New Testament teaching about evil and suffering in relation to Jesus. But before we do so we need to summarize and review the main elements of our study so far, as we have looked at the relationship between God and evil and suffering.

God is good – wholly, perfectly good. He is light and in him is no darkness at all.[1] In the world as he made it there was no evil, and in the world that he will one day bring into being there will be no evil. All that he makes and all that he does is good.

The essence of evil is the refusal to accept God as God. All evil arises from the rejection of his lordship, disobedience to his word, and the setting up of other gods in his place. To reject God is to reject goodness and truth and beauty and wholeness, and so to embrace evil and falsehood and ugliness and brokenness. Evil spoils and destroys, perverts and corrupts the good things that God has made and given.

Suffering arises from evil. In a universe where evil is present, suffering is inevitable and universal. Not only do the perpetrators of evil suffer; their innocent victims suffer as well, and, most of all, God suffers. His heart is broken over his broken world. And because God suffers, those who are identified with him, his people, suffer too.

God is sovereign. Evil and suffering, horrific and mysterious though they may be to us, are in no way an insoluble problem, for God is still the sovereign King over all the universe and is continuing to work out his purposes of righteousness and grace in

---

[1] 1 John 1:5.

the world, not so much despite the activities of the powers of evil as actually using them, as in the case of the cross, to bring about his great purposes of good.

The whole, picture. How this can be, how evil can be overwhelmed by good, remains a mystery to us, but we can be confident that it is not so to God, and that when we see the whole picture we will acknowledge his great wisdom and righteousness. Indeed, it is only by keeping the whole-picture perspective and especially the Bible's future focus that we shall be able to cope with the evil and suffering in the world in which we live. At the end of the age, when all the ways of God have been made clear, everyone will see and acknowledge the justice and rightness of all that God has done.

The eradication of evil. God is committed to purging his creation of all evil, and so to destroying all evil. God and evil cannot ultimately coexist; since God is God and eternally will be God, every effort to reject him as God must fail; every act of rebellion must be put down. Confronted with an evil world, God's obvious and righteous reaction would be to destroy it forthwith. This is what he did in the flood, bringing to an end a totally evil world. But after the flood he has chosen a different path, a longer road, involving the calling out of a people to live his goodness and holiness in an evil world, and choosing to take himself the awesome steps that would ultimately redeem and transform it.

Purposes of grace. Because God is sovereign, all history, good or bad, is purposeful; our universe is not ruled by chance or meaninglessness or chaos or the powers of evil. In particular, God is committed to bringing his people safely through all evil and suffering and using even the darkest experiences to show his glory and to further his purposes of grace.

Love and punishment. God not only allows men and women to go through suffering as a result of the evil that is in the world; on occasion, perhaps as a last resort, he will choose to inflict suffering as a punishment; but he only ever does this in compassion and love and grace and with a view to final good.

The ultimate answer. God's reaction to the damage done by sin and evil to his creation includes both sorrow and anger; but his power and wisdom are such that he can deride all attempts to cast him off the throne of the universe; the powers of evil may rage for a time, but their days are numbered; God has his ultimate answer ready: the Lord Jesus Christ.

Part 2
Evil and suffering – and Jesus

Luke 4:14–30
5. The coming of God

1. Morning worship at Nazareth (4:14–30)

The atmosphere in the synagogue was tense.[1] The place was crammed to overflowing. They all knew he would be there, and that he would have something to say. But whereas, when Jesus sat down to speak in Capernaum and all the other towns and villages of Galilee, his audiences praised his every word (Luke 4:15), here in Nazareth things were far less predictable. Some, doubtless, believed in him; others may have been uncertain; but others already had their minds made up: however impressive he may be, in no way could Joseph's boy be someone specially sent by God (22).

Jesus knew. He had to choose. He could cool it, tone down his claims, withdraw. Or he could face the rejection and wrath of his own people by making it perfectly clear who he was and why he had come.

He stood up to read from the scroll of Isaiah. Precisely what passage he read we do not know, but we can safely assume that it was considerably longer than the short section Luke quotes. Since Luke's quotation includes a phrase from Isaiah 58:6 as well as the opening verses of Isaiah 61, it seems very likely that Jesus read several chapters from that part of Isaiah, probably climaxing in chapter 61. However much he read, the context of the verses Luke specifically quotes would have made them particularly significant for the crowd in the synagogue at Nazareth, and for us as we explore the response of God to suffering and evil.

Like those in the synagogue at Nazareth, the people to whom the last few chapters of Isaiah were addressed believed in God but did not have much experience of him. For the most part, that did not worry them; they were reasonably happy as they were. But God

---

[1] This the 'oldest known account of a synagogue service'; I. H. Marshall, *The Gospel of Luke* (Paternoster, 1978), p. 181.

was not happy. He was profoundly concerned for at least two reasons: the prevalence of evil in the land, and the absence of any possibility of anyone being able to deal with it.

> The LORD looked and was displeased
>> that there was no justice.
> He saw that there was no-one,
>> he was appalled that there was no-one to intervene.[2]

It was not that God had chosen to ignore his people; the problem was not with him; it was with them.

> Surely the arm of the LORD is not too short to save,
>> nor his ear too dull to hear.
> But your iniquities have separated
>> you from your God;
> your sins have hidden his face from you,
>> so that he will not hear.[3]

In graphic passages the prophet describes the many evils rampant among the people, from sorcery, adultery, prostitution, lust, sexual immorality and idolatry (chapter 57) though religious hypocrisy (chapter 58) to all forms of injustice and unrighteousness (chapter 59). Such evil appalled God and was the reason for his seeming remoteness. But it did not thwart his purposes of mercy and grace. His arm was still powerful; since there was no-one else capable of dealing with the mess that evil had made of the world, he would do it himself.

> So his own arm worked salvation for him,
>> and his own righteousness sustained him.
> He put on righteousness as his breastplate,
>> and the helmet of salvation on his head;
> he put on the garments of vengeance
>> and wrapped himself in zeal as in a cloak...
> 'The Redeemer will come to Zion,
>> to those in Jacob who repent of their sins,'
>>> declares the LORD...

> 'Arise, shine, for your light has come,
>> and the glory of the LORD rises upon you.

[2] Isa. 59:15–16.
[3] Isa. 59:1–2.

> See, darkness covers the earth
>> and thick darkness is over the peoples
> but the LORD rises upon you
>> and his glory appears over you.
> Nations will come to your light,
>> and kings to the brightness of your dawn.'[4]

God will come; in glory and grace he will come to judge and to redeem, to save and to make righteous.

> Then you will know that I, the LORD, am your Saviour,
>> your Redeemer, the Mighty One of Jacob...
> I will make peace your governor
>> and righteousness your ruler.
> No longer will violence be heard in your land,
>> nor ruin or destruction within your borders,
> but you will call your walls Salvation
>> and your gates Praise...
> the LORD will be your everlasting light,
>> and your days of sorrow will end.[5]

These were the promises that climaxed in the verses recorded by Luke. *Today*, said Jesus, *this scripture is fulfilled in your hearing* (Luke 4:21). Today God has come. When there was no other to deal with evil, to set right the wrongs, to be the Saviour and the Redeemer, God himself in Jesus has stepped forward to be the answer.

It was too much for the people of Nazareth. Sensing the rising mood of his hearers, Jesus, so far from tempering his claims, continued to insist that he was sent from God, comparable to Elijah and Elisha. In response to his audience's taunting demand for miracles at Nazareth such as he was reputed to have done at Capernaum, he pointed out that Elijah and Elisha's most spectacular miracles were done for Gentile foreigners (24–27). Perhaps it was the mention of the offer of grace to the Gentiles that finally sparked the furious reaction that very nearly killed Jesus here at the start of his ministry (28–30).

The events on that Sabbath in Nazareth provide a pattern for the whole of his ministry: eager crowds with their fascination with miracles, a tenacious commitment by Jesus to remain faithful to the purposes for which he had come, and the ultimate inevitable clash

---

[4] Isa. 59:17, 20, 60:1–3.
[5] Isa. 60:16–18, 20.

which took him to the cross. Equally, the passage Jesus chose to quote from Isaiah in effect became the basis on which his ministry was built. For those with ears to hear, it declared both who he was and what he had come to bring.

2. Who he was (4:18–21)

Jesus, the one who came, was more than *Joseph's son* (22), more even than one of the prophets. He was the one on whom rested *the Spirit of the Lord* (18). On the day the anointing of the Spirit had come, at his baptism, the voice of God himself spoke those words that picked up Psalm 2:7, 'You are my Son, whom I love; with you I am well pleased.'[6] Here is God himself coming in the second person of the Trinity to work salvation, clothing himself in righteousness and salvation and vengeance and zeal, coming to Zion, rising upon his people, showing his glory. The one who has come to deal with the evil of the world is God himself.

Jesus came 'to proclaim the year of the LORD's favour and the day of vengeance of our God'.[7] Though Luke omits the phrase 'the day of vengeance of our God', we are not to conclude from this that judgment upon sin was specifically excluded from the ministry of Jesus. The Old Testament prophecies certainly anticipated that the coming of the Lord would be both wonderful for those who would welcome him and terrifying for those who hated him;[8] the coming of the light would show up and put to flight the evils of the darkness, even though the total destruction of evil would be delayed until the final Day of the Lord. But Luke certainly puts the stress on the favour and grace of Christ's ministry, the coming of God to bless rather than to destroy. In Christ God comes primarily as Saviour.

3. What he came to bring (4:18–19)

The emphasis of the ministry of Jesus, as outlined in Luke 4:18–19, was on people, not issues. Though in many senses the two cannot be separated, it is worth noting that where we might tend to think in terms of abstracts, Jesus' focus was on people. We talk about

---

[6] Luke 3:22. See also John 1:32–34, where John the Baptist adds his testimony that 'this is the Son of God'.

[7] Isa. 61:2. There may be echoes of the year of Jubilee here (Lev. 25:8–55); more certainly there is reference back to Isa. 49:8 and the promise of restoration arising from the ministry of the Servant of the Lord.

[8] See, for example, Amos 9:11–15; 5:18–20.

making poverty history or eliminating oppression; Jesus spoke of bringing good news to poor people, and giving freedom to those who are oppressed.

As he ministered in Galilee and Judea and Samaria, Jesus encountered all sorts of people, rich and poor, healthy and ill, successful and broken, good and bad. Every one of them, in one way or another, had first-hand acquaintance with evil and suffering and their results in their lives and the lives of others. To each of them the coming of God in Jesus brought something radical, a new opportunity, a different way of living.

a. For the poor, good news (4:18)

Luke, more than any of the Gospels, contains passages which warn against the dangers and evils of riches.[9] Most of these are unique to Luke; where other Gospels have parallel passages, Luke heightens their impact, as in his version of Matthew's 'Blessed are the poor in spirit', where Luke writes simply, 'Blessed are you poor.'[10] Most commentators point out that the concept of 'the poor' in Luke and elsewhere in the Old and New Testaments has a religious as well as an economic significance. 'The poor' are those who are economically or socially oppressed because of their faithfulness to God.[11] Jesus himself chose to be poor in order to fulfil God's purposes.[12] Most Christians in the first century knew very well what it was to be poor, not only because many of them came from the lower social classes, but also because any Christians who did have money were likely to lose it through prejudice and persecution. Though there can be no doubt that Christians must be committed to working to eliminate poverty throughout the world, it seems very unlikely that the 'good news' in this passage includes a promise of material prosperity for the poor. Rather, the good news that Jesus brings to the poor is that 'the kingdom of God' is theirs.[13] Though economically and socially poor, and destined to remain so, they have all the riches of the kingdom of heaven.

---

[9] Luke 1:53; 6:20, 24–25; 7:22; 12:13–21; 12:33–34; 14:33; 16:19–31.

[10] Matt. 5:3; Luke 6:20.

[11] The 'poor' are 'the people who are most in need of divine help and who wait upon God to hear his word'; Marshall, *The Gospel of Luke*, p. 183. 'Those of low status ... diminished honor ... those who are for any of a number of socio-religious reasons relegated to positions outside the boundaries of God's people'; J. B. Green, *The Gospel of Luke* (Eerdmans, 1997), p. 211.

[12] 2 Cor. 8:9.

[13] Luke 6:20.

b. For the broken, healing

Luke does not specifically quote Isaiah's phrase about binding up the broken-hearted,[14] but there can be no doubt that Christ had a special ministry to those who were hurting inwardly, who mourned and grieved and despaired.[15] The specific feel of 'broken-hearted' is 'crushed in spirit', 'disheartened'; here are people who not only suffer but are being crushed and destroyed by their sufferings; it is to these God comes, the God who lives in a 'high and holy place, but also with him who is contrite and lowly in spirit, to revive the spirit of the lowly, and to revive the heart of the contrite'.[16] Again, the ministry Jesus brings does not so much take away the circumstances that bring suffering or sorrow or mourning as reverse their destructive influence, bringing 'a crown of beauty instead of ashes, the oil of gladness instead of mourning, and a garment of praise instead of a spirit of despair',[17] so that, as Paul put it, they could 'delight' even in their sufferings.[18]

c. For the prisoners, freedom (4:18)

Are we to interpret 'freedom for the prisoners' literally or metaphorically? In chapter 7 Luke records how John the Baptist, now in prison, sent to Jesus with questions about who he was. As in Luke 4, Jesus used prophetic passages in Isaiah to repeat his claim that he was the promised one.[19] But though he quotes from Isaiah 61:1 about the good news being preached to the poor, he does not mention to John freedom for prisoners. In fact, John never was freed. At least part, then, if not all of the meaning of the promise in Luke 4 of freedom for prisoners is to be taken metaphorically.

d. For the blind, sight (4:18)

Jesus' ministry included both the giving of sight to those who were literally blind, and the bringing of light to those who were in 'darkness' and 'thick darkness'.[20] The light in particular is the light of God, of his glory and his presence.[21] While the Gospel writers

---

[14] Isa. 61:1.
[15] Isa. 61:2–3.
[16] Isa. 57:15.
[17] Isa. 61:3.
[18] 2 Cor. 12:10.
[19] Luke 7:22; see Isa. 29:18–19; 35:5–6.
[20] Isa. 60:1–2.
[21] Isa. 60:19–20.

clearly differentiated between conditions such as 'disease', sicknesses', 'evil spirits' and blindness,[22] they were not generally as concerned as we are to distinguish between 'literal' and 'metaphorical' illness and healing. The coming of the kingdom and the presence of the King meant 'power' and 'healing' for them all.[23] The early church's focus was the power and the healing, not an analysis of the disease.[24]

e. For the oppressed, release (4:18)

Again, this promise was fulfilled in a range of ways in the ministry of Jesus.[25] The woman who had been bound by Satan for eighteen long years was released through physical healing;[26] the rejects of society, from lepers to prostitutes, were accepted and welcomed into the kingdom. But, equally, though he lived among a politically oppressed people, right to the end Jesus insisted that he had not come to cast off the Roman yoke and 'restore the kingdom to Israel'.[27]

f. For everyone, transformation, restoration and hope[28]

Throughout the section of Isaiah from which Luke quoted the picture is one of the presence of God transforming every situation for those who welcome and receive him. In place of brokenness and despair he will bring hope and praise; in place of injustice and sin he brings righteousness and goodness; in place of disgrace and

---

[22] For example Luke 7:21.

[23] Luke 6:19. For a thorough study of the relationship between demonic-inspired conditions and physical illness in the New Testament see J. C. Thomas, *The Devil, Disease and Deliverance: Origins of Illness in New Testament Thought* (Sheffield Academic Press, 1998). Thomas, a Pentecostal scholar, stresses the variety in the New Testament teaching: some illnesses are the result of sin, others are not; illness can come from God or from demons or from Satan himself; God shows his power both by healing and by giving grace to suffer. Luke in particular blurs the lines between illness and demonic activity (p. 227).

[24] 'The early church did not seek to formulate a theory of illness; instead it healed the sick. It did not attempt to explain how the demonic could exist in a good world made by a good God; instead they cast out demons'; W. Wink, *Engaging the Powers* (Fortress Press, 1992), p. 316.

[25] Green specifies three elements: first, forgiveness, that is release from sins; second, setting free from the 'binding power of Satan ... freedom from both diabolic and social restrictions'; third, release from debts, the proclamation of Jubilee: 'the announcement of the eschatological epoch of salvation, the time of God's gracious visitation, with Jesus himself presented as its anointed herald' (Green, *The Gospel of Luke*, p. 212).

[26] Luke 13:16.

[27] Acts 1:6.

[28] Isa. 61:3–11.

desolation he gives healing and restoration. To all he brings hope: a new beginning, a new life with God at the centre, enriched by his presence, secure in his grace and goodness, and kept by his power.

4. What his coming demanded (4:22–30)

There is a staggering contrast between Luke 4:22 and 4:28: *All spoke well of him ... All the people in the synagogue were furious* – furious enough to kill him. The change, in just a few minutes, was caused by Jesus' teaching that those who benefited from the ministry of Elijah and Elisha, the widow and the leper, were outsiders, Gentiles; what is more, God chose to bypass the widows and lepers of Israel in order to minister to them. The implication was clear. God was indeed coming to bring good news and healing and freedom and hope. But these things were not the privilege of the favoured few. Already the words specifically quoted by Luke had stressed that it was the poor and hurting rather than the rich and comfortable to whom God was coming; now the point is made all the more sharply with the observation that God's concern for widows and lepers, two further categories of the poor and hurting, reached out and showed itself to those outside the pale of God's favoured people.

It was too much for the people of Nazareth. For us it is not a problem; most of us are, after all, the Gentiles he is appearing to favour, even if we are not particularly poor and hurting. But the underlying point is as relevant for us as it was for the people of Nazareth. They had specific and clear ideas of how God should deal with the evils of their world. There were ill people among them; God came to bring healing; therefore he should heal them. There were hurting people among them; God came to bring blessing; therefore he should bless them. On a broader scale, the Jewish nation was suffering oppression; God came to release the oppressed; therefore he must release the Jewish nation from Roman domination.

But their clear and specific ideas were wrong. It was not that God had no concern for widows and lepers in Israel; in the event Jewish widows and lepers and Gentile widows and lepers were alike blessed by the ministry of Jesus. But in his response to the evils of the world God was not going to be limited by the ideas and expectations of the people of Nazareth. He was coming to bring salvation and righteousness to the earth, and he would bring it his way. The agenda and method were his to decide. Not even the 'Never, Lord' of Peter[29] could be allowed to deflect him from his chosen way.

[29] Matt. 16:22.

The point is one we need to bear in mind constantly. God works to his own agenda and according to his own chosen method. His thoughts and his ways do not have to conform to our thoughts and ways. We see evil and suffering around us and in the world at large, and we readily decide what God ought to do about them. When he fails to do what we expect, we begin to question his wisdom or sovereignty or love. We are at a loss to explain why he does not do the thing that seems so obvious to us.

It is no problem for us to look back and see where the people of Nazareth went wrong; their understanding of God's ways was far too narrow, and far too dominated by their own way of seeing things. They needed a large dose of humility, of the willingness to let God be God and to do things his way, even though it ran counter to their ideas. However good their logic, however convincing their arguments, they had to give way and submit their ideas to those of God.

Though we can see the need for humility and submission in the thinking of others, we still find it hard to accept it for ourselves. Indeed, remnants of Enlightenment humanism still make us believe that it is an intellectual virtue to demand that God conform to our way of seeing things, that he fit into our horizon and obey the rules of our personal logics. But the real God is much too big for that. In no way will he fit into our little boxes, however neat they may be. The coming of God demands nothing less than the surrender of our claim to know the answers, the giving up of our right to decide the way the problems are going to be solved, and the willingness to say, 'Not my will, but yours be done.'[30]

The Bible states that God has come in Jesus to deal with the evil and suffering of the world. Because God is God, the impact of his coming is inevitably great. Light comes into darkness, life to the dead, transformation to every situation. Perhaps because that impact is so great and so Godlike, and certainly because our horizons and understanding are so limited, God's way of working will often be very different from what we expect. In particular, he may choose not to remove evil and suffering, but instead to allow it, knowing that this is the pathway to the fulfilment of his wise purposes, or that their removal would itself give rise to greater evil.[31]

In our day the impact of the fact that 'God has come' seems much smaller than during Jesus' earthly ministry, or, indeed, during the time of the New Testament church. We are less ready to let the truths of the gospel and the power of the Holy Spirit transform

[30] Luke 22:42.
[31] The suggestion that Jesus should avoid the suffering of the cross was seen by him as Satanic (Matt. 16:23).

our attitude to our own personal sin or to the evils of the world or to the suffering we have to bear. Childlike trust in the wisdom of God's purposes and ways tends to be overwhelmed by our culture of unbelief and cynicism; the willingness to suffer and even rejoice in sufferings so that God may be glorified through them[32] has been replaced by the 'I have a right to be happy' mentality of our age. As a result, we have not just a watered-down concept of who God is and of his ways; we also have a watered-down experience of his presence among us, much to our loss.

[32] Rom. 5:3; Phil. 1:20.

1 John 3:15
6. The incarnate God

If we are children of God, says John, we should be like our Father. One day he will 'appear', and when he does *we shall be like him, for we shall see him as he is. Everyone who has this hope in him purifies himself, just as he is pure* (1 John 2:28 – 3:3). Precisely who the 'he' is who will 'appear' John does not specify. Grammar and context would demand that it is the Father, but theology would indicate that it is Christ. It is interesting and significant that John can virtually merge the two;[1] the Father and the Son are one. Two verses later, using the same verb, John speaks of God's first 'appearing' in Christ: *But you know that he appeared so that he might take away our sins. And in him is no sin* (5). Then, in verse 8, he makes a parallel statement, again using the same verb: *The reason the Son of God appeared was to destroy the devil's work.* Our God is the God who 'appears',[2] who manifests his presence, who comes, whether in the incarnation or at the end of the age; and when he comes, says John, he comes as the God who is pure, who takes away sin, and who destroys the devil's work.

1. He did no evil (3:5)

No-one knew Jesus better than John. For three years and more he followed him and watched him. He saw him in every sort of situation, including his weak moments, when weary or caught off his guard. He saw how he responded to pressure, criticism and violence. Like everyone who encountered him, he struggled with the implications of who he was and how he lived. But his verdict

---

[1] Note that a similar merging is seen in Rev. 11:15, where 'he' refers equally to 'our Lord' and to 'his Christ', and in Rev. 22:3, where God and the Lamb are together referred to as 'him'.

[2] The Greek verb is *phainomai*, which gives us the word 'theophany'.

was unequivocal. Jesus was sinless: *in him is no sin*. John's verdict is confirmed by another who was very close to him, Peter, who used the words of Isaiah 53:9 to express his sinlessness: 'He committed no sin, and no deceit was found in his mouth.'[3] The incarnate Son of God did no evil.

That is not to say he did not do things that to some may have seemed evil. He did not live on a desert island; he lived in the real world and interacted with all the complex situations that life in the real world brings. Inevitably, many of the issues he had to face were far from straightforward; many of his actions would have seemed less than perfect to some of those around. He upset people.[4] He disappointed his friends and angered his enemies.[5] He used a whip on the animals in the Temple and caused chaos for the traders and money-changers.[6] He said harsh things about his own family and even harsher things about the religious rulers.[7] He refused to answer the pleas of a suffering mother;[8] he caused a fig tree to wither.[9] John and Peter witnessed all these incidents and heard all the criticisms. And yet they were still quite sure that Jesus never did evil.

Years ago I tried sea fishing. For the most part I enjoyed it, sitting in the boat and waiting for a tug at the line. But what I did not enjoy was watching the fish that I had caught gasping for breath in the bottom of the boat. That, I felt, was cruelty to dumb animals. So I decided that fishing was not for me, although, inconsistently, I continued to eat fish that other people had caught. Jesus was nowhere near as squeamish. Both at the beginning and at the end of his ministry he was responsible for the landing of a huge haul of fish.[10] So, though the Bible is quite clear that some forms of maltreatment of animals is wrong and so evil,[11] killing for food is not. Similarly, though in some circumstances it would be evil to refuse to help a desperate mother, on that occasion it was not. Though it may be wrong for you or me to smash up the local supermarket, for Jesus to purge his Father's house was not. Causing a fig tree to wither was the expression of righteous judgment on the people of God who had failed to produce the fruit that God required. Doing things that upset and angered people was all part of his Father's perfect will.

[3] 1 Pet. 2:22.
[4] Matt. 13:57.
[5] John 6:66; 9:28–29.
[6] John 2:14–16.
[7] Matt. 3:32–35; 23:13–36.
[8] Matt. 15:22–26.
[9] Mark 11:21.
[10] Luke 5:4–7; John 21:6.
[11] Deut. 22:4; 25:4; Prov. 12:10.

Here, as in all our dealings with the Bible, we have to be ready to let our concepts of what is right and wrong, or good and evil, be shaped by what we read and what we see in Christ, rather than trying to reshape reality by imposing our preconceived ideas. When Christ appeared he lived a sinless life.

2. He suffered evil

Even before he was made man, God was no stranger to suffering. We have already seen the grief he experienced when his heart was broken by the evil of the world.[12] If, as Jesus stated, God rejoices over each individual sinner who repents, then it would surely follow that he sorrows over each individual sinner who has not yet repented.[13] If we feel pain at the evils of a fallen world, how much more must the One in whose image we are made feel pain at what the enemy has done.[14]

a. Choosing to suffer

So suffering was no new experience for the incarnate God. But perhaps there were two aspects to his suffering that were new, or, at the least, particularly significant. The first is the element of deliberate choice. If I am injured in a road accident I will suffer pain and have to spend time in hospital. If I choose to give one of my kidneys for someone else I will similarly have to spend time in hospital and suffer pain. In the first case I have no option but to suffer; in the second case I choose to suffer. When the sin of the world causes God pain, there is a sense in which he does not choose to suffer; suffering is forced upon him by the combination of our sin and his character. But in his earthly ministry, and especially in his death, God incarnate chose to suffer, to take on more suffering than he had previously borne. Though it would be untrue to say that during his earthly life Jesus specifically courted suffering and evil in themselves, it is clear that he deliberately put himself into situations where he would suffer and encounter evil. He was born into poverty and rejection rather than into wealth and comfort; he refused the path of popularity and acclaim.[15] He chose to be an outsider, to belong to an oppressed nation, to mix with outcasts and

---

[12] Gen. 6:6.

[13] Luke 15:7. 'Rejoicing in heaven' in this passage is almost certainly a reverent periphrasis for 'rejoicing by God', though in keeping with the context the joy of God is shared with his 'friends and neighbours' round his throne.

[14] Matt. 13:28.

[15] Luke 4:12; Mark 1:36–39, 44.

sinners, to be harassed and eventually destroyed by his enemies. In no way did he seek to avoid evil; rather, he chose to walk the way of suffering, darkness and pain. He did not have to do it; he deliberately chose to bear our griefs and carry our sorrows, and, supremely, to take upon himself the sin of the world.

Perhaps we should not make too much of the contrast between God choosing to suffer in Christ and God suffering as a result of the sin of the world. Though there was a special element of choice in God coming in Christ to suffer and die, in an ultimate sense God also chose to carry the pain of seeing a world spoilt by sin and evil, since he knew at the moment when he created it that it would be marred by evil, and thus he knew the pain it would bring him. As a result of this knowledge he could, as far as we can understand, have chosen not to create the world at all, or to create it such that evil would not be able to mar it. But he chose to create it as it is, and so, in that sense, chose to suffer the pain of its evil.

b. Suffering as a man

A second aspect of suffering that was new when God became incarnate in Christ was that the Son of God in his life and ministry suffered, not just as God, but as man as well. The writer to the Hebrews stresses in two passages that 'Jesus, the Son of God', was 'tempted in every way, just as we are', and so is able to 'sympathise with our weakness', since he has been 'made like his brothers in every way', so that he 'shared in their humanity' and 'himself suffered' as they do.[16] The word he uses for 'tempted' includes more than just moral temptations to do evil; it could well be translated 'tested' or 'tried', and it means that Jesus was subject to all the pressures and stresses and pains that are the experience of the human race. Not just on the cross but throughout his life he knew at first hand what it was to suffer evil.[17] The 'man of sorrows' who was 'acquainted with grief'[18] was a refugee in Egypt, and knew the pain of losing his earthly father and being misunderstood and rejected by his mother and brothers. He struggled with demonic temptation; he had nowhere to lay his head. He was criticized and maligned. His friends were fickle, his enemies relentless in their attacks. He knew weariness and hunger, sorrow and tears. Well

---

[16] Heb. 4:14–15; 2:14–18.

[17] To say that Jesus faced all the evils we face need not imply that his experience was identical to what ours would be in the same situation. He faced death by drowning in the storm without the panic the disciples felt; conversely, he felt the awfulness of Israel's rejection of its God with an intensity the disciples never knew.

[18] Isa. 53:3.

before Gethsemane and Calvary, he tasted the bitterness and darkness of evil.

How did he react? However powerless we may be to prevent bad things happening to us, how we react when they do happen is still largely our responsibility. We do not have to respond to anger with anger, or to injustice with resentment; we can choose whether to respond to evil with evil, or to counter it with good.[19] We can respond to anger with grace, or to injustice with mercy. In every situation of encounter with evil Jesus responded 'without sin'.[20] Faced with temptation, he stood firm on the word of God.[21] When in danger, he trusted his Father.[22] When criticized and attacked, he responded with grace and wisdom. Despite poverty and rejection, he showed no signs of self-pity or resentment.

c. The impact of evil

Jesus was fully human, and he knew the power of evil. He felt the pain. He knew the sadness. His tears as he wept over Jerusalem or at the grave of Lazarus were real. Though he knew that the destruction of Jerusalem was part of the holy and righteous purposes of God, and that Lazarus was about to be raised from the dead, he still knew the pain of sorrow and grief. We can surmise that in many ways he felt the awfulness and hurt of evil much more than we do. Most if not all of us have built up defences that in some ways shield us against the raw impact of evil; we have seen so much injustice and suffering and pain we have become hardened to it. It would seem unlikely that Jesus had such self-protection. Quite apart from the times when he openly wept at the presence of evil and suffering, there are occasions when the Gospel writers speak of his being 'deeply distressed' or 'deeply moved in his spirit and troubled'.[23] Others could look on comparatively unmoved, but the holy Son of God felt the impact of evil and sin very deeply. But though evil had power over him, it did not master or control him. In him was a greater power. In the face of evil he responded with good.

3. He highlighted the central feature of evil (3:2–15)

Cain, says John, *belonged to the evil one and murdered his brother. And why did he murder him? Because his own actions were evil and*

---

[19] Rom. 12:21.
[20] Heb. 4:15.
[21] Matt. 4:1–11.
[22] Matt. 8:24–26.
[23] Mark 3:5; John 11:33.

his brother's were righteous (12). The phrase *Cain belonged to the evil one* is literally 'Cain was from the evil one' and the NEB justifiably translates it, 'was a child of the evil one'. It is in sharp contrast to the wealth of phrases John uses in this passage about his readers, who are *born of* God (2:29; 3:9), *children of God* (3:1, 2, 10), *like* God (3:2), living in God (3:6), seeing and knowing God (3:6) and indwelt by *God's seed* (3:9). The argument of the passage is simple: either we are children of God or we are children of the evil one. If we are children of God, our lives will be holy as he is holy. If we are children of the evil one, our lives will be evil. John, of course, was well aware that in practice this simple logic was not always worked out in the lives of his readers. Until the day comes when God in Christ appears and we are finally and totally *like him* (3:2), the hangovers of our former allegiance to the evil one will keep on appearing; we will need to keep confessing our sin and receiving God's forgiveness.[24] But, fundamentally, the child of God has a relationship with evil that is radically different from that of the person who is not a child of God. Once we are born of God, living in him, with his life in us, we cannot have an ongoing relationship with evil; we cannot keep on sinning or continue in sin (3:6).[25] The wellspring of our lives will be the nature of the one who is in us; we will purify ourselves just as he is pure (3:3). But those who have no relationship with God will demonstrate by their evil deeds that they are of the evil one.

John's teaching here is rooted in the teaching of Jesus during his ministry. More than any Gospel writer, John highlighted the violent clash in the ministry of Jesus between light and darkness, between Jesus as the embodiment of the holy God and those who opposed him as the embodiment of the evil one. As Cain killed his brother because Cain was intrinsically evil, and Abel was accepted and so made holy by God, so the Jewish leaders rejected and killed Jesus because he was the holy one, and they were from their father, the devil.[26] Equally, the followers of Jesus were to expect hatred and rejection from those in 'the world', since those in the world do not know the one who sent him.[27] 'If I had not come and spoken to them,' said Jesus, 'they would not be guilty of sin. Now, however, they have no excuse for their sin. He who hates me hates my Father as well ... They will put you out of the synagogue; in fact, a time is coming when anyone who kills you will think he is offering a

---

[24] 1 John 1:8–10.
[25] The Greek of verse 6 lacks words for 'keep on' and 'continue', but their force is implied in John's use of the present tense *hamartanei* and *hamartanōn*.
[26] John 8:37–38, 41, 44.
[27] John 15:18–21.

service to God. They will do such things because they have not known the Father or me.'[28]

Our natural tendency when seeking to understand what evil is is to seek a definition that has us personally or the human race at its heart.[29] Evil, we tend to feel, is what hurts us. Evil is what threatens the quality of life of a human individual or group. Evil is something that brings suffering or death to human beings. We might broaden our horizon and define evil in terms of the well-being of planet Earth, but even then our judgment of what furthers the well-being of planet Earth tends to be very human-centred. When we list threatened species that we are concerned to preserve we rightly include the giant panda, but pointedly exclude the MRSA bacterium. The Bible knows no such anthropocentrism. Though it never attempts the kind of dictionary definition of evil that we would like to find, its foundational assumption, as seen here in the teaching of Jesus and of John, is that we can understand what evil is only if we define it, not in terms relative to ourselves, but in terms relative to God. The central feature of evil is the rejection of God, particularly as he has come to us in Christ. The devil is evil because he rebelled against God. We are evil if we choose to reject God and so become 'of the devil' rather than 'of God'. Similarly, a deed or an event is evil if it is contrary to the nature of God and so 'of the devil'.

At this point we need to mention another aspect in which our definitions of evil differ from the understanding of the nature of evil in the Bible. Philosophers have tended to draw a firm line between moral evil and physical or natural evil. Moral evils arise in the context of moral beings, physical evil from non-moral sources. Greed and prejudice and hatred are moral evils because they are evil attitudes or stances adopted by moral beings; poverty, discrimination and oppression are moral evils because they result from such evil attitudes or stances. But an earthquake or a cancer or a plague does not arise from a moral being; they are 'natural' or 'physical', so the evil that they are and that they cause is to be seen as distinct from moral evil.

Though the Bible writers would have been well aware of the distinction between a moral act and a physical act, the biblical approach to evil does not divide it into two clear categories. There is a simple reason for this: the Bible does not accept our Enlightenment

---

[28] John 15:22–23; 16:2–3.

[29] 'The basic reference of good, as a notion required by the human mind, in its interaction with its environment, is to that which we like, welcome, desire, seek to gain or to preserve, whilst bad refers to that which we dislike, fear, resist, shun and to which we are accordingly averse. As Hobbes said, "Every man, for his own part, calleth that which pleaseth, and is delightful to him, good; and that evil which displeaseth him"'; J. Hick, *Evil and the God of Love* (Collins, 1968), p. 12.

concept that the world functions as a non-moral machine. 'Natural' and 'physical' events, according to the Bible, are not non-moral, since all that happens in the universe is the result of action by moral beings, that is, to use the language of the section above, by God or the devil or their agents. An earthquake or a storm is a moral act, since God or the devil causes it, or, at the least, is morally responsible for it.[30]

The Bible's approach, which defines evil not in terms of its impact on the human race but in terms of the nature of God and the rebellion of Satan, together with the consequent merging of moral and physical evil, has several implications which we shall be looking at in chapters 12 and 13. For our purposes in this chapter, as we explore the relationship between the incarnate Son of God and evil, we need to accept that for Jesus, and so for John, the essence of evil was the rejection of God, the refusal to accept his lordship and the breaking of relationship with him. Thus, conversely, the essence of good is God himself, the acceptance of his lordship, and life in relationship with him.

4. He confronted evil (3:8)

The appearing of the holy God in a world of evil was inevitably confrontational. *The reason the Son of God appeared was to destroy the devil's work.* It was an assault on the strongholds of the powers of evil.[31] 'The Lord you are seeking will come to his temple,' said Malachi. 'But who can endure the day of his coming? Who can stand when he appears? For he will be like a refiner's fire.'[32] John describes the coming of the Messiah to his Jerusalem Temple right at the start of Jesus' ministry.[33] This is none other than the Lord who

---

[30] It is noticeable that the distinction between moral and physical evil is often blurred even in secular thought. When the tsunami of December 2004 struck, it was quickly pointed out that many of the deaths could have been prevented had an early-warning system been used; no such system was in place because the vulnerable countries were too poor to set one up, so, in a sense, those who were responsible for the unfair distribution of the world's resources and technology were morally responsible for the deaths.

[31] Mark 3:27; Matt. 16:18.

[32] Mal. 3:1, 2.

[33] John 2:13–17. Westcott comments: 'The first step in Messiah's work was the abolition of the corruptions which the selfishness of a dominant and faithless hierarchy had introduced into the divine service'; B. F. Westcott, *The Gospel according to St John* (James Clarke, 1958), p. 40. The assumption that John's account of the cleansing of the Temple at the start of Jesus' ministry must be unhistorical because the Synoptics describe a similar cleansing at the close of his ministry is unconvincing; there is no reason why there could not have been two cleansings, and the prophetic symbolism of the cleansing of the Temple both at the start and at the close of his ministry is particularly powerful.

is coming, and he is coming to his Temple in holiness and so in judgment on all that is unholy. The cleansing of the Temple, in John, marks the beginning of the confrontation with 'the Jews'[34] which continues as a key motif of the Gospel and climaxes in the crucifixion; it prefigures the ultimate judgment of God on Jerusalem and its temple in AD 70. The heart of Christ's confrontation was 'zeal' for his 'Father's house', which Westcott describes as 'the burning jealousy for the holiness of the house of God, and so for the holiness of the people who were bound by service to it, as well as for the honour of God himself'.[35]

Besides the clash with corrupt religion and religious leaders, the ministry of Jesus was marked by confrontation with the powers of evil. The overall conflict with Satan is graphically pictured in Revelation 12:1–6, 13–17. The Synoptics each start their Gospel account with the story of Satanic temptations.[36] Mark and Luke describe an early confrontation when an evil spirit cries out in the synagogue at Capernaum, 'What do you want with us, Jesus of Nazareth? Have you come to destroy us? I know who you are – the Holy One of God!'[37] Confrontation continued throughout Christ's ministry: each act of healing or deliverance was in effect a confrontation; when Jesus healed the crippled woman on a Sabbath he spoke of her condition as being bound by Satan for eighteen long years.[38] The final conflict at the cross was one between Jesus and 'the prince of this world'.[39]

As well as confronting the powers of evil and their works, Jesus specifically confronted sin. This is implicit in his foundational call to repentance,[40] though the emphasis there is more on turning to God and accepting the good news of salvation rather than on a detailed denunciation of specific sins. It is seen in his conversation with the woman at the well, and in his dealings with the teachers of the law and the Pharisees.[41] The seriousness of sin, and especially of causing others to sin, is graphically stressed in Mark 9:42–49. Again, his teaching emphasized that sin was a matter of the heart much more than of outward actions, a point that even his disciples found difficult to appreciate.[42]

[34] John 2:18.
[35] Westcott, *The Gospel according to St John*, p. 42.
[36] Matt. 4:1–11; Mark 1:12–13; Luke 4:1–13.
[37] Mark 1:21–27; Luke 4:31–36.
[38] Luke 13:16.
[39] John 12:31; 14:30; 16:11.
[40] Mark 1:15.
[41] John 4:16–18; Matt. 23:13–32.
[42] Mark 7:14–23.

5. He destroyed evil (3:5, 8)

The appearing of God in Christ, says John, did more than just confront sin and evil. It dealt decisively with them. *He appeared so that he might take away our sins ... The reason the Son of God appeared was to destroy the devil's work.*[43] The word John uses for 'destroy' (*lysē*) has a wide range of meanings in the New Testament, from 'undo' in the sense of 'untie',[44] through 'set free'[45] and 'break' the law,[46] to 'kill' or 'demolish' when referring to the 'temple' of Christ's body.[47] Destroying the devil's work, therefore, can be pictured in several ways: the breaking of the devil's power, the setting free of his captives, the demolishing of the kingdom of darkness, the destruction of all that is evil, and the undoing of the damage that the devil has done.

Jesus took away sin and destroyed the works of the devil during his ministry. He declared forgiveness;[48] he healed broken bodies; he restored broken minds and broken relationships; he destroyed the hold of fear, anger, worry, falsehood, prejudice, greed and godlessness on the lives of his hearers; the 'strong man' was 'tied up' and his possessions carried off.[49] In Christ the kingdom of God came, and the hold of the powers of evil was broken. 'In him was life, and that life was the light of men,' wrote John, looking back on those years of ministry. 'The light shines in the darkness, and the darkness has not overcome it.'[50]

All this happened during his ministry. But the focal point of Christ's destruction of the works of the devil and of his removal of sin was the cross. It is to this that we now turn.

---

[43] 'John defines the purpose of the incarnation as destructive. Christ came to "loose" (NIV *destroy*) the works of the devil. The verb (*lyō*) means, at root, to untie and so to set free ... But it also came to be used of breaking something up into its component parts, tearing down a building, for example, and so destroying it. This gives us John's meaning here in terms of doing away with the devil's works, demolishing them and bringing them to an end'; D. Jackman, *The Message of John's Letters* (Inter-Varsity Press, 1988), p. 93.

[44] E.g. Mark 1:7.

[45] Luke 13:16.

[46] John 7:23.

[47] John 2:19, 21.

[48] Mark 2:5.

[49] Matt. 12:29.

[50] John 1:4–5, NIV margin.

Revelation 5:6
7. The scarred God

Revelation 4 is a glorious vision of God upon the throne of the universe, radiant in glory, worshipped by the great heavenly beings for his holiness and his eternity, and by the representatives of humanity as Creator and Lord of all. As we move to chapter 5 we see a scroll in his right hand, the scroll of his purposes for the world.[1] Tragically, no-one is found who is able to open the scroll; that is, to put God's purposes of wisdom and grace into operation. 'I wept and wept', writes John, 'because no-one was found who was worthy to open the scroll or look inside. Then one of the elders said to me, "Do not weep! See, the Lion of the tribe of Judah, the Root of David, has triumphed. He is able to open the scroll and its seven seals."'[2]

The 'Lion of Judah' and the 'Root of David'[3] are both Old Testament images of the conquering Messiah who would indeed bring in God's kingdom in power and glory. John looks to see who this mighty figure is; the Greek he wrote seems deliberately to make us wait, holding our breath: 'And I saw in the middle of the throne and of the four living creatures and in the middle of the elders . . . a Lamb standing as slain.'[4] 'Looking as if it had been slain' (NIV) is an unhelpful rendering of the Greek 'as slain' (*hōs esphagmenon*). If we

---

[1] Numerous suggestions have been made about the scroll. Beale lists five suggested identifications: a book of redemption to be identified with 'the Lamb's book of life' (Rev. 13:8), the Old Testament, a book containing events of the future 'Great Tribulation', a book containing God's plan of judgment and redemption, and a 'testament'. Beale opts for the last two, commenting, 'The "book" is best understood as containing God's plan of judgment and redemption, which has been set in motion by Christ's death and resurrection but has yet to be completed'; G. K. Beale, *The Book of Revelation* (Eerdmans, 1999), pp. 339–340.

[2] Rev. 5:1–5.

[3] Gen. 49:9–12; Isa. 11:1 – 12:6.

[4] Rev. 5:6, my translation.

see a notice on an item, 'As advertised', we conclude that it has been advertised, not that it just looks as if it had been advertised.[5] The Lamb most certainly was slain, and he bears the marks of slaughter clearly on him.

1. The scarred God

The promise of the coming God, the one who would come in glory and power to deal with the evil of the world and to establish his kingdom for ever, runs all through the Old Testament. But alongside it, and in contrast to it, was the prophecy of one who would come as a suffering servant, who, so far from conquering in glory, would be 'despised and rejected', 'a man of sorrows, and familiar with suffering', who would be 'crushed for our iniquities' and would carry 'the iniquity of us all'. 'Oppressed and afflicted', he would be 'led like a lamb to the slaughter' and stricken 'for the transgression of my people'. Like the sacrificial lamb, the Lord would make 'his life a guilt offering'; he would bear the iniquities of many, and through him they would be justified, 'because he poured out his life unto death' and 'bore the sin of many'.[6]

The contrast between the two promised figures was total; yet when John turned to see the Lion of Judah and the Root of David, he saw not only the conquering Messiah but the slain Lamb. In a way that the readers of the Old Testament prophecies could never have imagined, God had brought the two together in Christ.[7] The Lion of Judah, the Root of David, has indeed conquered, but the key to his victory is not force, but rather suffering and sacrifice and death. The ascended and glorified Christ, the Son of God, the Messiah, the one worshipped as equal with the Father by the heavenly hosts,[8] God himself, is 'as slain'. Our God is scarred. True, he 'stands' in the middle of the throne since he is the one who has risen from death and is alive for evermore.[9] True, his power and wisdom are total, symbolized by his *seven horns and seven eyes* (6). But he is scarred.

[5] Beale comments, 'The translation "as *though* slain" is unnecessary and misleading, as if the Lamb only looked slain, but was not; "as slain" is best'; Beale, *The Book of Revelation*, p. 352.

[6] Isa. 53:3, 4, 5, 6, 7, 8, 10, 11, 12.

[7] Beasley-Murray points out that there was a tradition in late Judaism of a messianic conquering lamb (G. R. Beasley-Murray, *The Book of Revelation* [Oliphants, 1974], p. 125), but no connection was made between him and the lamb of suffering and sacrifice.

[8] Rev. 5:12–14.

[9] Rev. 1:18.

Almost certainly the scar that John saw was the Lamb's slashed throat, since that was how the Old Testament sacrifices were slain; but Revelation's symbolism is given for us to apply and not to picture, as is evident from the concept of seven horns and seven eyes on a lamb. Matthew Bridges and Godfrey Thring quite legitimately adjust the imagery:

> Crown him the Lord of love;
> behold his hands and side,
> those wounds yet visible above
> in beauty glorified.
> No angel in the sky
> can fully bear that sight,
> but downward bends his burning eye
> at mysteries so bright.[10]

2. The eternal scarring

Our God is scarred; he will continue to carry the scars of Calvary for ever.[11] But a few pages later John tells us another profound truth about the Lamb. In the central interlude of his vision (Rev. 12 and 13), he gives us a bird's-eye view of the conflict between evil and God, the rebellion of Satan, and his attempts to destroy the Messiah and the people of God, particularly through a beast, the Satanic alternative to Christ. For a limited time this bestial Antichrist would be allowed to 'make war against the saints and to conquer them' and to rule 'every tribe, people, language and nation'.[12] 'All inhabitants of the earth will worship the beast – all whose names have not been written in the book of life belonging to the Lamb that was slain from the creation of the world.'[13]

Under the influence of Revelation 17:8 ('written in the book of life from the creation of the world'), some commentators and translators have linked the phrase 'from the creation of the world' with the writing of the Lamb's book of life; the NEB, for example, translates: 'All on earth will worship it, except those whose names the Lamb that was slain keeps in his roll of the living, written there since the world was made.' Such a translation is a major perversion

---

[10] From the hymn 'Crown him with many crowns'.
[11] 'The perfect participle *esphagmenon* ("having been slain") expresses an abiding condition as a result of the past act of being slain'; Beale, *The Book of Revelation*, p. 352.
[12] Rev. 13:5–7.
[13] Rev. 13:8.

of the Greek;[14] although 17:8 clearly states that the names of God's people have been known to him since the creation of the world, 13:8 equally clearly states that the Lamb was slain 'from the founding of the world'. Twelve words come between 'written' and 'from the founding of the world'; no words at all come between 'slain' and 'from the founding of the world'. It would seem quite clear that John meant us to understand that the Lamb was slain from the foundation of the world. At the very least, we can say that if it was not true that the Lamb was slain from the foundation of the world John would have rephrased the verse to remove its obvious suggestion that he was. In fact, the writing of the book of life is dependent upon the slaying of the Lamb, and the conclusion must be that John teaches that both events were 'from the foundation of the world'.[15]

The Lamb, then, was slain from the founding of the world. This in no way denies the historicity of the cross as an event in time on a specific Friday round about AD 33. But it stretches our understanding of the implications of that event. The sufferings of the Son of God, from our perspective, were focused into some thirty years of incarnate life and very specifically into six hours of crucifixion. But from the perspective of God, who is outside the time-frame of planet Earth, the sufferings and death were not limited to a few earth years or a few earth hours. The cost of redemption was far greater than that; it was being paid by God from the moment of determining to bring our universe into being. The marks of death, inflicted from our perspective on a grim Friday afternoon, have been carried by the Redeemer from the founding of the world. Not only is he now scarred for ever; he has been scarred throughout all the history of creation.

I find this stunning. It shatters for ever the image of a God who dwells in eternal bliss, who created a universe that unfortunately went wrong, but who continues much the same, apart from a brief period of thirty years or so, enjoying all the riches of heaven while we struggle with the ravages of sin and evil here on planet Earth. Never, throughout the story of our universe, has God been free from scars. The creation of the world profoundly affected God. It

---

[14] Beasley-Murray writes: 'It may safely be said that no group of translators would have come to such a decision were it not for the statement in 17:8': *The Book of Revelation*, p. 213.

[15] There is a parallel concept to the Lamb slain from the founding of the world in 1 Pet. 1:18–20: 'you were redeemed … with the precious blood of Christ, a lamb without blemish or defect. He was chosen before the creation of the world' (lit. 'known beforehand before the founding of the world'), 'but was revealed in these last times for your sake'.

changed him for ever. It introduced something into the Godhead that had never been there before. Somehow, in a way we have yet to begin to explore, he took into himself the realities of suffering and death, and he has known them ever since. From the moment of the founding of the world, God was scarred.

3. The slain God

The concept of a crucified God has been highlighted by Jürgen Moltmann[16] and taken up by many since. Though concerned to remain faithful to the teaching of the Scriptures, Moltmann's starting point was not biblical exegesis but Auschwitz and the desire to offer a theology that was able to cope with its horrors. He did so by stressing that on the cross God in love chooses to suffer in solidarity with a suffering world. The suffering of the cross was not just the suffering of the Son; the Father suffered too. Supremely, in the cry of dereliction, 'My God, my God, why have you forsaken me?', God chooses to experience suffering at its most terrible, that of Godforsakenness.

The understanding of the cross as the suffering and death of God did not originate with Moltmann. Several before him explored the idea; at the beginning of the twentieth century P. T. Forsyth had written: 'The victory over evil, cosmical or ethical, cost ... God his life.'[17] The theological development of this concept had been hampered in earlier centuries by an almost universal adherence to the traditional doctrine of the immutability and impassibility of God.[18] Nevertheless, under the influence of the Bible's teaching, several orthodox theologians seem to have managed to combine their acceptance of the doctrine of the immutability and impassibility of God with the belief that it was God himself who suffered at Calvary. Charles Hodge, for example, a pillar of nineteenth-century evangelical orthodoxy, wrote:

Although the divine nature is immutable and impassible, and therefore neither the obedience nor the suffering of Christ was the obedience or suffering of the divine nature, yet they were nonetheless the obedience and suffering of a divine person ... The

---

[16] J. Moltmann, *The Crucified God*, trans. R. A. Wilson and J. Bowden (SCM, 1974).

[17] P. T. Forsyth, *The Justification of God* (Duckworth, 1916), p. 151.

[18] Bauckham states: 'The idea that God cannot suffer [was] accepted virtually as axiomatic from the early Greek Fathers until the nineteenth century'; R. Bauckham, '"Only the suffering God can help": divine passibility in modern theology', *Themelios* 99 (1984), p. 6.

obedience of Christ was the righteousness of God, and the blood of Christ was the blood of God.[19]

Despite the reservations of the theologians, the belief that it was God himself who gave his life for us on the cross was central to much popular thought. In the middle of the eighteenth century Charles Wesley wrote with joy and wonder:

> And can it be that I should gain
>   an interest in the Saviour's blood?
> Died he for me, who caused his pain?
>   For me, who him to death pursued?
> Amazing love! How can it be
>   that thou, my God, shouldst die for me?

> 'Tis mystery all! The immortal dies!
>   Who can explore his strange design?
> In vain the first-born seraph tries
>   To sound the depths of love divine!
> 'Tis mercy all! Let earth adore,
>   Let angel minds inquire no more.

It is in the profound mystery of a slain God that we come to the heart of the Christian response to evil and suffering.

a. What was being done on the cross was huge

If there is one thing that has been emphasized again and again by the events of the last hundred years it is that the problem of evil and suffering is a huge one, and that therefore any answer to it in the cross has to be equally huge. Tragically, under the influence of nineteenth-century German philosophy, many theologians in the early years of the twentieth century held an optimistic view of human nature and so were able to minimize our need of drastic action by God; the cross could be accepted as little more than an expression of the love of God, or an example of how we should undergo suffering. Ironically, and maybe significantly, it was what the world experienced in two world wars focused on Germany, and particularly in the concentration camps such as Auschwitz, that destroyed such superficiality. The world's problem is not simply the need of love or of an inspiring example. It is that sin and evil and suffering are huge and horrific, so great that some thinkers have

---

[19] C. Hodge, *Systematic Theology* (Charles Scribner, 1871–3), vol. 2, p. 395.

been forced to conclude that no concept of atonement or salvation can ever answer them. Sartre, reflecting in 1947 on his experiences in the Second World War, wrote:

> We heard whole streets screaming and understand that Evil, fruit of a free and sovereign will, is like Good, absolute. Perhaps a day will come when a happy age, looking back at the past, will see in this suffering and shame one of the paths which led to peace. But we were not on the side of history already made ... Therefore, in spite of ourselves, we came to this conclusion, which will seem shocking to lofty souls: Evil cannot be redeemed.[20]

Sartre's atheism meant that he could not look to God for an answer; in any case, the answers being offered by the liberal theologians of his day were woefully inadequate. Only something very drastic would be sufficient to match the enormity of the problem. The size of the problem of suffering and evil can never be exaggerated; if it is going to be solved it must be by something that is even greater. That something was the cross.

b. What was being done on the cross was being done by the triune God

Perhaps our reaction to the concept of a slain God is to point out that the Bible does not state that God was crucified, only that Jesus was crucified. We might point to verses such as Romans 3:25, 'God presented [Christ Jesus] as a sacrifice of atonement', or 1 John 1:10, 'God ... sent his Son as an atoning sacrifice for our sins.' The picture, we might claim, is one of God the Son giving his life on the cross, while God the Father remains as he is, more or less an uninvolved onlooker.

Such a picture drives an unacceptable wedge between the persons of the Trinity. Though our understanding of the relationships between the Father, the Son and the Holy Spirit is necessarily only partial, it seems inconceivable that the cross, the most significant event of all history, should involve just one of the three persons of the Godhead. In no way could the Father remain uninvolved. Forsyth has to be right when he states, 'The Father suffered in his Son.'[21] And the suffering is more than the pain of seeing a dearly loved one going through awful suffering, great though that may be. The unity between Father and Son is such that the suffering of the

---

[20] J.-P. Sartre, *What is Literature?*, trans. B. Frechtman (Methuen, 1950), 161–162.
[21] Forsyth, *The Justification of God*, p. 169.

Son is the suffering of the Father; if the Son went through death the Father also went through death. The interpretation of 2 Corinthians 5:19, which in the Greek states that 'God was in Christ the world reconciling to himself' (*theos ēn en Christō kosmon katallassōn heautō*), has been debated through the years. The NIV avoids the bold statement that God was in Christ by translating, 'God was reconciling the world to himself in Christ.' Most other versions stick closer to the Greek and follow the example of the AV, 'God was in Christ, reconciling the world unto himself.' Calvin states:

> Some take this to mean simply 'God was reconciling the world to Himself in Christ', but the meaning is fuller and richer than that, for he is saying, first, that God was in Christ and then that by this intervention he was reconciling the world to Himself. This is said of the Father, since it would be unnatural to say that the divine nature of Christ was in Christ. Thus he is saying that the Father was in the Son, in agreement with John 10.38, 'I am in the Father and the Father in me.'[22]

The word order and sentence construction clearly favour the interpretation adopted by the majority of the versions and by Calvin. If Paul had intended to say 'God was reconciling', he could have used the straight imperfect indicative *katēllassen* and so removed any ambiguity; instead, he used the imperfect of the verb 'to be', putting it before 'in Christ' and then added 'reconciling' as a participle; at the very least we can say with confidence that if Paul had not believed that God was in Christ he could never have written the words in the way he did; the ambiguity, such as it is, while allowing us to accept the NIV interpretation, requires us to accept the other as well: God was in Christ, and in Christ he was reconciling the world to himself.

What was being done on the cross was being done by the whole Godhead. The work of saving and redeeming the world is the work of Father, Son and Holy Spirit.[23] The price that had to be paid was paid by the complete Godhead. The suffering was the suffering of the Father as well as of the Son. The life that was poured out was the life of the Father as well as the life of the Son. Since the unity of the Godhead is indivisible, we can safely say that what was done

[22] J. Calvin, *The Second Epistle of Paul the Apostle to the Corinthians*, trans. T. A. Smail (Oliver and Boyd, 1964), p. 78.

[23] This is pictured at that great Trinitarian moment when Jesus was baptized and the 'dove' descended on the 'Lamb of God' and the voice from heaven spoke. For the watchers, the primary significance of both the Lamb and the dove was atoning sacrifice (John 1:29–33; Matt. 3:16–17; Lev. 5:7).

at the cross was done by the triune God, God the Father, God the Son and God the Holy Spirit.

c. What was being borne on the cross was being borne by the triune God

There has been a long tradition, when meditating on what was borne on the cross, of focusing on the physical sufferings of Christ. These were indeed horrific, but it is vital to remember that they were not all that was borne at the cross. I well remember being very disturbed some years ago, when reading Richard Wurmbrand's *Tortured for Christ*, to come across the account of a priest who, in the agony of the persecution and torture he was going through, declared, 'I have suffered more than Christ!'[24] Perhaps there was some justification for his cry if he was thinking in terms of physical or even mental suffering. But the physical and human sufferings of Christ, great though they were, were nothing compared with his real suffering. For the cross was infinitely more than a man suffering and dying. It was the holy God bearing the sin of the world. It was the sinless God being made sin.[25] It was the triune God taking upon himself and into himself the appalling evil of a fallen world. It was Light taking into itself darkness. It was Life suffering death. It was the righteous God allowing himself to be made a curse.[26] Never could we overstate what God bore for us on the cross. Never could we fully understand what it meant for him to bear our suffering and carry our sorrows.[27] Never can we grasp what it meant for the thrice-holy God to take the evil of the world upon his shoulders, to suffer sin's penalty, to be subject to its condemnation, to become sin, to taste the awfulness of death, to suffer hell. What God did on the cross was huge, far greater than going through physical suffering and death; what he bore there was nothing less than the whole sum of evil of a fallen world, and the cost of such an act was infinite.

d. What was done on the cross is for ever in the triune God

If the cost to God of dealing with the evil of a fallen world was infinite, I suggest that there is a very real sense in which it is also eternal. The Lamb is 'as slain'. The cross is 'from the founding of the world'. What God bore at Calvary he still bears. Somehow, evil in all its forms – sin and suffering and death – has been taken eternally

[24] R. Wurmbrand, *Tortured for Christ* (Hodder and Stoughton, 1967), p. 35.
[25] 2 Cor. 5:21.
[26] Gal. 3:13.
[27] Isa. 53:3–4.

into the Godhead; the marks of slaughter on the Lamb are eternal; there is blood on the throne of heaven. The price that was paid for our redemption is an eternal price; despite the glory of the resurrection it was not refunded on Easter Sunday morning. For ever God bears the cost of Calvary. Of course, what he has taken into himself has been transformed. Somehow, in a way that is far beyond our grasp, because our God has suffered evil the evilness of evil has been broken, the sting of death has been drawn, the sinfulness of sin has been overcome. Just as the resurrection transformed the darkness of death, so that the scars that Christ for ever carries are now both hideous and radiant with beauty, so what God bore for us at the cross is both still infinitely costly and gloriously transformed.

This is the heart of the Christian response to evil and suffering, and it is very big. It is a huge answer to a huge problem. Because the answer is God himself, the answer is greater than the problem. Infinite wisdom, infinite grace, infinite love have paid the infinite price, have given nothing less than God himself. God has done much more than just sympathizing with our sufferings, much more than sending a Saviour. He has given himself to be the Saviour, his life to redeem a lost world. He has taken upon himself sin and evil and pain and suffering; he has borne them, suffering the full extent of their raw awfulness; he has lifted them and carried them, overcoming their darkness with his light, breaking their power, shattering their awfulness.

How he has done this and what it means are the theme of our next chapter.

Ephesians 1:9–10; 19–23
8. The conquering God

If you keep your mouth shut and try to say something you will probably make a noise something like *mmm* or *moo*. Even if you don't, the Greeks did. So they invented a word *moo-oh*, spelt *myō*, which meant to 'shut your mouth'. If there's something about which we can say nothing, either because there's nothing to be said, or because we're sworn to secrecy, we *my*, we keep our mouth shut about it; it is a *mystērion*, a word that came into English as 'mystery'.

There is plenty that is mysterious about evil and suffering. Confronted with the 'Why?' that demands an instant and adequate explanation for a disaster or a death, we all too often can only remain silent. Equally, there is plenty that is mysterious about God; faced with his infinity or eternity, we soon run out of words and are forced to shut our mouths. If God himself is a mystery, it is hardly surprising that his ways are a mystery as well; how can we expect to understand the vastness of his purposes, or the incredible complexity of the detailed events through which he achieves them? Again, words fail us and our mouths are shut.

But the Greek word *mystērion* developed a special meaning which was firmly attached to it by the time of the New Testament. It was linked particularly with the secret rituals and teachings of certain religions such as the Eleusinian cult or the worship of the Egyptian goddess Isis or the Persian god Mithras. These 'mystery religions' offered their followers secret knowledge and swore them to silence. In this context, then, the 'mystery' was mysterious only to some; for those in the know there was nothing mysterious, in the sense of hidden, about it.

In no way did Christianity see itself as another 'mystery religion'. Its teachings were to be proclaimed from the housetops, not kept a closely guarded secret. Yet in at least two ways it was appropriate to refer to its teachings as 'mysteries' in the sense that they were clearly accessible to some but not to others. The first arose from the fact that Christian truth was revealed truth; God had spoken in Christ and through the Holy Spirit, telling and showing us things that we could not otherwise discover; these things, now known clearly to us, remain a mystery to those who have not yet heard the gospel. Secondly, even when the gospel truth is proclaimed, the work of the Holy Spirit is needed to enable us to understand and to grasp it; if we're operating just on the 'natural' level we shall be unable accept God's truth; it will be mysterious foolishness to us. It is only through the Spirit that 'we have the mind of Christ' and so can discern 'the deep things of God'.[1]

We have seen that the power of evil is great, and can be dealt with only by a power that is greater still. In a similar way, we can say that the mystery of evil and suffering is great; if it is going to be answered it must be answered by some mystery that is greater still. And that is precisely what has happened; in response to the mystery of evil, the Bible presents us with the mystery of God's will. And because the mystery of God's will is an 'open' mystery for those who receive it, instead of the two mysteries combining to plunge us into even deeper darkness, the second mystery is great enough to deal with the first.

1. The mystery of God's will (1:9–10)

Hardly has he started writing his letter to the Ephesians[2] when Paul bursts out in a great hymn of praise for all that God has done.[3] God has blessed us, he says, with every spiritual blessing in Christ; he has chosen us, predestined us for adoption, redeemed us, forgiven us, revealed his purposes to us, and given us the Holy Spirit; all this he has done in Christ, and he has done it for Gentiles as well as for Jews, for the praise of the glory of his grace.[4] All this, and more, Paul packs into a single breathless sentence, pouring out one phrase

---

[1] 1 Cor. 2:6–16.

[2] It is generally agreed that the lack of the words 'in Ephesus' (Eph. 1:1) in the oldest manuscripts, together with a degree of internal evidence such as the lack of personal greetings, indicate that this letter's destination was not just the church at Ephesus. Very possibly, like the book of Revelation, it was a general letter designed to be circulated to all the churches in Asia Minor or even further afield. However, even if this is correct, it still seems likely that the Christians of Ephesus were among those to whom the letter was sent, so, for ease of expression, I shall refer to the recipients of the letter as 'the Ephesians'.

[3] Eph. 1:3.

[4] Eph. 1:3–14.

after another in excited exultation at what God has done. Armitage Robinson writes:

> He seems to be swept along by his theme, hardly knowing whither it is taking him. He begins with God, – the blessing which comes from God to men, the eternity of his purpose of good, the glory of its consummation. But he cannot order his conceptions, or close his sentences. One thought presses hard upon another and will not be refused. And so this great doxology runs on and on: 'in whom ... in Him ... in Him, in whom ... in whom ... in whom'.[5]

In the middle of it all comes the phrase *the mystery of his will* (9), a phrase which covers the whole hymn, or, indeed the whole of God's revelation in Christ, but which Paul specifically unpacks in verses 9 and 10.

a. The staggering fact (1:9)

If the Bible did not tell us, we would never dare to believe it. After all, God's thoughts and ways are vastly different from ours, as high above them as the heavens are above the earth.[6] That may well still be true of the details and complexities of our God's ways, but, says Paul, now that God has come to us in Christ he has done nothing less than *made known to us the mystery of his will* (9). No longer is the big picture obscure; no longer do we need to call it a hidden mystery; no longer do we need to say we do not understand. Indeed, since Paul wrote this great sentence without punctuation, and the word translated 'he made known' is an aorist participle following immediately after 'with all wisdom and understanding',[7] Paul may well be saying that the gift of this knowledge is accompanied by nothing less than divine wisdom and understanding so that we can receive it.[8] So here is the staggering fact: the glorious and sovereign God, who is all-wise, whose purposes are far beyond anything the human mind could ever discover, has chosen to make known to us his overall plan, to tell us, in a way that we can understand, what it is he is doing, where he is going, what his answer is to our fallen world with all its evil and suffering, and what he will do to set it all right.

---

[5] J. Armitage Robinson, *St Paul's Epistle to the Ephesians* (Macmillan, 1914), p. 19.
[6] Isa. 55:8–9.
[7] Eph. 1:8–9a (*en pasē sophiai kai phronēsei gnōrisas, hēmin to mystērion tou thelēmatos autou*).
[8] See NIV margin. Moffatt translates: 'granting us complete insight and understanding of the open secret of his will'.

b. The divine favour (1:9)

God has made known to us the mystery of his will, says Paul, *according to his good pleasure* (9). Again, so condensed is Paul's thought, and so rapid his transition from one idea to another, that it is very possible that this phrase is to be linked with 'his will', as in verse 5; God's 'good pleasure' is a way of unpacking 'his will'. Even if that is so, it still shows us the driving force both for his will and for making his will known to us: it is his pleasure and it is good. Just as God delights in the amazing universe that he has created, so he delights in his purposes of grace and salvation for it, and he particularly delights in revealing to us those purposes. When God became incarnate, the angels used the same word as Paul writes here (*eudokia*) as they spoke of the heart of God towards the fallen human race; the AV translated it 'good will toward men'; the NIV has 'men on whom his favour rests'.[9] God's heart goes out to a broken world, and he delights to declare his good purposes of grace towards it.

c. The divine method (1:9–10)

All through this hymn of praise in Ephesians 1, Christ is centre stage; it is in him that we have every spiritual blessing, in him we were chosen, through him we have been adopted as God's children, in him he pours out his grace, in and through him we have redemption and forgiveness; and it is *in Christ* that he focuses his will and purposes (9). God's answer to the evil and suffering of a fallen and broken world is Christ; his plan for the world centres on Christ; the implementation of the plan is through Christ;[10] the achievement of the plan is Christ's. Book after book has been written on the problem of evil; all sorts of answers have been proposed: the free-will defence, the 'best possible world' theodicy, the character-building argument, and many others.[11] All these approaches have something helpful to contribute to the issue, but none of them takes us to the real answer, the one that God himself has given, the Lord Jesus Christ.

[9] Luke 2:14.

[10] Compare the imagery of the scroll in Rev. 5 as the book of the purposes of God which Christ alone can open.

[11] For a brief outline of some of these approaches see below, chapter 13, section 3, 'Theodicies'.

d. The ultimate fulfilment (1:10)

Like God himself, the purposes of God are big. What God does he does on a grand scale. So perhaps it is not surprising that the timing of his purposes should be on a grand scale too. After all, he who could have brought the complete universe into being in a split second in fact chose to spread its creation over millions of years. No oak tree springs up full grown overnight. No child of God achieves sinless perfection of life in just a few days. God has his timescale, and though the Bible teaches very clearly that we are already in the end times, we have not yet reached the moment of ultimate fulfilment. Still we wait for the mystery of his will and purpose *to be put into effect when the times will have reached their fulfilment* (10).[12] The NIV translation accurately reflects the meaning, but obscures the force of Paul's word *oikonomia*, the standard word for the management of household affairs, from which we get 'economy'. Just as the wise head of the house plans ahead for the well-being of all who belong there, and then implements his plan stage by stage, so God is working out his purposes, 'towards the implementation (*eis oikonomian*) of the fullness of the times', or, as Wyclif put it, 'in to dispensacioun of plente of tymes'. We naturally want it now, if not yesterday. But God works according to his timing. Does that mean we are back to square one, that until the time of fulfilment we have nothing to enable us to cope with evil and suffering? Most certainly not; so far from having nothing, in at least two ways we have everything – apart from the final consummation of God's amazing purposes. First, we have, as we have been seeing, the full revelation of what his purposes are, and on that we can build our lives, we can anchor our sure and certain hope. And, secondly, though the final consummation is still in the future, the unfolding purposes of God are already gloriously effective, as we shall be seeing in a moment. But first we need to unpack just what the revealed mystery of God's purposes is, the great climax of Ephesians 1:9–10.

e. The mystery revealed (1:10)

God, then, has a purpose, a great overarching purpose, into which he fits all the details of planet Earth and the wider universe, which he is accomplishing in Christ and will complete in the fullness of time; this great mystery of his will he has made known to us; it is

---

[12] *Eis oikonomian tou plērōmatos tōn kairōn*: '"Moment of intense significance", "at just the right moment", "when the time was ripe"'; C. L. Mitton, *Ephesians* (Oliphants, 1976), p. 55.

nothing less than *to bring all things in heaven and on earth together under one head* (10). When Paul writes 'all things', he means just that.[13] He uses the definite article (*ta panta*) to stress the point; he writes 'all *things*' to make it clear that it is not just humankind or living creatures that he is describing; and he adds 'in heaven and on earth' to make sure that nothing is excluded. Though 'all the things on earth' must include evil and suffering and all the devastation they have produced, we can safely say as well that the phrase 'things in heaven' (*ta epi tois ouranois*) includes the powers of evil as well as heavenly angelic beings. Parallel phrases come later in the letter: 'the rulers and authorities in the heavenly realms',[14] and 'the rulers ... the authorities ... the powers of this dark world and ... the spiritual forces of evil in the heavenly realms'.[15] 'All things' includes all things, personal and inanimate, on earth and in heaven, in the past and in the future, good and bad.[16]

The great problem, of course, is that as we see them now, 'all things' are in a hopeless mess. The world is characterized by conflict, by alienation, by discord, by rejection, division, brokenness and corruption. We are hurt, we are alienated; we shake our fist at a world that does not make sense, and even at a God whose ways seem unacceptable. But, says Paul, whatever the world may be now, God has made known to us the mystery of his will, that he is going to bring everything in this broken, warring world *together under one head*. Just as the thousands of pieces of a jigsaw puzzle, fragmented and meaningless, jumbled into a hopeless mess, can, with wisdom and perseverance, be brought together to form one coherent and beautiful whole, so God is going to take every one of the broken fragments of our world and universe and bring them together into one.

The word Paul uses to express this great purpose of God is *anakephalaiōsasthai*. It pictures the bringing together of things under one head; it was used in rhetoric of bringing together and summing up the points of an argument. Translators bring out the meaning in various ways: 'gather together in one all things in Christ' (AV), 'unite all things in him' (RSV), 'be brought into a unity in Christ' (NEB), 'that all human history shall be consummated

---

[13] Westcott comments, 'It is altogether arbitrary to introduce any limitation into the interpretation of *ta panta*'; B. F. Westcott, *Saint Paul's Epistle to the Ephesians* (Macmillan, 1906), p. 14.

[14] Eph. 3:10.

[15] Eph. 6:12.

[16] Compare the parallel thought in Rom. 8:28, 'in all things God works for the good of those who love him, who have been called according to his purpose', and the subsequent list of things that are powerless to thwart that purpose (35–39).

in Christ' (Phillips), 'to bring all creation together ... with Christ as head' (GNB), 'bring everything together under the authority of Christ' (NLT), 'to bring all things ... together under one head, even Christ' (NIV). Everything, every person and every power, every object and every event, things good and things bad, things on earth and things in heaven, will be fitted together into a perfect beautiful picture by the nail-pierced hands of our Lord Jesus Christ.

A little later in this letter Paul illustrates this concept by what was for him, the former strict Pharisee, the amazing miracle of Jew and Gentile being brought together in unity under the one head.[17] Christ, he says, 'is our peace, who has made the two one and has destroyed the barrier, the dividing wall of hostility'.[18] We can almost hear him adding, 'And if he can do that, he can do anything!'

So here is the 'mystery' of God's will, the truth about his purposes that he has made known to his people, but which everyone else simply cannot grasp. Everything is going to be brought together into one glorious whole, all divisions ended, all barriers broken down, all suffering made meaningful, all hostility removed, all evil destroyed. For those around us this seems like an impossible dream; with Sartre, they can see no answer to evil and suffering, no hope for the future. But for those of us who know how great our God is, this is our confident assurance. Evil will not have the last word; Christ will.

2. The mastery of God's Christ (1:19–23)

The second half of Ephesians 1 contains the first of the two great prayers Paul prayed for his readers. It picks up the theme of God's revelation to his people, praying that the Ephesians may be given 'the Spirit of wisdom and revelation' so that they may know God better, and may have the eyes of their heart enlightened so that they may know the hope to which God has called them, the riches of God's inheritance, and the power that is theirs in Christ.[19] This is a prayer that revealed truth will become living truth in the experience of God's people; however great the truth that God has revealed, however explicit his revelation, it will benefit us not one bit unless, with the aid of the Holy Spirit, we let it change our thinking and our living. Sadly, we all know Christians who, say, hold firmly to the doctrine of the fatherhood of God as described by Jesus in Matthew 6:25–34, but then fail to apply it and spend their time worrying.

[17] Eph. 2:11–22.
[18] Eph. 2:14.
[19] Eph. 1:17–19.

Equally, it is very possible for us to have a theoretical knowledge of the great 'mystery of God's will' that we have been looking at, and still slide into despair when we face suffering or see the evil in the world around us. It is for this reason that we need to reinforce our study of the mystery of God's will with the stirring truths of the final verses of Paul's prayer, where he describes the mastery of God's Christ.

a. Over-the-top power (1:19)

I want you to get a real grip, both in theory and in experience, on the size of God's power, says Paul, *his incomparably great power for us who believe.* I want you to realize how big it is. It is huge. It is 'over the top'; the word translated by the NIV as 'incomparably great' is one of Paul's favourites, *hyperballō*, which various versions translate as 'surpassing' 'exceeding', 'beyond measure' and the like. Its basic meaning is 'to go beyond'. Think of the greatest, most fantastic power you could ever conceive. It goes beyond that. It is over the top, beyond, surpassing.

This is God's power. This is the power that called everything into being, that flung the universe into space, that sustains every sub-nuclear particle in its orbit and every galaxy in its path. Does doing that wear God out? Does he get exhausted from all that effort? No way![20] When he has exerted his great power creating and upholding the universe, he has still got tons and tons of power left, enough to create and uphold another universe, and another, and others, millions of them...

But what if problems arise in one of the worlds he has made? Will he have enough power to sort them out? Of course! Power enough and to spare. Power enough to sort out a million problems, billions of problems, power to work all things together for good – and still have tons of power left over.

b. Clear demonstration (1:20)

Do you still find it hard to grasp? Then look, says Paul, at the resurrection of Jesus. God *raised him from the dead and seated him at his right hand in the heavenly realms.* All the powers of darkness joined forces: sin and evil and death and hell, all the rebellion of Satan and his hosts, all the rejection of God by the human race – everything was brought together to destroy Christ. And was God struggling? Was it touch and go whether evil or God would come

[20] Isa. 40:28.

out on top? Never! It is Psalm 2 all over again. The powers may rage and plot and do their worst. But God is still totally in control of the situation. In his great power and wisdom all the machinations of evil have become only what his 'power and will had decided beforehand should happen'.[21] When the powers of evil had done their utmost and for a moment might have seemed to have won, in stepped the glorious power of God.

> Up from the grave he arose
>   with a mighty triumph o'er his foes.[22]

Either the resurrection happened or it did not happen. If it did happen, then it demonstrated once and for all that the power of God is greater than any other power. If ever you begin to doubt God's ability to sort out any and every problem, look again at the resurrection.

c. 'Far above' lordship (1:20–22)

Once he gets going, there is no stopping Paul. Or, to put it more correctly, God is so concerned that we should grasp the greatness and totality of his lordship over every other power, that the Holy Spirit, the author of Scripture, continues to pile phrase upon phrase to make sure there is no possibility of any doubt whatever. This Christ, whose resurrection demonstrates total victory over every other power, is now seated on the throne of the universe, in the position of honour and glory at God's right hand, reigning as sovereign Lord over all (20). And where are the other powers – sin and evil and pain and suffering and rebellion and Satan and darkness? Are they in a comparable position of power, perhaps at God's left hand? No way! Verse 22 picks up again the 'all things' of verse 10: *God placed all things under his feet*, every *rule and authority, power and dominion, and every title that can be given* (21); you name it: it is under Jesus' feet. And not just a bit under. Not such that Jesus has to struggle to keep them under. Instead, they are a long way under, completely under, such that Christ is *far above* every one of them (21). Again, Paul's word here (*hyperanō*) is an over-the-top word. *Anō*, 'above', would have made perfect sense. But Christ's mastery isn't just mastery – it is hyper-mastery.

---

[21] Acts 4:28.
[22] From the hymn 'Low in the grave he lay' by Robert Lowry.

THE MESSAGE OF EVIL AND SUFFERING

d. Where we fit in (1:19, 22)

Does all that blow your mind? I hope so. But there is still one more amazing thing. It comes in two phrases, one in verse 19 and one in verse 22. It tells us that though God's tremendous power, Christ's total victory, has effect everywhere, in every situation and at all times, God has chosen to focus it and all that it means on one particular spot. Just as the sun on a brilliant day shines with power on everything spread below it, but with a magnifying glass its rays can be focused even more powerfully on a small area, so in his wisdom and love God not only works in power to ensure that all things are brought under the headship of Jesus Christ, but he focuses his power and all it means on one particular spot. His 'incomparably great power' is *for us who believe* (19), the lordship of Christ is *for the church* (22). All the wisdom, all the might, all the purposes of God are brought together for the good of his people, for those who put their trust in him, for the body on earth of the reigning Lord Christ, the church.

Listen again to Paul as he picks up the theme in chapter 3:

> Although I am less than the least of all God's people, this grace was given me: to preach to the Gentiles the unsearchable riches of Christ, and to make plain to everyone the administration of this mystery, which for ages past was kept hidden in God, who created all things. His intent was that now, through the church, the manifold wisdom of God should be made known to the rulers and authorities in the heavenly realms, according to his eternal purpose which he accomplished in Christ Jesus our Lord.[23]

God has a tremendous purpose: to bring all things in heaven and on earth under one head, the Lord Jesus Christ. All his wisdom and power is working towards this one goal: all that is broken healed; all that is marred restored; all that is evil conquered and transformed; every knee bowing, and every tongue confessing that Jesus Christ is Lord. The fulfilment of this purpose in God's time is certain; it is as certain as the fact that God's power is far greater than all the other powers put together; it is guaranteed by the resurrection of Christ from the dead; it is already being implemented because Christ is even now on the throne of the universe with every other power far beneath his feet. And in his people God is demonstrating that power and victory; he is shattering the hold of evil on their lives; he is sending them into the fallen and broken

---

[23] Eph. 3:8–11.

world to declare his kingdom, to bring good news to the poor, freedom to the prisoners, healing to the broken, salvation to the lost. As they do it the angels wonder; in particular the dark rulers and the authorities in the heavenly realms see their own hold broken and their purposes thwarted; they see 'the manifold wisdom of God' and are shattered.

But, you say, it is not like that. The people of God are not exhibiting the power and victory of the Lord Jesus Christ. We are ineffective, powerless. Instead of manifesting the wisdom of God we have tried to function according to our own wisdom; instead of expressing God's power we have tried to operate according to human power structures, and as a result we have fallen flat on our faces.

Sadly, there is truth in this; but it is certainly not the whole picture. Though statisticians seem to delight to tell us that structured church activities in Britain are in decline, the church of Jesus Christ worldwide, the true people of God whose names are known only to him, is still gloriously alive, still experiencing the power of God, often in incredibly difficult situations, still conquering despite suffering and evil and persecution, still demonstrating the reality of the living God and the power and wisdom of his purposes to the rulers and authorities in the heavenly places. If your personal experience and way of seeing things are limited to a few weak local congregations and struggling Christians, remember that, on the human level, Paul, when he wrote to the Ephesians, could see little more; all that there was in those early days of Christianity was a sprinkling of small and weak persecuted congregations scattered round the eastern Mediterranean: no great powerful church of Christ marching forwards 'like a mighty army'. Yet, behind the weak, struggling façade, Paul knew there was something very different: the church of God, the body of Christ, empowered by the Holy Spirit, and called to bring in God's kingdom and transform the world. Others may not be able to see it; certainly the 'rulers of this age' have no idea of the real situation; but, says Paul, we are able to look at things the way God sees them, the way they really are. 'God has revealed ... to us by his Spirit' his 'secret (*en mystēriō*) wisdom, a wisdom that has been hidden and that God destined for our glory before time began.'[24]

So that is why Paul kept praying that the Spirit of wisdom and revelation would enlighten his readers' hearts.[25] However hard it may be to see it on the human level, through the power of the Holy

---

[24] 1 Cor. 2:10, 7.
[25] Eph. 1:17–18.

Spirit all God's people are able to look beyond the immediate appearances and see and experience the amazing underlying facts, the wonderful purposes of God in the mystery of his will to bring everything together in Christ, and the overwhelming power that guarantees that in God's time it will all be brought about through his total lordship and mastery.

Mark 1:14–15; Luke 6:20–36; Matthew 12:24–37
9. The teaching of Jesus on evil and suffering

It is impossible in one chapter to explore all the passages in which Jesus taught about evil and suffering. Nevertheless, by looking at three key passages we shall be able to draw out the main elements of his teaching.

1. The gospel in a nutshell (Mark 1:14–15)

The first passage is Mark's summary of the whole of Jesus' teaching:

After John was put in prison, Jesus went into Galilee, proclaiming the good news of God. [15]*'The time has come,'* he said. *'The kingdom of God is near. Repent and believe the good news!'*[1]

The key to Jesus' teaching about evil and suffering is his declaration of the coming of the kingdom of God. The time of fulfilment has come; at last all the prayers for God to intervene, to save his people, to scatter his enemies, to break the hold of evil, to inaugurate his kingly rule on earth, are about to be answered. All the promises of a Saviour, a Messiah, a Redeemer, of God himself coming to bring righteousness and healing and justice and truth, are being fulfilled. Now, the kingdom is coming.

The essence of the kingdom is the King. The kingdom is coming because the King has come, Emmanuel, God in Christ with us. To receive the kingdom we receive the King. To reject the King is to

---

[1] 'This passage [Mark 1:15], set by Mark as the climax to his prologue to the ministry of Jesus, is intended to supply a summary of the gospel preached by Jesus, of which the teaching of Jesus in the body of the gospel can be viewed as an exposition'; G. R. Beasley-Murray, *Jesus and the Kingdom of God* (Eerdmans, 1986), p. 71.

reject the kingdom. To reject the King is to reject God, and that, as we saw in chapter 6, is the very essence of evil.

If the time is fulfilled and the kingdom is now coming, that must presuppose that until now the kingdom has been at least largely absent. Instead of being in a relationship of love and obedience with God, men and women have been in rebellion against God. So the primary need is for repentance, a radical turning to God that is the beginning of a new relationship of obedience and love. To turn to God means turning away from evil, both the specific sins that we have committed and, most significantly, from bondage to evil and its powers. But this is something that is far beyond our unaided ability; we cannot deal with our sin or break the power of evil over our hearts and minds and lives. That is why Jesus did not just announce the coming of the kingdom and call for repentance: he also brought 'good news'.

For centuries the people had been waiting for the coming of the good news:

> How beautiful on the mountains
>   are the feet of those who bring good news
> who proclaim peace,
>   who bring good tidings,
>   who proclaim salvation,
> who say to Zion,
>   'Your God reigns' ...
> The LORD will lay bare his holy arm
>   in the sight of all the nations,
> and all the ends of the earth will see
>   the salvation of our God.[2]

Now, says Jesus, the good news has come. In him God comes as Saviour. Where men and women are helpless to deal with sin and evil, God has stepped in to break their power and release their captives. Through his teaching and preaching and healing and miracles the kingdom of darkness is having to give way to the coming of the kingdom of God.

As his ministry went on, it became clearer how he was to do this, how much it was to cost him, how the great prophecies of redemptive suffering in the passage that immediately follows those verses in Isaiah 52[3] were to be fulfilled in the cross of Calvary. But, right from the start, for those who knew the great promises of the

[2] Isa. 52:7, 10.
[3] Isa. 52:13 – 53:12.

Old Testament, it was clear that his teaching and ministry had radical implications for evil in all its forms. In him the holy God was coming in grace and salvation to establish his kingdom. To each person he presented a choice: acceptance or rejection. Accepting the kingdom meant accepting the King and turning from all that was evil. For those willing to do so there was forgiveness and cleansing, not through religious ritual or personal effort but as a free gift from God. Then, even more wonderfully, there was a whole new way of living, as those in whom the kingdom had come, who had a living relationship with the King, and, as a result, a radically new relationship with the world around.

Though the relationship of each disciple to Jesus was the heart of the coming of the kingdom, so great an event inevitably spilled over into every part of life. Each was specifically called to a radical change of life;[4] the kingdom demanded a total rejection of sin and a life that expressed the goodness and holiness of the King. It taught a new way of viewing the world, with radical kingdom values and a new understanding of what was right and wrong, good and bad. It shed new light on suffering, how we should view it and how we should face it. It offered a new vision for a broken and suffering world and a new mission to change it. All this those early disciples must have learnt as much from living with and watching Jesus as from his specific teaching. Nevertheless, all of Jesus' teaching related to the kingdom; his parables illustrated principles and aspects of the kingdom; his great 'Sermon on the Mount' taught the radical nature of life in the kingdom. It is to part of Luke's parallel summary of this body of Jesus' teaching we now turn.

2. Kingdom teaching (Luke 6:20–36)

The teaching of Jesus in Luke 6:20–36 is completely in keeping with the revelation of God in the Old Testament. Many of the phrases, for example, in Luke's account of the beatitudes (20–23) refer back to Isaiah 58:6–7 and 61.1–3. Jesus' summary command, *Do to others as you would have them do to you* (31), is itself a summary of 'the Law and the Prophets'.[5] God has not changed; the principles and values of the kingdom are the principles and values of his nature, and they are consistent with all that he has ever revealed of himself.

Yet at the same time the teaching of Jesus about the kingdom was shatteringly radical. The reason for this was simple: though his hearers claimed to be the people of God, in fact their concepts

[4] Mark 1:17.
[5] Matt. 7:12.

and values had become those of the world around them. Holiness and love and mercy were in short supply; the enjoyment of riches and good food had become more important to them than their relationship with God. To such Jesus' message was stark: the receiving of the kingdom for them would mean nothing short of revolution.

a. Happy are the sad (6:20–26)

For our culture today the words of Jesus are even more radical. Asked to list evils current in our twenty-first-century world, we would readily include poverty, hunger, tears, discrimination and persecution. Yet these are the very things that Jesus lists as blessings (20–22). Quite legitimately we could translate him as saying, 'Happy are you poor', 'Happy are you hungry', 'Happy are you who weep',[6] 'Happy are you who are hated and persecuted.'

It is vital we allow these revolutionary sayings of Jesus to have their full force. Commentators and preachers have offered all sorts of ways of dulling their impact, so that we can, after all, continue to believe that happiness consists of riches, plenty of food, pleasures, popularity and so on. But, though there may well be ways in which we need to develop our understanding of his words, in no way must we seek to escape from their revolutionary impact.

With Isaiah 61:1–3 and Luke 4:18–19 in mind, we see that Jesus is stating that where the kingdom comes worldly values are reversed. Poverty plus the kingdom is blessedness. Hunger and tears and rejection and persecution plus the kingdom are a matter for rejoicing and leaping for joy.[7] Two factors underlie this radical truth. The first is that poverty and hunger and suffering are the doors into the kingdom; that is, those who are rich, contented, and self-satisfied will be the ones who will miss out on the kingdom: riches and food and pleasures will prevent them seeking and finding God; by filling their lives with a few tawdry 'good things' they miss out for ever on what is truly good (24–26). The second is that the possession of the kingdom, that is to say, the presence of the King, is so radical and so glorious that it transforms everything; bathed in the light of his presence even poverty, hunger and suffering become beautiful.

---

[6] The reference is to 'mourning and sorrow of all kinds ... no restriction in meaning should therefore be sought'; I. H. Marshall, *The Gospel of Luke* (Paternoster, 1978), p. 251.

[7] 'In that day' (23) is to be taken as referring to the present, the day when the people of the kingdom experience hatred and persecution, not to the end of the age. See Beasley-Murray, *Jesus and the Kingdom of God*, pp. 161–162.

But at this point we need to make a very significant qualification. We could do this by picturing three people. The first is rich and well fed and happy. The things he values are money, food and pleasures. As a result he has no time for God and his kingdom, and in God's eyes, so far from being blessed or truly happy, he is a helpless captive of evil. The second is poor and hungry and suffering. But she welcomes the kingdom and the King; in the light of his presence everything is transformed; filled with his riches and goodness and joy, she can even 'delight in'[8] her poverty and hunger and suffering, so great is the blessedness she now knows in Christ. The third is equally poor and hungry and suffering. But he shares the values of the first man; for him money, food and pleasures are what matter; he is driven by the desire to escape poverty and hunger and suffering so that he can enjoy wealth and rich living and the world's pleasures. This person in his heart is no different from the first person; the only difference is in their outward circumstances. And, like the first person, he has no time for God and his kingdom, and God sees him as an equal captive of evil.

It is in this context that we can understand the differences between Luke's beatitudes and those given by Matthew in the Sermon on the Mount.[9] Commentators agree that Luke's account is the most likely to be what Jesus actually said; but we are not to conclude that Matthew is trying to blunt the impact of Jesus' words by spiritualizing away their meaning. Rather, he is bringing out the necessary qualification: the poor are blessed, not simply because they are poor, but because with their poverty goes poverty of spirit, that is, they have a 'humble and a contrite heart'[10] that welcomes the coming of the King; if they are outwardly poor but inwardly have the same values as those whose god is riches, then they will miss out on God's gift of blessedness. It is the welcoming and possessing of the kingdom of God that are the key issues.[11]

So here, at the heart of the teaching of Jesus, is an urgent corrective to our values. Our culture is quick to assume that poverty

---

[8] 2 Cor. 12:10.

[9] Matt. 5:3–6.

[10] Isa. 57:15.

[11] Matt. 5:3; Luke 6:20. 'The saying is addressed to those who are literally poor, or who share the outlook of the poor ... Yet, as the sequel makes clear, it is not poverty as such which qualifies a person for salvation: the beatitudes are addressed to disciples, to those who are ready to be persecuted for the sake of the Son of man. It follows also that poverty as such is not a state of happiness. The happiness is because of the promise made to the poor ... Theirs is the kingdom of God ... The thought is undoubtedly spiritual – not that the poor will become rich instead of poor; a simple reversal of worldly position is not envisaged'; Marshall, *The Gospel of Luke*, pp. 249–250.

and hunger and sorrow and suffering are necessarily evil in themselves; as we have seen earlier, the criterion for evil is seen as anything which detracts from immediate human happiness. Jesus' view is very different. For him the criterion for evil is the rejection of God, the refusal to accept the coming of his kingdom. Poverty without the kingdom is evil, but it is evil because it lacks the kingdom, not because it is poverty. Riches without the kingdom are equally evil; conversely, poverty with the kingdom is blessedness.

The implications of such radical teaching on how each of us should be living in the twenty-first century are great. But we need to note that Jesus' words, 'Happy are the poor', 'Happy are the hungry', and 'Happy are those who suffer', are not to be taken as negating the value of all we are doing to alleviate suffering in our world today, to feed the hungry, and to 'make poverty history'. What they do remind us is that, valuable and Christ-like though these endeavours are, if they are all that we offer to the poor and hungry and suffering we are drastically failing in our calling as the people of God. God's purpose for our world is not that everyone should be rich and well fed and free from suffering – and at the same time Godless. It is that his kingdom should come. But the coming of the kingdom, as long as we give it its key central place, will inevitably affect the way we live in a world that is full of evil, and it is to this we turn as we look at the next section.

b. Responding to evil (6:27–33)

As in the parallel sections in the Sermon on the Mount, in these verses Jesus is setting the standard for the behaviour of the children of the kingdom in an evil world. Confronted with enmity, hatred, curses, ill-treatment, violence, robbery, theft, ingratitude and wickedness, the standard for our response is nothing less than God himself; our mercy must be as rich as his mercy (36); our goodness must be as perfect as his.[12]

It hardly needs pointing out that in all his teaching Jesus anticipated that his hearers would be the victims of evil: they would have enemies, they would be hated and cursed and ill-treated and so on (27–29). In the previous section he anticipated they would be excommunicated, insulted and reviled 'because of the Son of Man' (22). When he sent out his disciples on mission Jesus warned them that they would suffer: they would be handed over to local councils and flogged in the synagogues; they would be arrested and brought before governors and kings. 'Brother will betray brother to death,

---

[12] Matt. 5:48.

and a father his child; children will rebel against their parents and have them put to death. All men will hate you because of me.'[13] Later, at the end of his ministry, he listed the evils his people would continue to live with: wars and rumours of wars, nation rising against nation and kingdom against kingdom, and famines and earthquakes in various places. Christians would be persecuted and put to death and 'hated by all nations because of me'. 'But see to it that you are not alarmed. Such things must happen, but the end is still to come.' There will be apostasy and betrayal and false prophets. 'Because of the increase of wickedness, the love of most will grow cold.'[14] The picture is a grim one, clearly stating that the experience of evil and suffering would be the norm, especially for the followers of Jesus.

'If the world hates you, keep in mind that it hated me first. If you belonged to the world, it would love you as its own. As it is you do not belong to the world, but I have chosen you out of the world. That is why the world hates you. Remember the words I spoke to you: "No servant is greater than his master." If they persecuted me, they will persecute you also. If they obeyed my teaching, they will obey yours also. They will treat you this way because of my name, for they do not know the One who sent me ... In this world you will have trouble. But take heart! I have overcome the world.'[15]

Evil and suffering will continue in the world for as long as it rejects the kingdom and the King; all will suffer as a result, but those who will suffer the most will be those who go against the stream, those who are the children of the kingdom and follow in the footsteps of the King.

Faced with all this, Jesus calls his disciples to a response that is as radical as his teaching on kingdom values. In place of what the world would see as the natural response to evils, Jesus calls for the kingdom response – effectively a polar opposite. When life gets tough we are not to react with grumbling or resentment or self-pity, but we are to rejoice and leap for joy. To our enemies and those who hate us we are to return, not enmity and hatred, but rather love and goodness. When people curse us we call down a blessing on them; when someone ill-treats us we pray for their good. If we are victims of violence, not only do we not retaliate, we do not even run away – we allow them the opportunity of doing it again. If they rob us of our

---

[13] Matt. 10:17–22.
[14] Matt. 24:6–12.
[15] John 15:18–21; 16:33.

coat we let them have our shirt as well (27–29). Of course it sounds crazy; of course we can see lots of ways in which we can claim it is impractical in the real world. But it is the teaching of Jesus, profound and radical. If we water it down – if we, for example, argue that doing good to our enemies will only encourage them to do more evil, and so we choose simply to cold-shoulder them instead of demonstrating active love and kindness to them – we shall lose the dramatic impact of the kingdom, the radical edge of the teaching of Jesus, and obscure the huge difference that there is between the ways of our holy God and the ways of a fallen world (32–33).[16]

3. The great controversy (Matthew 12:24–37)

This, the third passage we are looking at in this limited survey of Jesus' teaching about evil and suffering, is one that is notorious for the number of problems of interpretation it contains. Our purpose in studying it, however, is not so much to solve these, as to draw from it six further elements of the teaching of Jesus about evil.

a. The impossibility of neutrality (12:30)

'*He who is not with me*', says Jesus, '*is against me, and he who does not gather with me scatters.*' Though we have rightly learnt in these days to accept that the process in which a person turns from evil to God and receives the kingdom and finds Jesus Christ as Saviour and Lord can often be a slow and long one, even taking a number of years, we must not lose sight of the clear teaching of Jesus that every person is either part of the kingdom of God or part of the kingdom of evil. By nature we are 'evil', even though we can point to good deeds that we do.[17] Until we turn to God and receive the kingdom and its King we are outside of it. Until we are with him we are against him.

b. The heart as the source of good and evil (12:33–35)

One of the most radical elements of Jesus' teaching was his insistence that good and evil were a matter of the heart rather than

---

[16] In a park in Huyton, Liverpool, in August 2005, Anthony Walker, a black teenager who was a Christian and a youth leader at Grace Family Church, Liverpool, was subjected to a torrent of racial abuse and then viciously attacked with an axe. His head was split open, and he died some hours later. The radically Christian response of his family and church, who, for all their pain and suffering, refused to respond to evil with evil and insisted on forgiving the murderers, made a profound impression on the media and the nation.

[17] Matt. 7:11.

of outward actions. This was not to say that outward actions were unimportant (36–37); Jesus demanded of his followers standards of behaviour higher than those of the Pharisees and teachers of the law.[18] But it did mean that the condition of the heart was foundational to everything else; outward words and actions come from *the overflow of the heart* (34). *'The good man brings good things out of the good stored up in him, and the evil man brings evil things out of the evil stored up in him'* (35). It is the heart that has to be put right if the *fruit* of our lives is to be good (33). Again, changing our heart is something beyond our human abilities; it can be done only by God,[19] by the power of his Spirit.

c. The abundance of forgiveness (12:31–32)

Discussions of these verses generally spend so much time exploring the one unforgivable sin that they virtually ignore the amazing statements of the abundance of forgiveness: *'Every sin and blasphemy will be forgiven men'*, *'Anyone who speaks a word against the Son of Man will be forgiven.'* Whatever difficulties this passage may contain, this at least is very clear: through Christ God offers forgiveness for 'every sin', even sin explicitly in the teeth of the Lord Jesus. He who cried, 'Father, forgive them', when they were nailing the Son of God to a cross,[20] assures us that no sin, apart from blasphemy against the Holy Spirit, is unforgivable. There is no life so marred with sin and evil that it cannot be made clean and holy through the blood of Christ and the power of the Holy Spirit. Not even major sins, not even deliberate sins, not even repeated sins, not even sins that we commit after we have vowed we will never commit them again – none of them is beyond the abundance of our God's forgiveness.

d. The unforgivable sin (12:31–32)

So what is the one and only unforgivable sin? In the context of Matthew 12 it has to be linked with the determined refusal of the Pharisees to accept that Jesus' ministry was 'by the Spirit of God' (28). Jesus does not say that by attributing his work of driving out demons to Beelzebub the Pharisees were committing the unforgivable sin. After all, the best-known Pharisee of the first century, who played a leading part in all the opposition to Jesus and his teaching,

---

[18] Matt. 5:20.
[19] Ezek. 36:26–27.
[20] Luke 23:34.

was later able to write that, though he was 'the worst of sinners', 'the grace of our Lord was poured out on me abundantly'.[21] Rather than accusing the Pharisees of committing the unforgivable sin, Jesus was warning them that they were in danger of doing so if they continued on their present path. The unforgivable element was not their implacable opposition to Jesus; that continued (and Paul shared in it), yet when that opposition reached its climax and they got him nailed to a cross he still prayed for their forgiveness. So it must be an implacable opposition to the Holy Spirit, a total and final refusal to accept his work. Such a refusal inevitably means that forgiveness, for which the work of the Spirit is essential, becomes impossible.[22]

e. The reality of Satan (12:26–27)

Jesus did not spend much of his time teaching about Satan; he had many better things to talk about. But from time to time he referred to him, making it quite clear that he is very real and a force to be reckoned with, relentlessly opposing God and his purposes, especially those in Christ and his people. Again, there is no neutral ground between the kingdom of God and the kingdom of Satan; anything that is not good 'comes from the evil one'.[23] Right from the start Jesus' ministry was opposed by Satan; Jesus must have described to his disciples his own experiences in the wilderness.[24] Whenever the seed of the gospel is sown, he said, Satan seeks to snatch it away from people's hearts.[25] It is Satan who has sown 'weeds' in the field of the world;[26] these are in fact 'the sons of the evil one', a description applied by Jesus in John 8:44 to those who opposed him. Equally, when, at Caesarea Philippi, Peter opposed the purposes of God in the cross, Jesus spoke to him as to 'Satan'.[27] It was Satan who later sifted Peter as wheat;[28] Jesus prayed for protection for all his disciples from 'the evil one'[29] and taught them to pray the same.[30] The climax of the conflict came in the cross when 'the prince of this world' made his supreme attempt to destroy Jesus

---

[21] 1 Tim. 1:13–16.
[22] For a further comment on the unforgivable sin see pp. 26–27.
[23] Matt. 5:37.
[24] Matt. 4:1–11.
[25] Mark 4:15.
[26] Matt. 13:39–40.
[27] Matt. 16:23.
[28] Luke 33:31.
[29] John 17:15.
[30] Matt. 6:13.

but was himself finally 'condemned' and 'driven out';[31] his ultimate fate is eternal destruction.[32]

f. The binding and burgling of Satan (12:29)

The coming of the kingdom of God in the ministry of Jesus is graphically pictured in Matthew 12:29 as a threefold process. First of all Jesus *ties up* Satan, the *strong man*.[33] Then he enters his *house*. Then he burgles it, carrying off Satan's *possessions*. Here is the other side of the coin to Satan's implacable opposition to the work of God's kingdom in Christ and his people. This is the assault on the kingdom of darkness by God himself, predicted by Jesus when he spoke of building his church and said that 'the gates of Hades will not prove stronger than it'.[34] This is light chasing away darkness, the kingdom of God destroying the works of the devil. Debates continue between those who wish to pinpoint the exact moment at which Jesus bound the strong man, just as debates continue over the binding of Satan for a thousand years.[35] Whatever arguments may be put forward, the key truth remains the same: now, and through all the time of the coming of the kingdom of God,[36] Satan is bound; this means not just that his power is limited, but that he is under the control of the one who has overcome him and bound him. Because he is bound, Christ, and with him his people, can enter his house, can go on the offensive against evil. In the incarnation God came to the dark planet; in his ministry he mixed with sinners and shared the experience of evil and suffering; on the cross he went through into the deep darkness of hell. Though we are not called to do all that he did, we too are sent as his people into an evil world and our task is the same as his: to plunder it, to seize as many of Satan's possessions as we possibly can and bring them out of the darkness into the light of the kingdom of God. Once again, the power and authority to do this do not belong to us; it can only be through *the Spirit of God* (28), the Spirit who empowered Jesus and who has been poured out on us.

---

[31] John 12:31; 14:30; 16:11.

[32] Matt. 25:41.

[33] Gundry interprets the 'strong man' as Jesus, and 'his possessions' as the disciples, who are 'carried off' through persecution; R. H. Gundry, *Matthew* (Eerdmans, 1982), p. 236. But this seems hard to sustain in view of the parallel passage in Mark (3:27), which even Gundry concedes 'obviously' equates the strong man with Satan.

[34] Matt. 16:18, NIV margin.

[35] Rev. 20:2.

[36] Except, possibly, for 'a short time' immediately before the return of Christ (Rev. 20:2).

Interlude
Evil and suffering – and Jesus

God's ultimate answer to evil and suffering is the Lord Jesus Christ. He is the fulfilment of the promises in the Old Testament that God himself would come to judge and destroy what was evil and establish for ever his kingdom of righteousness. Yet when he came he did not do what most were expecting God to do. True, he lived a sinless life; he brought healing and hope to those who suffered; he radiated truth and love. But he did not strike dead their enemies; he did not destroy the wicked; he did not bring heaven on earth; he did not restore the kingdom to Israel. As a result, many rejected him. They turned elsewhere to find the answer they wanted to the problems of their day.

But some did receive him. Doing so required something very big, a whole new way of relating to everything, a radical *metanoia*, a reversal of thinking, a turning around, an all-embracing repentance. Foundationally, this meant a turning away from the evil that underlies every other evil, the rejection of God as God. But to accept God as God meant far more than simply finding a place for religion in their lives. It meant letting God be God, submitting everything to his lordship, including their ideas of good and bad and right and wrong. It meant seeing the world his way, understanding life his way, living his way, responding to evil his way, facing suffering his way. It meant accepting his way of dealing with evil and suffering, a way that was so alien to their expectations that even his closest friends found it almost impossible to cope with.

For the heart of his response to evil and suffering was the cross. And on the cross God in Christ took upon himself all the evil and suffering of the world. All the sin, all the darkness, all the pain, all the hell, all the destruction, all the death. Such an amazing answer to the problem of evil and suffering no-one could have imagined. And our amazement grows even greater when we realize that for

God the cross is not just a moment in time. The cost of it and the implications of it extend back to the foundation of the world and forward into eternity. Our God is scarred for ever.

Out of the cross came the resurrection. From death came life, not just the restored life of Jesus of Nazareth, but fullness of life, God's life, resurrection life, transforming life, eternal life opened up and freely available for all who will receive it. From submission to suffering and death and hell came victory, the shattering of the powers of evil, the ransacking of the strong man's house, deliverance for his prisoners, the redemption of his possessions, the reversal of all his plans.

And so the magnificent plan of God was augmented. Instead of writing off and destroying the broken and spoilt universe, marred by sin and evil and suffering, his purpose is to redeem it and remake it and restore it, to fit all the broken pieces back together again, to heal its hurts, to transform its darkness into light, to turn its sorrow into joy, to bring everything together into one beautiful whole under the headship of Christ.

In Part 3 of our study we are going to continue to explore what the Bible teaches about the nature of evil and suffering, but before we do so, we shall draw some conclusions from our survey in Part 2 of God's answer in Christ to evil and suffering.

Our God is involved. We can banish for ever any thought of God standing helplessly or disinterestedly by while the world struggles with evil and suffering. Equally, we can reject any image of a God who did something about evil and suffering two thousand years ago, but is now no longer involved. Rather, he is the timeless God who suffers both with us and for us today; the cross, though a real event at a fixed point in history, is now.

Our God is love. We can banish for ever any thought that God does not care. The cross is the measure of his love. The price he paid, his very life, is the value he places on us.

Our God is in control. There is one who is far above every rule and authority, power and dominion, and every title that can be given; all things have been placed under his feet; and his name is the Lord Jesus Christ.

Our God does things his way. In our more sober moments we would all agree that this has to be. For all our frustration and bewilderment and protest, every one of us knows that we are incapable of running the universe or of solving its problems. Only the one who has infinite wisdom and infinite resources is capable of doing that.

The end of the journey is Christ. We have a God who is capable of solving every problem, healing every hurt, righting every wrong, destroying every evil; and his chosen method is Jesus, the Man of Galilee. We can banish any concerns about the justice of the last judgment, the rightness of the Day of the Lord, or the way all things will work out; for the Judge is Jesus, the Lord who will come is Jesus, all things will be worked together by Jesus. He is our peace. In him we can have absolute trust.

Part 3
What on earth? The nature of evil and suffering

Genesis 3:1–24
10. The paradigm evil

We have already seen[1] that when we come to the question 'What is evil?', there is a radical difference between the answer we would naturally give and the answer the Bible gives. The Bible makes God the key to the nature of both good and evil; we replace God with ourselves.

In this part of our study we are going to turn to a range of passages to help us unpack the biblical teaching. But, first, we need to spend a bit of time looking at the implications of the difference between the two approaches. In particular, we need to become aware of a deep fallacy that is often committed when we try to approach the issue of evil and suffering with a combination of both of them.

1. The great divide

a. No God – no problem

It is fairly easy to accept that if there is no God there is no problem of evil. If the world is not created, not designed, not watched over by an all-powerful and all-loving God, then the question 'Why evil?' makes no sense. That is not to say that atheists do not have to face moral choices or suffer pain; but it is to say that they do not have to try and reconcile the evil they experience with the ultimate goodness of reality, since they do not have to believe that reality is ultimately good. Reality for them is the world around them and what they experience, and nothing more. If it is evil and painful it is evil and painful. They do not have to ask why it is evil and painful;

[1] Page 69.

what is, simply is; it is the result of a chance, meaningless process; there is no way we can demand meaning for it.

b. No God – no ultimates

So an atheist is spared the agony of the question 'Why evil and suffering?' An atheist, equally, is required to define evil without any reference to God. It has to be, to update Hobbes's phrase, what we do not like; or, to be less self-centred, what is detrimental to the well-being of our community or society; or, to be less anthropo-centric, what is detrimental to the well-being of planet Earth; or, to be even more broadminded, what is detrimental to the well-being of the universe. These definitions, of course, illustrate the slippery nature of atheistic definitions. If we take the commonest, what is somehow harmful or unpleasant to me, we are immediately faced with the problem that what is harmful and unpleasant to one person is helpful and pleasant for another: two men go for a job; the decision is announced; for one it is good news, for the other bad news. If we enlarge our definition and state it in terms of com-munity, we have to face the fact that what may be good for one community is bad for another; trade tariffs protect jobs and the standard of living in rich nations, but push poor nations deeper into poverty. If we are more environmentally conscious we may well concede that what is good for the human race, for example the exploitation of fossil fuels to heat our homes and drive our cars, is bad for planet Earth; if we are very broadminded we might have to concede that, given our destructive bent, what is good for planet Earth might even be the extinction of the human race, something that we would probably decide is a very bad thing for us.

Overshadowing all these questions is another, even more signifi-cant issue. If we, say, define good and evil in environmental terms, and decide that evil is to be defined as what destroys the ecological balance of our planet, or something similar, we then have to face the question, 'Why is the destruction of the ecological balance of our planet an evil?' After all, we could say, its current ecology is very different from the ecology of four billion years ago; presumably nobody wishes to argue that it is evil that things have changed in the past four billion years; why, then, do we assume that it would be evil to change our current ecology for a different one? The fact is that if we try to define good and evil in terms of anything within the universe, such as what I enjoy, the maximization of human well-being, or the preservation of the environment, it is always possible to question whether or not this thing is good. Why is human happiness or the maximizing of human well-being or the preservation of the environmental status quo a good? Always we seem to be pushed out to a further, broader, more fundamental criterion, from ourselves to our community, from our community to the human race, from the human race to the world, from the world to the universe. And where next? For those who reject God there is nowhere else, no ultimate basis for good and evil, no final answer to the question 'Why is this a good and that an evil?'

Faced with issues like these, the atheistic thinkers of our generation have been forced to abandon any ultimate concept of good and evil and take refuge in relativism. There are no ultimate answers, they say; there are no fixed standards of good and evil. What is good for one person is bad for another; what I call evil you call good; though, in order to live in community, we have to agree to act as though some things are good and some things are evil, their goodness and evilness are totally confined to our own attitudes and points of view; nothing is intrinsically good or intrinsically evil.

Atheists, then, do not have a problem with evil on two counts; in a relativistic age we can dismiss both good and evil as purely subjective and therefore of no substance; and in an uncreated and so meaningless universe the question 'Why evil?' is itself meaningless.

c. But God makes all the difference

In contrast, the Christian locates the key to the definition of evil, not in the individual or the human race or the environment, but in God. This has profound implications. It provides an ultimate reference point that solves the problem of relativism. Just as God is the basis for meaning and truth and for the material existence of the universe, so he is the basis for goodness. And if he is the basis for goodness a whole new approach to the issue of evil and suffering is opened up to us. Not only is our starting point different from the atheists'; all our subsequent discussion is based on fundamentally different presuppositions, and that makes all the difference.

We accept, then, that the true criterion for good and evil lies not in our happiness or the preservation of the status quo of the environment of planet Earth, but rather in God. Thus the only test of whether a specific thing is good or bad has to be with reference to him. We can only ever say, 'This thing seems evil to me, in that it makes me unhappy; or that thing seems good to me because it preserves the ecological balance; but its true goodness or badness can be understood only in the context of God and his overarching purposes for his creation.'

You may wonder if this is in practice no better than saying, 'We don't understand, but one day we will', and whether in reality it gets us any further than the atheists who have to retreat into relativism because they will not admit the existence of an ultimate being. But it is different from the retreat to relativism in two very significant ways. First, it accepts that there is an ultimate good purpose behind everything even though we may not at present be able to see it. This is in strong contrast to the relativists' defeatist acceptance that everything is ultimately meaningless. It is the difference between being confident that the pieces of the jigsaw can and will be put together to form a beautiful picture and the conviction that they never can be. Secondly, we do not remain totally in the dark over God's purposes. Though he has not revealed to us all that he is doing, and though there are many details of our lives and of our world that we are at present unable to fit into the big picture, he has shown us enough to enable us to begin to fit things together and to understand something of his ways.

d. God and no God

Exploring those ways will occupy us for much of the rest of this book, but we need at this point to be clear on one very significant issue in order to avoid a major mistake which discussions of the problem of evil and suffering almost invariably make. We could put it like this: if we start with a definition of good and evil that, like that of the atheists, assumes there is no God and so is based totally in the world, then our subsequent discussion should consistently operate with that definition and according to that worldview. If we start with a definition that, like the Bible's, accepts the existence of God and roots the concepts of good and evil in him, then our subsequent discussion should consistently operate with that definition and according to that worldview. What we should not do is to start with one definition and then discuss it in the context of the other worldview. In particular, we should not, as Christians, be required to defend our belief in God and at the same time accept that good and evil are to be defined in terms of human happiness. Most discussions of the problem of evil make this mistake, and as a result make the issue far more difficult than it really is. The Bible does not make this mistake; it starts with God, gives us an understanding of good and evil that is based on God, and then goes on to face, in the context of God and his purposes, the issues and problems that arise.

This is a point that we shall be picking up a number of times in the next few chapters. Meanwhile we are going to look at what many would claim is the foundational passage in the Bible's teaching on the nature of evil.

2. Back to the beginning (Genesis 3:1–24)

a. Evil, the garden and the fall

It is important to emphasize that Genesis 3 is not giving us the answer to the question, 'Where did evil come from?' It is not describing the origin of evil. It is not even saying that evil and suffering are the result of the fall, the sin of Adam and Eve. Both existed before the fall. God's words, 'It is not good', occur before we get to chapter 3;[2] it would seem possible to speculate that, if it was not good for Adam to be alone, he 'suffered' the 'evil' of loneliness well before the fall. The serpent, Satan,[3] has clearly rebelled against God before he appears in the garden; before the woman and the man commit their sin of disobedience he is challenging God's lordship, questioning his word and telling lies,[4] things which would seem to be clearly evil.[5] We could also surmise that the Satanic rebellion which resulted in the devil being 'hurled down' from heaven[6] would have involved not just sin and evil, but at least some sort of suffering that was experienced by Satan, and also, in keeping with our discussion of Genesis 6,[7] in the heart of God himself.

Was the garden of Eden itself entirely free of pain and suffering? It is hard to imagine that it could have been so. Quite apart from the fact that the words of God to the woman in Genesis 3:16 spoke not of the introduction of pain but of the increasing of pain, it is hard to conceive of life in any garden that could be pain-free. Did not Adam stub his toe against tree roots? If he slipped when climbing a tree, would he not fall and bruise himself? Did his muscles not ache after a long walk through the garden, or his skin feel sore after a day in the sun? If he experienced loneliness before the forming of the woman, did he not also feel other emotions, both pleasant and

---

[2] Gen. 2:18.

[3] Rev. 12:9.

[4] Gen. 3:1–5. In his analysis of Gen 3:1–5 Milne perceptively lists nine areas of doubt or wrong understanding of God, along with 'covetousness', which Satan sowed in Eve's mind before the act of taking the fruit; B. Milne, *The Message of Heaven and Hell* (IVP, 2002), pp. 62–63.

[5] Paul's comment that 'sin entered the world through one man' (Rom. 5:12) does not have to imply that no sin was committed in the world before the sin of Adam and Eve, but rather that their disobedience was the point when sin polluted the human race and through it the world at large. Commenting on Rom. 5:12, Stott writes: 'Paul is not concerned with the origin of evil in general, but only with how it invaded the world of human beings. It entered through one man, that is, through his disobedience'; J. Stott, *The Message of Romans* (IVP, 1994), p. 150.

[6] Rev. 12:10–12; Luke 10:18.

[7] Chapter 2 above.

unpleasant? Surely Eden was not free from pain and suffering; but what made it Eden was the presence of God. We have all watched it happen: a child falls over and bangs his knee; for a moment he does not know how to react; we wait, expecting tears. But tears do not come; he looks round and sees his Dad; he knows his Dad admires him for his courage – after all, he is his son. So he is brave; he rejects the tears, and he smiles; the pain may be there, but the presence of the father makes all the difference. Pain and suffering there were in the world before the fall; but the presence of God transformed them into something beautiful.

b. The tree of the knowledge of good and evil (3:3–7, 22)

The word 'good' (*ṭôb*) occurs seven times in the first chapter of Genesis, with the climax, 'God saw all that he had made, and it was very good.'[8] But in chapter 2 a new word appears, the word 'evil' (*raʿ*): 'The LORD God had planted a garden ... In the middle of the garden were the tree of life and the tree of the knowledge of good and evil.'[9] Again, this mention of evil comes before the account of the fall; in a perfect garden where he himself walks, God places a tree whose name includes the word 'evil'. The fruit of this, alone of the trees, God prohibits.

How are we to understand 'the tree of the knowledge of good and evil'? Many suggestions have been made. Some have suggested there is no particular significance in the character of the tree; the important thing is God's prohibition. He could as well have said, 'You may eat of any tree, except a fig tree', or 'except a pear tree'; the issue was obedience to a command, not the variety of tree.[10] It is undoubtedly true that the basic issue is a command of God to be obeyed, but that does not have to preclude the possibility that the choice of command was not arbitrary, but meaningful. Perhaps, say some, the tree's significance is to be found in the fact that the phrase 'knowing good and evil' can in Hebrew indicate moral maturity.[11] Adam and Eve, as God placed them in the garden, were morally unsophisticated, even naive; eating the forbidden fruit would catapult them into maturity, with both an intellectual and experiential (the Hebrew concept of

---

[8] Gen. 1:31.

[9] Gen. 2:8–9.

[10] C. S. Lewis, in his masterly account parallel to Gen. 3, which he sets on the planet Venus, chooses a seemingly arbitrary issue, the spending of a night on the Fixed Land, as the test piece for obedience. See C. S. Lewis, *Voyage to Venus* (Pan Books, 1960), p. 66.

[11] See the discussion in J. Skinner, *A Critical and Exegetical Commentary of Genesis* (T. & T. Clark, 1910), pp. 95–96.

knowing includes both elements) awareness of the nature of good and of evil. Others, for example von Rad, suggest that the meaning of the title of the tree is much wider than moral knowledge; to know good and evil is to know everything; to eat the fruit of the tree is to grasp at omniscience, something that belongs to God alone.[12] These insights are helpful, and allow us to interpret the title as implying both moral and general knowledge and experience. We might take issue with von Rad, however, in that human minds are simply not capable of omniscience; I may know many things, and I may have a very broad range of knowledge, but I have not and never will have the capacity to know everything there is to know. A further helpful suggestion is made by H. Seebas, 'The fact that man was not allowed to approach [the tree of the knowledge of good and evil] and take of its fruit suggests that though evil existed, God desired at first to spare him the knowledge of all that was involved, for only God himself could overcome it.'[13]

I suggest the best key to our understanding of the significance of the tree of the knowledge of good and evil lies in the words of God in Genesis 3:22, *'The man has now become like one of us, knowing good and evil.'* This reflects the words of Satan, *'God knows that when you eat of it your eyes will be opened, and you will be like God, knowing good and evil'* (3:5). The temptation implicit in the fruit was that of becoming like God; the outcome of eating it was exactly parallel to the act of disobedience by which the woman and the man ate it. Both were a refusal to let God be the one and only God; both were an assertion of the right of humans to be more than creatures, to grasp at divinity, to set themselves up as God, to determine for themselves good and evil, right and wrong, true and false. Here again we are confronted with the basic essence of sin and evil, the refusal to allow God to be God.

The rejection of authority is a hallmark of our culture. 'Man come of age' no longer needs to be told what to do. We can at last cast off the chains of tradition and structures. Metanarratives are to be abolished. Authorities (with the probable exception of science and technology) are to be questioned and rejected. Each of us is to become our own authority. We make the rules; we decide what is true and what is false, what we will believe. We create our moral principles and we decide how to apply them. And we can do these

[12] 'The pair of terms (good and evil) is not at all used only in the moral sense, not even especially in the moral sense. In the great majority of cases it means ... simply "everything" ... Knowledge of good and evil means, therefore, omniscience in the widest sense of the word'; G. von Rad, *Genesis*, 2nd edn (SCM, 1963), p. 79.

[13] H. Seebas, 'Adam, Eve', in C. Brown (ed.), *New International Dictionary of New Testament Theology* (Zondervan, 1975–8), 1, p. 85.

things because we have what it takes to do them. We have put out our hand and taken the fruit of the tree of the knowledge of good and evil; we are supreme in our lives; we have set ourselves up as God.

c. The paradigm evil (3:8–24)

There has been debate over how the words of God in Genesis 2:17, that death would be the result of eating the fruit, were fulfilled. Some, pointing out that Adam and Eve lived on for many years, interpret 'death' as spiritual death, that is, separation from God. This interpretation seems to be borne out by Paul's discussion in Romans 5:12 – 6:11, where his references to death through sin and life in Christ are referring to spiritual, not physical, death and life. Others would take it more literally and conclude that it means physical death, even though it was deferred.[14] I would suggest that both interpretations are valid: spiritual death and physical death are each the result of sin; when he sinned, physical death became the inescapable destiny of Adam; but, much more immediately, his living relationship with the God who is the source of all true life was broken.

The climax, then, of the events in Genesis 3, what we could call the paradigm evil, is the break between the human race and God, graphically described at the end of the chapter:

So the LORD God banished him from the Garden of Eden to work the ground from which he had been taken. [24]After he drove the man out, he placed on the east side of the garden of Eden cherubim and a flaming sword flashing back and forth to guard the way to the tree of life (23–24).

It is this appalling break, this shattering of the unity of God and his creation, this cutting off of human creatures made in the image of God and alive with the breath of God from God himself, the source of all that we are – it is this that sets the scene for all the rest of the Bible account, and for the whole of human history. Whatever happens from now on is shaped by this moment. The human race has decided to dethrone God and to take his place. As a result, what was 'very good' becomes the arena for evil and suffering:

To Adam he said, 'Because you listened to your wife and ate from the tree about which I commanded you, "You must not eat of it,"

---

[14] So Milne, who cites Rom. 5:12, 14, 17, as supporting this view; Milne, *The Message of Heaven and Hell*, p. 64.

> *'Cursed is the ground because of you;*
>   *through painful toil you will eat of it*
>   *all the days of your life.*
> *It will produce thorns and thistles for you,*
>   *and you will eat the plants of the field'* (17–18).

From this moment the human race is on its own in a fragmented world. The immediate presence of God is a thing of the past; instead of unity and harmony there is separation and alienation. Life no longer rests in the security of the will of God; rather, it is to be wrested from a hostile world around. Pain and suffering are no longer transformed by the presence of the Father; they are to be borne alone; worse still, they no longer have meaning, for meaning now rests in humanity, and humanity is not adequate to provide meaning for them. In a deep and meaningful relationship of unity and love with the One who made us and gives meaning, not just to us, but to everything, everything indeed has meaning, nothing is alien. But, when we are severed from him, strangers in a broken world, things are very different. Perhaps this is maturity; perhaps the pain and the experience of alienation and meaninglessness are the knowledge of good and evil.

In his famous lines, Milton pictures the man and the woman going out from the garden, sad but yet heroic:

> Some natural tears they dropped, but wiped them soon;
> The world was all before them, where to choose
> Their place of rest, and Providence their guide.
> They, hand in hand, with wand'ring steps and slow,
> Through Eden took their solitary way.[15]

Doubtless there is deep insight in this description. But Milton lived at the start of the Age of Enlightenment, when confidence in the abilities of the human race to live in a broken world, and not just to survive but to conquer it and turn it back into a paradise, was strong. We, well over three hundred years later, are wiser and sadder. We know that the high hopes of the Enlightenment have been shattered; we have lived through its fruits in the evils and darkness of the twentieth century. The dreams of heaven on earth built by human endeavour have faded. The result of the human race taking its solitary way out from a relationship with God has been Auschwitz and Pol Pot and 50,000 children dying every day through starvation or readily avoidable disease.

[15] John Milton, *Paradise Lost*, XII.645–649.

Revelation 12 – 14
11. The cosmic battle

The book of Revelation uses symbolism to teach deep truth. It is always a mistake to seek to understand such symbolism literally. Jesus is not literally a lamb with seven horns and seven eyes;[1] the devil is not literally an enormous red dragon with seven heads and ten horns and seven crowns;[2] heaven is not a literal cube;[3] Armageddon is not a literal earthly battle with swords or tanks.[4] But if it is a mistake to understand the symbolism literally, it is an even greater mistake to dismiss or play down the underlying truths that lie behind the symbolism. The key feature of Christ in heaven is that he is the Lamb, both slain and conquering; he has complete power and complete wisdom. Satan is hideous and horrifically destructive, with overwhelming (though not complete) power and great authority on earth; the dimensions of heaven are absolutely perfect; the story of planet Earth is one of conflict between the powers of evil and God, a conflict that will end in a great climax when in a moment all God's enemies will be destroyed.[5] These are profound truths, and if we ignore them because they are presented to us in a genre we find difficult to cope with we will be unable to grasp the richness of the Bible's teaching.

In the great central interlude of the book of Revelation (chapters 12 – 14), we are given an overview of all history, an insight into the cosmic conflict between evil and good in which we are involved. From seeing only our own situation and its problems it enables us to

[1] Rev. 5:6.
[2] Rev. 12:3.
[3] Rev. 21:16.
[4] Rev. 16:16.
[5] See my brief discussion of the symbolism in Revelation in P. Hicks, *Discovering Revelation* (Crossway, 2004), pp. 49–51, 119–120, and the lengthier treatment in G. K. Beale, *The Book of Revelation* (Eerdmans, 1999), pp. 50–69.

see the bigger picture, why the world is as it is, why evil is so awful, and where we fit in. In particular we are given a glimpse of the dark powers of evil, headed up by the satanic parody of the Trinity, and their inexorable war on God and his purposes and his people.

1. Jesus and his people (12:1–2, 5–6, 13–17)

The first few verses of chapter 12[6] introduce us to the main actors in this cosmic drama. The most important is Jesus. He is clearly identified in verse 5 by the use of the quotation from Psalm 2 that says he *will rule all the nations with an iron sceptre*. Jesus is born of *a woman* (1, 2, 5), the second actor in the drama. We might think this is Mary, but the other details given in the chapter (6, 14–17) make it clear that something more than Mary is meant here. The clue comes in verse 17: *the rest of the offspring* of the woman are *those who obey God's commandments and hold to the testimony of Jesus*. So the woman represents the community of God's people, Israel in the Old Testament and then the church in the New Testament (of which Mary was part), out of whom Jesus was born, and to which we belong. Later verses highlight the persecution and suffering of the people of God symbolized by the woman (6, 13–17), but verse 1 stresses the glory. This is how the people of God appear in heaven, in God's eyes, wrapped in brilliant light, reigning over the universe (1). This is the reality of which we have as yet only a taste.

2. Satan and his schemes (12:3–5)

The third actor is the loathsome dragon or serpent, specifically identified in verse 9 as 'the devil, or Satan, who leads the whole world astray'. Verse 3 tells us he is *enormous* and hideous, *red* with the blood of destruction, frighteningly powerful (*ten horns*) and exercising despotic rule (*seven crowns*). The first part of verse 4 adds that he is horrifically destructive. His avowed intention is to destroy Jesus (4b).

But God wonderfully intervenes (5). Jesus is rescued; God gives him the protection of heaven and *his throne*, ensuring that he lived despite all Satan's schemes to destroy him, whether by the killing of

---

[6] 'It is widely agreed that the story told in chapter 12 is an adaptation of an ancient myth, known throughout the world of John's day. His use of it is an astonishing example of communicating the Christian faith through an internationally known symbol, comparable in a fashion with the Evangelist's exposition of the incarnate ministry of the Lord in terms of the Logos, also an internationally known symbol in his day'; G. R. Beasley-Murray, *The Book of Revelation* (Oliphants, 1974), p. 192.

the baby boys by Herod, or through other attempts to silence or kill him before he had completed his work.

3. The defeat of Satan (12:7–12)

In verses 7–12 the scene shifts, and we see the cosmic conflict from a different angle. This is war between heaven and hell, good and evil, God and the devil. We probably do not need to date verse 7 specifically, locating it in prehistory, or at the incarnation, or the cross, or the resurrection or ascension. Heavenly events are outside of earthly time, and this is the cosmic conflict of the ages, spanning the whole of time, yet supremely focused in the whole work of Christ, and in which we play a key part.

The passage draws on imagery from Daniel, especially Daniel 2:31–45; 10:12–21; 12:1–4. Michael (Rev. 12:7) is there described as a great angelic guardian of God's people. Satan and his hosts of evil seek to take control of the universe by casting God off his throne. But there is no way he can do that (8). Michael, the heavenly representative of the people of God here on earth, is too strong for him. His defeat is dramatic and total; he is *hurled down* (9), and for ever forfeits whatever access he had to the presence of God (8).[7]

4. Holy people in a tough place (12:10–17)

The defeat of Satan has two contrasting outcomes: victory for the kingdom of God is certain (10), but Satan's fury is now directed at planet Earth (12). Having failed to destroy Jesus or cast God off his throne, and knowing that his final destruction is not far off, he directs all his energies at destroying God's creation and especially God's people. This is why the world is such a tough place for holy people to live. There is only one way the people of God can possibly survive in such a situation: by living out the salvation that Christ has won for us on the cross, and by standing firm in our commitment to Jesus, even if it means martyrdom (11).

We may be tempted to feel that there is a bit of a raw edge to verse 12. The angels in heaven have much to rejoice about, but we down here have to put up with hell on earth. But we need to remember three things: first, we share in the responsibility for creating hell on earth; secondly, hell on earth is only for a limited time, and then come all the glories of heaven for ever; and, thirdly, when verse 12 talks about those who dwell in heaven rejoicing, that includes us.

[7] The reference here may be to Job 1:6–9; 2:1–6; Zech. 3:1–2, picking up the meaning of his name, 'accuser' (see verse 10); no longer can he even accuse us before God.

We are already citizens of heaven[8] and seated with Christ in the heavenly realms.[9] We do not have just the agony; we can share in the ecstasy as well.

Michael is the heavenly representative of God's people on earth, and verse 11 makes it very clear that the defeat of Satan is not something of which we are just spectators. It is something in which we are closely involved. We are the ones who overcome him *by the blood of the Lamb and by the word of* our *testimony* (11). We are called to share in casting him down. We are not just victims of the devil; we are his destroyers.

From verse 13 to verse 17 the scene changes again and we are back to the story started in verses 1–6. The picture is one of continual attempts by the devil to destroy God's people, and continual protection by the keeping power of God. In verse 6 we have been told that the woman, the people of God, will be protected from the power of Satan by God for the whole period of the last days, the age of the Christian church, symbolized by 1,260 days. This assurance is repeated in verse 14.[10] Not even Satan's manipulation of natural phenomena (15) can defeat us. Just as God gloriously triumphed when the Israelites seemed to be trapped by Pharaoh at the Red Sea,[11] so he will use every resource to rescue his people.

5. Antichrist (13:1–8)

But if God has resources, so has the devil. Two of them are described in chapter 13. The first is a beast out of the sea (1).[12] It too is a hideous monstrosity (1–2). Much of the imagery goes back to Daniel 7:2–7, where Daniel saw four kingdoms or empires presented as four beasts. Here the characteristics of Daniel's beasts are all rolled into one, suggesting that this beast is to be identified with earthly power structures in general. There can be no doubt, however, that those in the first century would have identified it with the power of Rome, especially since the reference to a *fatal wound* in verses 3 and 14 would readily have been applied to Nero, who committed suicide in AD 68, but who was widely expected to return from the dead.

The beast is the second person of the Satanic trinity. It thus corresponds to Jesus Christ and is Satan's rival to Christ. It is the

[8] Phil. 3:20.
[9] Eph. 2:6.
[10] 'A time, times and half a time' means a year plus two years plus half a year, which equals forty-two months or 1,260 days.
[11] Exod. 14:10–31.
[12] The sea probably symbolizes hell.

Antichrist, the devil's alternative to Jesus, the one through whom he seeks to conquer the world. The Antichrist is in fact hugely successful. Not only does he get the whole non-Christian world following him (8), he seems to be able to do what he likes with God's people (7), even to the extent of conquering them. But only for a time. God allows[13] the beast to do his evil work for *forty-two months* (5), not for ever. When the time is up, the beast will be destroyed and all his work undone. In the first century the savage opposition by the power of Rome to Christianity was a manifest expression of the beast; in other centuries the spirit of Antichrist has taken other forms, through other tyrannies and power structures. As John said, 'many antichrists have come',[14] and many no doubt will continue to come.

6. 'The false prophet' (13:11–18)

The third member of the Satanic trinity, the *beast* from the *earth* (11), seems to be a bestial copy of the Holy Spirit in a number of ways. He is the means by which the beast exercises his *authority* in the world, as Jesus works in the world through the Holy Spirit; he causes people to *worship the first beast*, just as the Spirit brings people to worship Jesus; he does *great and miraculous signs*; and he causes *fire* to *come down from heaven*, perhaps a copy of the Day of Pentecost (12–13).

His chief task is to deceive the inhabitants of the earth in order to make them worship the first beast or Antichrist. To help him in this, and in contrast to the grotesque hideousness of the first beast, he appears like *a lamb* (verse 11), attractive and apparently harmless. As a result, in the rest of the book he is called 'the false prophet'. He promotes the devil's false religion by making an idolatrous image in honour of the beast or Antichrist. He miraculously animates it so that it can condemn to death all those who refuse to worship the beast (14–15). This recalls Daniel 3:1–6, but very probably also refers to specific events in the Roman state religion that the Christians of the first century experienced.

[13] As elsewhere in Revelation, the phrase 'was given' (13:5, 7) implies that it is God who is doing the giving. The emphasis, however, is not that God gives power to the beast to make war against his people, but that God gives the beast permission to use the power that has been given to it by Satan (13:2). 'That God is the ultimate source of the beast's authority in these verses is implied by the decreed time limit and the predestined number of those who worship him in v 8 (the same implication is found in the authorization clauses of Daniel 7). Only God, not the devil, sets times and seasons. The devil would never want to limit his work against God's kingdom to a mere "three and a half years"'; Beale, *The Book of Revelation*, p. 695.

[14] 1 John 2:18.

In Revelation 7:3 the people of God are 'sealed' by having God's mark put on their foreheads. Not to be outdone, the beast and the false prophet decide that they will mark everybody, too (16). God's mark is a sign of his ownership and the guarantee that he will keep his people through all the pressures and suffering of life on earth. The beast's mark is also a sign of ownership, and it is essential if someone is going to be able to live comfortably in this present world order (17). Just as God puts his name on us as we are baptized 'into the name of the Father, the Son, and the Holy Spirit',[15] so the false prophet brands the beast's followers with the beast's name or its numerical value.[16]

7. God's people: agony and ecstasy (13:9–10; 14:1–5)

Little in chapter 13 seems calculated to encourage the people of God, least of all the parenthesis in the middle of the chapter:

He who has an ear, let him hear.

> [10] *If anyone is to go into captivity,*
> *into captivity he will go.*
> *If anyone is to be killed with the sword,*
> *with the sword he will be killed.*[17]

This calls for patient endurance and faithfulness on the part of the saints.

Chapter 14, however, as so often in Revelation, directs our attention away from the dark picture of earth with its evils and suffering to the realities of heaven. So far from bearing the mark of the beast, the people of God, pictured as the 144,000, have the *name* of the Lamb *and his Father's name written on their foreheads*; they stand already *before the throne*; they are holy; they are God's, and they *follow the Lamb wherever he goes*. Despite all their suffering on earth, their

---

[15] Matt. 28:19.

[16] Letters were used for numerals in the ancient world, so any word or name could be given a number. Through the centuries people have shown amazing ingenuity in getting names to fit 666; one scholar managed to make the names of all the early Roman emperors except two fit, a possible confirmation of 1 John 2:18. Significantly, the number of 'Jesus' is 888, exceeding at every point the most perfect thing we could imagine (777; '7' in Revelation stands for perfection). The Antichrist (666) falls short of perfection at every point.

[17] A reference to Jer. 15:2; 43:11, though 'the emphasis here, as in 6:2–8, is not on the punishment of the wicked, but on the suffering of God's people'; Beale, *The Book of Revelation*, p. 704.

place in heaven is secure; they are the people of God; nothing can separate them from him; whatever they go through, they sing (1–5)!

8. The eternal gospel (14:6–20)

Three angels with three messages follow, each of them vital for our dark world. The first is the message of *the eternal gospel* to be proclaimed to everyone on earth, *every nation, tribe, language and people* (6–7). The second is the pronouncement of the doom of the Satanic world order (8). The third is the warning of awful judgment on those who ally themselves with the beast, on the day when *the harvest of the earth is reaped* (9–20). The primary means of the proclamation of the gospel throughout the New Testament is the witness of the people of God, as is seen, for example, in Revelation 10 – 11. But here the fact that it is angels who proclaim both the good news of the gospel and the certainty of judgment could lead us to speculate that the primary reference of the passage is to those who have not heard the gospel through human agency. This would fit with the unusual expression 'the eternal gospel' and with the limited content of the summary given: *Fear God and give him glory, because the hour of his judgment has come. Worship him who made the heavens, the earth, the sea and the springs of water* (7). This is parallel to Paul's words in Acts 14:17; 17:24–28; and Romans 1:18–20, where he teaches that God has not left himself without witness even where the gospel has not yet been preached by human agency.[18]

We can list a number of conclusions from our survey of these three chapters.

1. *There is a war on.* Behind the evil and suffering of this world lies a great cosmic conflict. We see only part of the whole: our situation, our suffering, the evil that affects us. But the real picture is much bigger, nothing less than the war between evil and good. We do not choose to be caught up in this conflict; we are victims of it.

2. *The human race is divided into two.* Though we have no option but to be involved in the cosmic conflict, the fact that we are moral beings means that we have a choice over which side we fight on. Like Jesus in Matthew 12:30, the book of Revelation states that every person is either on the side of evil or on the side of good. The criterion is the mark we bear, either the mark of the Antichrist, or the name of Christ and his Father.

---

[18] Beale feels that 'the eternal gospel' here is primarily a declaration of judgment rather than an offer of salvation; Beale, *The Book of Revelation*, pp. 748–9. Like all preaching of the gospel it is surely both (2 Cor. 2:15–16).

3. *We are soldiers, not just victims.* Those who are on the side of Christ, the people of God 'who obey God's commandments and hold to the testimony of Jesus', have a key role to play in the conflict. So far from being passive sufferers, we share in the victory of hurling down Satan in at least three areas: the power of Satan in our lives is broken through the blood of Christ shed on the cross; we accept and declare the truths of the gospel; and we are totally committed to God and his Christ, even if it costs us our lives. Because of this we are more than just victims of the devil; in Christ we are his destroyers.

4. *Key to the cosmic conflict is Satan's determination to destroy Christ.* God's purposes of grace and salvation for his creation are focused in Christ. In order to prevent them Satan has to destroy Christ; or, failing that, to thwart his work; or, failing that, to prevent the coming of his kingdom through his people.

5. *The people of God are therefore the devil's special target.* We are to expect him to attack us at every opportunity and in every way. But we can be confident that, as with Job, he can exercise his power against us only as God allows, and for a limited time.

6. *The devil's goal is to prevent the human race from acknowledging and obeying God.* To this end he uses his agents, including worldly power structures, to speak out against God, to persecute and destroy God's people, and to get the world to worship him in place of God and Christ.

7. *These tactics are very successful.* If we feel that the powers of evil have the upper hand in the world of our own day, the situation must have looked even bleaker in the first century, when the Christian church was tiny and seriously threatened with extinction.

8. *Yet the ultimate reality is very different.* The church as God sees it is not weak and struggling. It is glorious and victorious, sharing and rejoicing in the overcoming of Satan. We are the people of the Lamb who sing the glories of our Saviour, who live holy and pure lives, and follow him wherever he goes, even to a martyr's death.

9. *Being the people of God means that suffering is not just inevitable but in a sense to be welcomed.* To follow the Lamb means to share the sufferings of the one who is scarred, and thus to partake richly of all that he is. There is a sum of suffering that has to be accomplished before the war is over; ours is the privilege to share in it.

10. *God cares for us.* Just as God ensured that Satan's designs to destroy Christ were thwarted, so he makes sure that whatever Satan may seek to do to destroy us is unsuccessful (12:14, 16). Ultimate and total victory for God's people is guaranteed by the ultimate and total victory already won by Christ (12:10–11; 14:1–5).

11. *Compromise will not do.* Essential to the survival of God's people in so tough a world are faithfulness and a total commitment to Christ. God has committed himself and will not fail us; we must not fail him.

12. *There is a gospel to be declared.* As elsewhere in Revelation, a key purpose of God is the proclamation of the gospel. Though God ensures that no-one is ignorant of the 'eternal gospel' that enables men and women to know enough of him through what they see in the world around us to respect and seek him, the full message of the good news as it is in Christ is entrusted to his people to declare, by who we are, what we say, and how we die.

13. *The proclamation of the gospel entails the judgment of God on those who reject it.* Those who ally themselves to the powers of evil will share their fate, which is horrific and certain.

12. Suffering evil

A substantial proportion of the Bible is narrative; in our study of what the Bible teaches about evil and suffering we need to learn from the stories of those who experienced or practised evil or went through suffering. To cover every instance would be impossible; we shall have to be content with a selection. We shall treat each situation as a case study, briefly outlining the story, then seeking to answer some basic questions, and ending with comments and conclusions.

1. Joseph (Genesis 37 – 50)

Joseph's story is one of strong contrasts and rapidly changing fortunes. He starts as his father Jacob's favourite son who has precocious dreams, and who is rejected and hated by his brothers (Gen. 37:3–11). Attempted murder by his brothers is followed by being sold into slavery in Egypt (37:24, 28). But *the LORD was with Joseph* (39:2) and he becomes a successful and trusted manager of Potiphar's house (39:5–6) until disaster strikes again when, after refusing to be seduced by Potiphar's wife, he is accused by her of attempted rape and thrown into prison (39:17–20). Again *the LORD was with him*; the pendulum swings once more, and he is trusted with responsibility by the warder (39:21–23). But he is still in prison, and, despite very successful dream interpretation and an attempt to get out, he seems to be stuck there for life (40:1–23). But after two more years the pendulum swings again and, after interpreting Pharaoh's dreams, he shoots from prison to being second in the land (41:1–45) and the means of bringing Egypt through seven years of famine. Then comes the long story of his dealings with his brothers and eventual reconciliation (chapters 43 – 45) and the settling of the whole family in Egypt (47:11), where Jacob eventually dies (49:33). Despite their reconciliation, Joseph's brothers are afraid that, once Jacob was dead, Joseph, in his all-powerful position, might exact revenge on them. So we come to the climax of the story:

> *But Joseph said to them, 'Don't be afraid. Am I in the place of God?* [20] *You intended to harm me, but God intended it for good to accomplish what is now being done, the saving of many lives.* [21] *So then, don't be afraid. I will provide for you and your children.' And he reassured them and spoke kindly to them* (50:19–21).

What evil is there in this account? Plenty, including a particularly unsatisfactory home background; victimization by his brothers; slavery; moral uprightness being rewarded with a totally unfair accusation; and sudden ruin, imprisonment, and being forgotten for two years.

What forms of suffering? All the above undoubtedly brought suffering both physical and emotional, though the narrative does not mention this; it rather stresses that God was with Joseph and so, despite the setbacks, he continued to prosper even in adversity.

How did Joseph react to evil and suffering? Very positively, presumably accepting that God was with him in each situation working out his purposes of good. This strong faith may well have been helped by the dreams of ultimate success given right at the start of the narrative.

Where was God in all this? Generally invisible, particularly when his brothers were seeking to kill him, or Potiphar's wife was bringing about his ruin. But he uses Joseph's gifts and hard work to prosper him and bless others. In order to avoid a disastrous famine he reveals the future through Pharaoh's dreams and their interpretation. At the end of the narrative it becomes clear that the whole story is being overruled by God to save Egypt, and Jacob's family among others, from famine.

Comment. A very encouraging story, right at the beginning of the Bible, that teaches that even major personal disasters can be used by God to work out his purposes of grace. Joseph is presented as a model of trust in God despite adversity and thus a man whom God was able to use. What Joseph suffers is eventually used to prevent suffering on a much wider scale.

What we can learn about the nature of evil and suffering. Evil and suffering, including serious sin and major personal disasters, are part of life; God does not generally intervene to prevent them, but he works through them, and sometimes supplements them, to fulfil his good purposes.

2. The plagues of Egypt (Exodus 7 – 12)

Many have argued that the first nine of the ten plagues of Egypt were a series of connected events arising from an unusually high inundation of the Nile.[1] But though we can thus view them as having a 'natural' explanation, the account in Exodus clearly states that God claims full responsibility for them: 'I will stretch out my hand and strike the Egyptians with all the wonders that I will perform among them.'[2] In a parallel way, Pharaoh and the Egyptians are determined not to let the Hebrews go and harden their hearts against them and their God, but at the same time God takes responsibility for their obstinacy.[3] The whole story is presented as a demonstration of the power and glory of the God of the Hebrews, as he confronts the cruel oppression of the greatest political power of the day and its awesome gods and wipes the floor with them in order to fulfil his purposes of grace and set his people free.

What evil is there in this account? The primary evil is the oppression of the Hebrews by the Egyptians, and their determination to oppose the true God and not let them go. If the scholars are right, the plagues themselves, apart from the killing of the first-born, are 'natural disasters'.

What forms of suffering? The Hebrews suffered slavery and oppression which got worse as God started to intervene;[4] the Egyptians suffered the plagues, though those who *feared the word of the LORD* were spared some of the suffering (9:20–21). God felt pain at his people's pain.[5]

How did they react to evil and suffering? Pharaoh, as the representative of his people, recognized the plagues as a contest between the Hebrew God and the gods of Egypt. He could view the outcome of the first two plagues as a draw, since his magicians could copy them (7:22; 8:7). After that he had to concede victory to God (e.g. 8:9), but still held out against him, willing to undergo further suffering rather than to give way.

Where was God in all this? Everywhere. The narrative is describing a conflict between God and the gods of Egypt, worked out on an earthly stage. God's involvement is therefore emphasized; even though the plagues were 'natural' events and Pharaoh's obstinacy was his own choice, God claims responsibility for them both.

---

[1] See, for example, the article by K. A. Kitchen in *The Illustrated Bible Dictionary*, 3rd edn (IVP, 1980), pp. 1234–1236.

[2] Exod. 3:20.

[3] Exod. 5:2; 4:21.

[4] Exod. 5:6–9, 21.

[5] Exod. 2:25.

Comment. The evil of the plagues arose out of a greater evil, the oppression of a people. The suffering undergone by the Egyptians can be seen as both a punishment for their cruelty and for their obstinate opposition to God, and as the price that had to be paid to rescue the Hebrews from their suffering.

What we can learn about the nature of evil and suffering. Evil and suffering as we experience them can be the outworking of the conflict between God and the powers of darkness. Evil gives rise to further evil. God's intervention to help may actually increase suffering rather than alleviate it. God uses natural events and people's choices, even when they are evil, in working out his purposes.

3. Elijah (1 Kings 17 – 19)

The context of these three chapters is the turning away of God's people, led by Ahab and his Tyrian wife Jezebel, from the worship of God to the worship of Baal. Elijah's mission is to counter this and turn the people back to God. Baal, basically a nature god, claimed lordship over the weather, so it is fitting that the first clash should be a demonstration that God's power over rain is greater than that of Baal: '*As the* LORD, *the God of Israel, lives, whom I serve, there will be neither dew nor rain in the next few years except at my word*' (17:1). For some time Elijah stayed with a Gentile widow in Zarephath near Sidon, saving her and her son from starvation, and raising the son from death (17:7–24). After three years of drought the definitive clash between God and Baal came on Mount Carmel, where Baal was shown to be an impotent deity, and God demonstrated his reality both by sending fire and by sending rain (18:38, 45). Following this setback, Jezebel was determined to destroy Elijah, and in fear and self-doubt he fled to the desert, where he was met by God who renewed and recommissioned him (19:1–18).

What evil is there in this account? The primary evil is the turning away of the people from God to Baal. Additionally, there are the natural evil of a drought, the savage opposition of Jezebel towards Elijah, and the personal evil of his fear and doubt. The slaying of the false prophets (18:40) is not looked on as an evil, but as a necessary purging of evil from the land.

What forms of suffering? The suffering that arose from the drought; the pain in the heart of God at his people's apostasy; Elijah's emotional struggles.

How did Elijah react to evil and suffering? The man who stood firm for God through the drought and fearlessly challenged Ahab and the prophets of Baal is portrayed in chapter 19 as a very human person, experiencing fear and doubt, linked, very probably, with exhaustion and reaction, and unable to cope with the pressures of life (19:3–4).

Where was God in all this? Right at the centre. The drought and its ending are clearly his work, as is the fire on Carmel. All three are, however, mediated through Elijah, in particular through his prayers. In chapter 19, given Elijah's weakness, God's intervention is more direct, providing for his physical need miraculously, and speaking in an audible voice.

Comment. No concern or sympathy is shown in the narrative for the fate of the prophets of Baal; their extermination would have been seen as an inevitable result of their defeat and the people's decision to follow the true God. Jesus points out that there were doubtless many Jewish widows in need during the years of famine, but Elijah was sent to a Gentile, who, we can assume, was the only one who was prepared to welcome him.[6]

What we can learn about the nature of evil and suffering. God uses a natural disaster, drought, to show his superiority to Baal and to persuade his people to turn back to him. He responds graciously and miraculously to the needs of a Gentile widow and the personal need of his servant.

4. The exile (2 Chronicles 36:15–21)

We have grown used in our day to seeing images of horrendous scenes of evil and suffering during times of oppression and war. Most writers on the theme of evil take the Holocaust as the most horrific of evils. But, sadly, the evils and suffering of the Holocaust and other atrocities of the twentieth century are nothing new, except, perhaps, for the number of people involved. Wartime atrocities and the extermination of peoples have been practised throughout history. When God warned his people that if they rejected him he would let their enemies destroy them, they knew that such a destruction would be horrific. How horrific it was can be gauged from the book of Lamentations:

> Those killed by the sword are better off
> than those who die of famine;
> racked with hunger, they waste away
> for lack of food from the field.
> With their own hands compassionate women
> have cooked their own children,

[6] Luke 4:25–26.

who became their food
    when my people were destroyed.
The LORD has given full vent to his wrath;
    he has poured out his fierce anger.
He kindled a fire in Zion
    that consumed her foundations.[7]

The Bible makes it quite clear that the defeat of God's people, the destruction of Jerusalem and the exile were the result of the people's apostasy. *Again and again* God sent messengers to warn them, *because he had pity on his people* (2 Chr. 36:15); but *they mocked God's messengers, despised his words and scoffed at his prophets* until the point was reached where *there was no remedy* and the judgment of God had to fall (16–17).

What evil is there in this account? The twin evils of the people's rejection of God, and the horrors of war.

What forms of suffering? Innumerable. The Babylonians *spared neither young man nor young woman, old man or aged* (36:17). The writer of Lamentations, presumably an eyewitness, especially recalled the suffering of the children. Alongside the suffering of his people went the suffering of God, both the pain caused by his people's sin, and the pain of seeing his chosen and loved 'son' destroyed, a pain pictured in the heart cry of Hosea 11.

How did they react to evil and suffering? Doubtless the reactions varied, but those we have, such as the writers of Chronicles and of the book of Lamentations, fully recognize the justice and goodness of God in allowing the exile.

Where was God in all this? When the armies of Nebuchadnezzar attacked the city, when the troops were killing the men and raping the women, when the children were starving to death, God did not intervene to prevent the horrors. Many times before he had intervened to rescue his people, but this time he allowed the atrocities to happen, because there was no other remedy for the apostasy of his people.

Comment. We have all heard well-meaning people say, 'I can't believe that a God of love would allow an innocent child to suffer.' The Bible makes it very clear that God, whose love and compassion are greater than anything we can imagine, passionately desires that no innocent child will ever have to suffer, but the Bible writers accept that the suffering of the innocent is the inevitable result of the existence of evil and sin in our world; though God may for a time protect the innocent (and the guilty) from the suffering that arises

[7] Lam. 4:9–11.

132

from sin, for him always to do this would be to ignore the seriousness of evil and so to deny his holiness and his righteous judgment.

What we can learn about the nature of evil and suffering. Evil, particularly the fundamental evil of refusing to let God be God, is far more serious than we like to think. The most drastic steps need to be taken to deal with it. Part of the awful evilness of evil is that it harms the innocent; it crushes not just the perpetrator but those around, and, on the cross, God himself.

5. 'Joseph, I'm pregnant' (Matthew 1:18)

We know the end of the story, that it was all infinitely worth while. But in those early months, and, indeed, until after the resurrection, the way was far from easy. A frightened girl, a suspicious Joseph, questions, doubts, gossip, misunderstanding, rejection, a strained relationship, a troubled birth, exile in Egypt, and much more. 'A sword will pierce your own soul too,' said Simeon to Mary.[8] To be the person God called her to be cost Mary dear.

What evil is there in this account? There is absolutely no evil in the incarnation; it was a beautiful and holy divine act. But, however perfect the act, its repercussions in an evil world inevitably included evils: fear, doubt, rejection, pain, exile.

What forms of suffering? Many and varied, from public disgrace to watching her son die on the cross.

How did Mary react to evil and suffering? Generally with humble acceptance: 'I am the Lord's servant ... May it be to me as you have said.'[9] But at times she struggled.[10]

Where was God in all this? Very, very close; occasionally clearly visible; more often obscured. He was giving Mary the greatest privilege conceivable, and he did not fail her as she struggled with its implications.

Comment. Most of the people in the Bible whom God chose and called to serve him suffered as a result. The choice to side with God in an evil world is a choice to be a victim of evil. We may wish to ask, 'Why could not God become incarnate in the world without causing suffering to an innocent young girl? Why could he not declare his word through a Jeremiah or a Hosea or a Paul and not allow them to get hurt in the process?' But alongside those questions we would have to ask, 'Why did God not give his life for the world on the cross without any pain or cost to him?'

[8] Luke 2:35.
[9] Luke 1:38.
[10] Mark 3:21, 31–5.

What we can learn about the nature of evil and suffering. Great gifts from God bring pain and suffering as well joy and privilege. The gift of any child, like the gift of the Christ child to Mary, will sooner or later bring pain as well as joy; the more we love someone the greater potential there is for hurt if the relationship goes wrong or is broken.

6. 'All the little boys he killed' (Matthew 2:16–18)

The slaughter of twenty or thirty young boys in an attempt to kill the Messiah was all in a day's work for Herod.[11] Contemporary accounts describe his savage cruelty and the hundreds if not thousands of men, women and children he butchered, including his own wife and sons. His motivation was power; anything that might have threatened his position was dealt with ruthlessly. Herod, though notorious for his cruelty even in his day, was fairly typical of ancient rulers; before he was twenty the emperor Augustus killed two thousand Roman knights and three hundred senators who threatened his position.[12] Such was the world into which was born a child who came to show us a very different model of kingship.

What evil is there in this account? The craving for power, ruthless cruelty, the savage murder of innocent children.

What forms of suffering? Sudden death, inconsolable grief.

Where was God in all this? He allowed it to happen, just as he allowed all the other savageries and sins of Herod and Caesar and Augustus and all the many tyrants great and small down through the centuries. If we are tempted to say, 'But it was OK for him; he made sure his Son escaped', we need to remember two things. First, that God loved those boys who were killed and grieved over their slaughter as much as their mothers did. Second, that God's Son, too, though saved at birth, was later savagely slaughtered, and his Father did not intervene.

Comment. This incident may seem like a dark stain on the delightful Christmas story, but it reminds us of the real world into which Jesus came, and, indeed, in which we live today. We need to set the cruel but swift death of twenty or thirty boys at Bethlehem alongside the slow and painful death of tens of thousands of children in our twenty-first century world who die of preventable hunger or readily curable disease every day.

---

[11] 'In the life of this ruler, a deed like the massacre of the children of Bethlehem is a small episode, such as may be required in the ceaseless struggle for power'; E. Stauffer, *Jesus and His Story* (SCM, 1960), p. 41.

[12] Ibid.

What we can learn about the nature of evil and suffering. They are real; they are part of our world. We may wrap ourselves around with tinsel and pretty stories, but the truth is that the impact of sin and evil on our world is horrific. We have just emerged from a century in which a hundred million 'innocent' people were killed in wars, millions of 'innocent' foetuses were aborted, and alcohol and drug abuse and bad driving caused millions of 'innocent' deaths, not to mention those who have suffered and died because of poverty and injustice. I have grieved over the death of my baby son; hardly a family in the world has escaped sudden and tragic loss. This is a world that desperately needs the coming of a Saviour.

7. John the Baptist (Matthew 11:2–6; 14:3–12)

'Among those born of women there has not risen anyone greater than John the Baptist,' said Jesus.[13] High commendation indeed, for a man who fearlessly declared the word of God and confidently pointed people to the coming one, and was not afraid to denounce the sin of those in power (Matt. 14:4). Yet, as those words were being spoken, John, in prison, was struggling with doubts about Jesus: *'Are you the one who was to come, or should we expect someone else?'* (11:3). Perhaps Jesus' reply (4–6), showing that his ministry was fulfilling the prophecy of Isaiah 61, helped him. Perhaps it did not, since central to that prophecy was a promise of 'freedom for the captives and release from darkness for the prisoners',[14] and Jesus did nothing to get John out of prison. There he stayed, rotting away in his cell, his fruitful ministry cut short, until his savage execution (6–12).

What evil is there in this account? Immorality, political oppression, corruption and manipulation, murder, a godly life unnecessarily and meaninglessly cut off in its prime.

What forms of suffering? The physical suffering of an ancient prison and eventual execution. The frustration of a fruitful ministry cut short. Supremely, the struggle with doubt, the horrible fear that he had got it all wrong, that all his ministry had been a mistake, that Jesus was not the Messiah. The logic was simple: 'Jesus claims to be the Anointed One, come to bring good news and set the prisoner free. I am a prisoner, and he specifically says he values me above all others. Therefore he will set me free.' But he did not, and in the end instead of freedom came death.

[13] Matt. 11:11.
[14] Isa. 61:1.

How did John react to evil and suffering? Like most of us, he struggled.

Where was God in all this? Not immediately obvious, particularly to John and his disciples. But very definitely there all the same, working out key elements of his purposes both for John and, through John and Jesus, for a lost world.

Comment. 'He must become greater; I must become less,' said John,[15] though he hardly realized the full implications of what he was saying. 'Take my life,' we say to God, unaware that we are giving him the right to lay us in an early grave. With the start of the ministry of Jesus, John's work was finished. From a human point of view, which tends to rate life on earth higher than life in heaven, he should have been granted a long and pleasant retirement. But God used the evils of Herod's court to take him to himself.

What we can learn about the nature of evil and suffering. Our logic may not be God's logic. We may produce an excellent argument why a God of love should do what we think is best, but he has reasons for doing something else. Our values may not be God's values; he may not agree with us that the early and cruel death of a good person is a disaster.

8. Ananias and Sapphira (Acts 5:1–11)

We have grown used to sin in the church. Division, self-seeking, gossip, prejudice, immorality, greed and the like are all too familiar to us in what is, after all, a community of sinners. The New Testament church was also made up of sinners, and sins of various sorts soon made their appearance: injustice and prejudice, false teaching, and 'sharp disagreement',[16] followed later by the divisions and disputes and immorality at Corinth.[17] So familiar are we with such human failings among the people of God that it comes as a shock to realize that God is nowhere near as complacent about them as we tend to be.

When the people of God entered the promised land God undertook that if they were faithful to him he would give them success in all that they did. But hardly had they started when they were defeated at Ai. The reason was that Achan had sinned, deliberately going against God's clear instructions and taking for himself things that were God's. It was the first sin of the newly consecrated people of God, the first refusal to obey him, the first rebellion against his

[15] John 3:30.
[16] Acts 6:1; 15:1; 15:39.
[17] 1 Cor. 1 – 6.

lordship; as such God could not ignore it and the punishment was severe.[18]

In a similar way God could not turn a blind eye to the first entry of deliberate sin into his newly consecrated people, newly filled with the Spirit of holiness, in the book of Acts. We may be profoundly grateful that not every sin in the church meets with such severe punishment; but we need to be aware that God views each one as seriously as he viewed the sin of Ananias and Sapphira. Without doubt, our complacency about the presence of sin in the church today is one of the chief reasons why, compared with the days of Acts, the presence and power of God in our midst are so limited.

What evil is there in this account? From our point of view the main evil is the sudden death of a man and his wife. From God's point of view, expressed through Peter, it was the evil of sin among his holy people, expressed in deceit and spiritual hypocrisy.[19] If God was to be among them in the fullness of his Holy Spirit, then his people must be holy. If they were not holy they could not have the presence of God; in effect they could not be his people.

What forms of suffering? Sudden death and *great fear* (11).

How did they react to evil and suffering? The summary account that follows the story of Ananias and Sapphira speaks of 'many miraculous signs and wonders', and 'more and more men and women' becoming Christians.[20] We can conclude that the demonstration of God's holiness and judgment on sin among the people of the Jerusalem church resulted in a new commitment to holiness, and so in new evidence of God's powerful presence among them.

Where was God in all this? Very obviously present.

What we can learn about the nature of evil and suffering. God takes evil and sin among his people very seriously indeed; if we want his presence among us we need to be prepared to face his judgment.

9. Paul (2 Corinthians 12:7–10)

When Ananias (same name, but a different person) was called by God to go to the newly converted Saul of Tarsus and pray for the healing of his blindness, God told him that two things were to be central to Saul's life from then on: evangelism and suffering: 'This

[18] Josh. 7:1–26.

[19] 'They wanted the credit and prestige for sacrificial generosity, without the inconvenience of it. So, in order to gain a reputation to which they had no right, they told a brazen lie. Their motive in giving was not to relieve the poor, but to fatten their own ego'; J. Stott, *The Message of Acts* (IVP, 1990), pp. 109–110.

[20] Acts 5:12–16.

man is my chosen instrument to carry my name before the Gentiles and their kings and before the people of Israel. I will show him how much he must suffer for my name.'[21]

Paul the evangelist is the hero of us all; but not many of us are prepared to follow in the steps of Paul the sufferer. Yet in the New Testament the two are virtually inseparable: if we are going to be in the front of the battle we shall get hurt.

Paul had an amazing theology of suffering. It was not a theology worked out in a comfortable library but in a life that was full of pain and hurt. Listen to some of the words he uses to describe himself: 'like men condemned to die in the arena', 'a spectacle', 'fools', 'weak', 'dishonoured', 'hungry and thirsty', 'in rags', 'brutally treated', 'homeless', 'cursed', 'persecuted', 'slandered', 'the scum of the earth', 'the refuse of the world', 'hard pressed', 'perplexed', 'struck down', 'always being given over to death', 'in troubles, hardships and distresses', 'in beatings, imprisonments and riots', 'in hard work, sleepless nights and hunger', being of 'bad report', 'regarded as impostors', 'dying', 'beaten', 'sorrowful', 'poor', 'having nothing', 'in prison', 'flogged', 'exposed to death again and again', 'beaten with rods', 'shipwrecked', 'in danger from rivers', 'in danger from bandits', 'in danger from my own countrymen', 'in danger from Gentiles', 'in danger in the city', 'in danger in the country', 'in danger at sea', 'in danger from false brothers'.[22]

That is by no means a complete list. One thing left off it was the *thorn* (or 'stake') in his flesh (2 Cor. 12:7). Many have speculated over the nature of the thorn,[23] but since Paul does not tell us, we simply do not know what it was. All we do know about it is what he says here: that it was *a messenger of Satan, to torment me*. On three specific occasions Paul pleaded with Jesus to take it away. But he answered 'No' (8–9).

What evil is there in this account? A 'messenger of Satan', something direct from the dark lord himself, that tormented Paul. The language is very strong; this was no fleeting pain or occasional problem. It was the devil's work, and it really hurt.

What forms of suffering? Plenty; physical pain, weakness, persecution, problems, and all the emotional reactions that go with them.

How did Paul react to evil and suffering? He asked Jesus to take it away. When Jesus said 'No', Paul accepted the evil and chose to

[21] Acts 9:15–16.
[22] 1 Cor. 4:9–13; 2 Cor. 4:7–11; 6:4–10; 11:23–26.
[23] Suggestions include neuralgia, malaria, eye trouble, rheumatism, leprosy, epilepsy, or something more emotional or spiritual such as his anguish for the unsaved Jews.

'delight' in the suffering – not just in the suffering of the thorn, but *in weaknesses, in insults, in hardships, in persecutions, in difficulties* (10). The word he uses (*eudokō*) is the word we met in chapter 8, where it refers to God's delight in revealing the mystery of his will to us, and the 'good will' or 'favour' in the angels' song. The pain still hurt, the weaknesses were still very real, the insults still stung, the hardships were still acute, the persecutions were still horrific, difficulties and setbacks and problems still kept coming one after the other. But Paul chose to have 'good will' and even 'delight' towards them.

Where was God in all this? The thorn was not his work; it was Satan's. So, too, presumably, were the weaknesses, insults, hardships, persecutions and difficulties. But the phrase *there was given me a thorn in the flesh* almost certainly entails that God was involved in the giving; that is, God allowed Satan to afflict Paul.[24] Certainly, though God had the power, in answer to prayer, to take the thorn away, he also had the right to allow it to stay there. Both the giving of the thorn and the unanswered prayer were for good reasons, *to keep me from becoming conceited* and *so that Christ's power may rest on me* (7, 9). But, in addition, God undertook to give Paul 'a continual supply of grace'[25] to enable him to cope with the suffering.

Comment. Our immediate reaction to suffering is to ask God to take it away. When our friends are ill, we pray for healing; if missionaries are taken hostage by terrorists, we pray for their quick release. This is undoubtedly right; Paul prayed for Jesus to take the thorn away. But often the Lord's answer is 'No'. Presumably Christian spectators prayed fervently that Stephen would not be martyred; when Paul was travelling we can be sure his friends prayed that he would be kept safe from dangers such as shipwreck or stoning or imprisonment. Perhaps our praying needs to be broader: not just for healing, but that the way our friends suffer their illnesses will be a blessing to others and glorifying to Christ; not just for release, but for a clear testimony to the gospel 'whether by life or by death'.[26]

What we can learn about the nature of evil and suffering. Evil is Satanic, but it is not outside of God's lordship. Confronted with it, God is not helpless; its power is broken; its effects are reversed;

---

[24] Cf. Job 1:11–12.

[25] J. C. Thomas, *The Devil, Disease and Deliverance* (Sheffield Academic Press, 1998), p. 73. Thomas accepts that the thorn was a physical illness, and adds, 'It is made extremely clear that the power of God is made manifest not only in the healing of the sick, but also in the faithfulness of those who suffer in obedience to Christ.'

[26] Phil. 1:20.

in amazing ways he uses it for good. As a result, our attitude to suffering can be turned inside out. Instead of resenting it or being defeated by it, we can 'delight' in it because God is bringing good out of it and we are 'more than conquerors'.[27]

[27] 2 Cor. 4:7–12; 6:4–10; Rom. 8:37.

Interlude
What on earth? The nature of evil and suffering

The Bible is not into giving neat definitions. Perhaps the nearest we get to one is the answer God gave when Moses asked him to tell him his name.[1] Neat it certainly was, but even 'I AM THAT I AM' could hardly be called a definition of our great God. If the heaven of heavens cannot contain him, there is no possibility of wrapping him up in a few defining words.

Nor does the Bible attempt to wrap up evil and suffering in neat definitions. Very probably we should follow its example, and avoid trying to tie the concepts down to simple formulas. So, as we come to the end of Part 3 and seek to sum up what we have found so far from the Bible about the nature of evil and suffering, we shall have to content ourselves with listing a number of insights without being so bold as to claim that even when put together they tell us all there is to be told.

Theocentricity. Central to the Bible's teaching on evil, as on just about every other subject, is the insight that, if we are going to understand it, we must start with God, and not with ourselves. Those who have no God are forced to produce definitions of evil that start with themselves: what they do not like, what makes them unhappy, what spoils their quality of life, and so on. Christians, by contrast, choose to turn away from themselves to God. Just as they make God and his truth the foundation of their lives, so they make God the key to their understanding of what is evil.

Rebellion. Since God is all that is good, to reject him and be separated from him must be the supreme evil. Thus the refusal to let God be God, to rebel against his lordship, to break fellowship with him by asserting our will over against his, is the paradigm evil, the evil from which all other evils come.

[1] Exod. 3:14.

Evil. If this is so, then a working definition of evil could be anything that takes us away from God; conversely, anything that brings us closer to God can be seen as good.

Seriousness. God takes evil and sin very seriously. We constantly tend to underestimate the evilness of evil and the gravity of sin.

Involvement. In contrast to the Enlightenment individualism that still profoundly affects our thinking, the Bible views things holistically. I am not just an isolated individual; I am part of a community, part of the human race, part of God's creation. Or, perhaps, to put the emphasis more accurately, the community or the human race or God's creation includes me. So, since the human race is in rebellion against God and the whole creation is caught up in a conflict between evil and good, each member of the human race will be affected; we cannot stand on the sidelines and claim that we are non-combatants. Whether we like it or not we are in the battle; everything we do is part of the conflict; it either furthers the kingdom of darkness or brings in the kingdom of God. Everything that happens to us is in the context of the conflict; in particular, since one of the major results of rebellion against God is pain and suffering, we shall get hurt as a result of the actions of others; we shall be 'innocent' sufferers.

Identification. God's answer to evil is Christ, and Christians are one with Christ. This means that we are right in the front of the battle against evil. Ours is the privilege and responsibility of being the means of hurling down Satan, through our faithfulness to Christ, the way we live and our testimony to his gospel. It also means that all our suffering is to be seen in that context; it is not random or meaningless. We are in Christ and Christ is in us; what we suffer he suffers; we are suffering with him and he is suffering with us. That enables us to view suffering in a completely different way from those around us.[2] Since Christ is Satan's special target, we too are particularly targeted by Satan, but in Christ we have all the resources of God to bring us through.

Reaction. We can react to evil and suffering positively or negatively. Like Joseph in Genesis, we can trust God through setbacks and suffering even though we are not able to understand his purposes until the end of the story. Or we can follow Pharaoh and harden our heart. Since we are human, our confidence in God will sometimes waver, as happened with Elijah and John the Baptist. But that does not change the fact that God is working out his purposes and that they are good.

[2] 'In the kingdom of Christ suffering for His sake is a sign of His favour and an earnest of His reward'; F. F. Bruce, *The Book of Acts* (Marshall, Morgan and Scott, 1965), p. 200.

Great saints of the Bible struggled with doubts, and so do we. And, gloriously, God was gracious to them and helped to answer their questions. There is a sense in which God has every right to ask us just to hang on in, to trust him though the darkness is total, to keep going even though we have no notion of his purposes. He is under no obligation to answer our anguished 'Why?' But, in his grace, he helps us when we are struggling; he does provide some answers to our questions. They are rarely the answers we want him to give. Nor should we expect them to solve all our problems; our heavenly Father still asks us to trust him. But they help us in our weakness. It is to some of these answers we now turn in Part 4 of our study.

Part 4
Why on earth? Reasons for evil and suffering

Genesis 32:22–32
13. Wrestling with God

1. From Jacob to Israel (32:22–32)

Jacob had a bad start in life. He was a twin; despite jostling in the womb and hanging on to his brother's heel, he was born second, so his brother Esau inherited the privileges of the firstborn. All Jacob got was the role of the number two, and a name that meant 'Heel' or 'Trickster'. Esau was the star, great at outdoor pursuits and all the things that mattered; Jacob was wet and weak, staying at home with the women when the men went out hunting. His father rejected him in favour of Esau; perhaps in reaction his mother doted on him and as a result spoilt him.[1] True to his name, and names shaped natures in those days, he became a manipulator and a cheat, craftily tricking Esau out of his privileges as firstborn, then running from him when he vowed to kill him, and spending twenty years with his uncle Laban, where he was on both the giving and the receiving end of cheating.[2]

We pick up his story as he is returning from his time with Laban, complete with wives and children and flocks, knowing that Esau is coming to meet him, with a force of four hundred men. In fear Jacob cried out to God for help, and sent his company on ahead.[3] Left alone, a man wrestled with him through the night. *When the man saw that he could not overpower him, he touched the socket of Jacob's hip so that his hip was wrenched as he wrestled with the man. Then the man said, 'Let me go, for it is daybreak'* (25–26). Perhaps when the man started wrestling with him, Jacob thought that he represented Esau, the brother he had wrestled with in the womb,

---

[1] Gen. 25:21–28.
[2] Gen. 25:29–34; 27:1 – 31:55.
[3] Gen. 32:1–21.

whom he had tricked, and whom he feared. But by the time he had finished he knew the man was much more than that. '*I saw God face to face*' (30).

All night they wrestled. All his life had been a struggle, a wrestling with circumstances, with others and with God. Neither side won. Jacob was not defeated by his life's experiences, but neither did he triumph over them. He could not get on top of God, nor, as yet, had God got on top of him.

Then the man touched his hip socket. He deliberately injured him. Not in order to win the fight, for the next thing he did was to ask Jacob to let him go. Rather, he injured him so that he would be damaged for life; from that day onward he walked with a limp.

> But Jacob replied, '*I will not let you go unless you bless me.*'
> ²⁷*The man asked him, 'What is your name?'*
> '*Jacob,' he answered.*
> ²⁸*Then the man said, 'Your name will no longer be Jacob, but Israel, because you have struggled with God and with men and have overcome*' (26–28).

'*Israel*', says the NIV footnote, 'means *he struggles with God*.' God chose a new name for Jacob, and in doing so chose a new name for his people. Amazingly, it is a name that talks not of divine blessing or grace but of human struggles. Israel, the man and the people, and through them the new Israel, the people of God today, have a name that speaks of struggling with God.

For Jacob the new name, and the explanation God gave of it, was hugely significant. No longer was he 'Heel'; now he was the man who has 'struggled with God and with men' and has 'overcome'. All his life he had struggled, apparently to no purpose; but now the promise was that although struggles, symbolized by his damaged hip, would continue, the outcome would always be positive; he would overcome.

As day broke, outwardly little had changed. Jacob was still the man who had had a raw deal in life and had given as good as he got; Esau was still waiting for him with four hundred men. What was different was Jacob himself. The struggles of that night, and so all the struggles of his life and potentially the struggles of all the people of God, had climaxed in victory. No longer were they unyielding and meaningless; no longer were the ways of God that brought pain and problems hopelessly dark and menacing. Now the struggling was infinitely worthwhile, for the God who causes us to struggle is the God who through the struggles makes us victors and who empowers us with his blessing.[4] Jacob went limping into the new day with a new relationship with his God and a whole new way of understanding evil and suffering (30–31).

2. Struggling with the issues (32:24)

Sooner or later everyone struggles with God over the pain and suffering he allows us and others to go through. Some struggle and overcome; others struggle and are overwhelmed. Job, suddenly thrust from prosperity to total disaster, cried:

> I will not keep silent;
>> I will speak out in the anguish of my spirit,
>> I will complain in the bitterness of my soul.
> Am I the sea, or the monster of the deep,
>> that you put me under guard?
> When I think my bed will comfort me
>> and my couch will ease my complaint,
> even then you frighten me with dreams
>> and terrify me with visions,
> so that I prefer strangling and death,
>> rather than this body of mine…
> Will you never look away from me,
>> or let me alone even for an instant?
> If I have sinned, what have I done to you,
>> O watcher of men?
> Why have you made me your target?
> Have I become a burden to you?
> Why do you not pardon my offences
>> and forgive my sins?[5]

More recently, John Roth called his contribution to a book of contemporary theodicies[6] 'A Theodicy of Protest' and started with a quotation from Elie Wiesel, the Jewish writer on the Holocaust: 'He is almighty, isn't He? He could use His might to save the victims, but He doesn't! So – on whose side is

---

[4] Brueggemann suggests a parallel with the woman who touched the robe of Jesus in the crowd and drew power out of him (Luke 8:43–48): 'Power has shifted between God and humankind'; W. Brueggemann, *Genesis* (John Knox Press, 1982), p. 268.

[5] Job 7:11–15, 19–21.

[6] Philosophical attempts to reconcile the existence of a good and all-powerful God with the existence of evil and suffering.

He? Could the killer kill without His blessing – without His complicity?'[7]

For many the struggle with God is on an emotional level; we are repelled by evil and suffering that seem so contrary to the nature of a loving and just God; if God really does allow such awful things to happen, then we are repelled by God himself; we feel we cannot relate to or trust a God like that.

For others the struggle is primarily an intellectual one. We refuse to abandon trust in God, but we find it desperately hard to reconcile what we believe about God with the evil and suffering we go through or see around us in the world. So we struggle to reconcile the two, seeking ways of understanding what God is doing, of justifying his actions, and so producing a theodicy.

3. Theodicies

a. A less than omnipotent God

The number of suggested theodicies is large, and there are several ways of classifying them. We could see them as falling into two main approaches. In the first are theodicies which concede that the existence of evil and suffering in the world makes it impossible to believe in an all-powerful and all-loving God. But, they say, we can continue to believe in God by accepting that he is not all-powerful; he is a limited God. This is the position adopted at the popular level by the rabbi Harold Kuschner in his bestseller *When Bad Things Happen to Good People*.[8] The best-known academic presentation of this argument is by process theologians, who argue that if God is all-powerful then no-one else would have any power; since it is clear that other beings do have power, God cannot be all-powerful. So, though God would wish to prevent evil, he is unable to do so; faced with evil he can only seek to 'persuade', never to coerce.[9]

Some evangelicals have been attracted to the view that God is less than all-powerful.[10] But most feel that to concede that is to go

---

[7] Elie Wiesel, *The Trial of God*, quoted by J. K. Roth, 'A Theodicy of Protest', in S. T. Davis (ed.), *Encountering Evil*, 2nd edn (Westminster John Knox Press, 2001), p. 1.

[8] Pan, 1982.

[9] 'God never has a monopoly on power ... This view of shared power implies, in turn, that divine power is persuasive, not controlling'; D. R. Griffin, 'Creation out of Nothing, Creation out of Chaos, and the Problem of Evil', in Davis, *Encountering Evil*, p. 122.

[10] Particularly as expressed by 'open theism'. See, for example, Clark Pinnock (ed.), *The Openness of God: A Biblical Challenge to the Traditional Understanding of God* (Paternoster Press, 1994).

against the clear teaching of the Bible.[11] So, instead, they follow a second approach: God could prevent all the evil and suffering in the world; but he has a good reason for not doing so, which justifies his allowing them, at least for the time being. A number of such reasons have been suggested, any one of which, philosophically speaking, would be adequate to explain why the world contains evil and suffering. But it is also possible to combine two or more of the suggestions and so build a composite and potentially stronger theodicy.

b. Retribution and reformation

What good reason might God have for allowing evil and suffering for a time in our world? One suggestion, not very popular today but going back to the Reformers and beyond, is as a just punishment for human sin. We have spoilt God's world by our rebellion against him; rightly and justly he allows us to experience the results of what we have done.

A development of this suggestion stresses not so much the element of punishment but the intention of God that experiencing evil and suffering would have the effect of turning us from our sinful ways back to him. If the outcome of our rebellion against him was a delightful world in which nothing unpleasant happened, it would seem unlikely that we would ever think of turning back to him. But if the result of rejecting him is a world of evil and suffering, then we would have much more motivation to seek to reverse things.

c. The free-will defence

Perhaps the commonest reason suggested for why God allows evil and suffering is the existence of human freedom. There are many ways of unpacking this. We might point out, for example, that among the things that God has chosen to create are beings, angelic and human, made in his image, who are able to have a deep relationship with him. Key to that relationship are love and obedience,

---

[11] Retaining a strong concept of God's omnipotence does not, of course, commit us to claiming that God can do just anything. No-one wishes to say that God can make two and two equal five in a standard mathematical system, or fall out of a tree, or commit a sin. Indeed, the implication of the Latin-based word 'omnipotent', that he 'can' do 'everything', is lacking in the biblical words *'ǎdônāy ṣěbā'ôt* and *pantokratōr*, which are both better translated 'ruler over all'. Bible writers were much more interested in God's overruling lordship than in the academic question, 'What could God do or not do?' Their response to the twentieth-century debate on whether or not God could create a stone too heavy for him to lift would simply be that he would never try.

both of which require the exercise of free choice; I cannot be said to be exercising real love or genuine obedience if I am forced to love and obey. The creation of such beings introduces the possibility that they would use their freedom to reject and disobey God, thus causing evil and suffering. God knew that this would happen, and that the price he would have to pay would be the cross, but he was willing to pay that price in order to have true and deep relationships with his creatures.[12]

d. 'Irenaean' theodicy

Another suggested reason why God allows evil and suffering is that he wants us to grow and develop as people during our lives on earth, and it is only in a world where evil and suffering exist that we are able to develop all our potential. We could never develop courage, say, unless confronted with danger, or compassion without encountering suffering; love of enemies is a deeper love than love of friends, so we need enemies who do evil things to us in order to develop depth of love. In a world without evil and suffering we would be weak and spineless creatures, never developing our capacities; in a tough world we grow into real people.[13]

e. The nature of the world

Yet another reason put forward for evil and suffering is that they are an inevitable part of the material world God has made. All that he created was very good, but even what is very good can, because of its nature, be the source of evil and suffering. Water is good to drink and to swim in, but we can also drown in it. Pain is good because it

---

[12] For philosophical presentations of the free-will defence see A. Plantinga, *God, Freedom and Evil* (Harper and Row, 1974), and S. T. Davis, 'Free Will and Evil', in Davis, *Encountering Evil*, pp. 73–107.

[13] For a philosophical presentation of the so-called Irenaean theodicy see J. Hick, *Evil and the God of Love* (Collins, 1968), and 'An Irenaean Theodicy', in Davis, *Encountering Evil*, pp. 38–72. Those who base their theodicy on an Irenaean approach have to face the question, 'If evil and suffering are needed to enable us to grow and develop as people, does that mean we won't grow and develop in heaven, where there will be no evil and suffering?' They could choose to answer that there is no need for further growth once we are made perfect in heaven. Or they could suggest that growth in heaven is in different areas from those on earth: we will be growing in wisdom, say, and skills, or some area we cannot at present even conceive of, rather than in things like courage and compassion. The difficulty this question raises warns us against adopting just one limited theodicy and making dogmatic statements such as 'God has to allow evil in our lives in order to enable us to grow.'

warns me not to put my hand in the fire, but it can also cause me much suffering.[14]

All of these suggested reasons involve the assumption that a world with the feature described, even though it entails evil and suffering, is better than a world without it. A world where we learn the evilness of evil is better than a world where we sin with impunity. A world where people can love and obey God freely is well worth creating, even if it involves evil and suffering for human creatures and for God himself. Better to develop our characters through evil and suffering than not to develop them at all. God is thus justified in allowing evil and suffering to exist, at any rate for a time. Another way of expressing the same point is to say that God allows evil and suffering because only by allowing them can he bring about something that is very good, so good, indeed, that it outweighs all the badness of the evil.[15]

Many have found one or other of these suggestions helpful as they struggle to understand why God should allow evil and suffering in our world; some feel the answer may well be a combination of more than one of these suggestions. We could also point out that, even if we cannot be sure exactly which of the several reasons is the true reason, it is helpful to know that there are possible reasons: the agony of struggling with an insoluble problem is removed.

4. Accepting the mystery (32:29)

There are some, however, who feel that the whole attempt to think of reasons why God may allow evil and suffering is misguided. We should not struggle with the issues, they say; we should admit that we cannot understand the ways of God; we should simply accept things as they are and bow before the mystery of God. In support of this approach we could quote Isaiah 55:8–9[16] or Romans 9:20,[17] or we might turn back to the story of Jacob in Genesis 32. Elated,

---

[14] For a consideration of this approach see C. S. Lewis, *The Problem of Pain* (Geoffrey Bles, 1940), pp. 19–23.

[15] Rom. 8:18; 2 Cor. 4:17.

[16] 'For my thoughts are not your thoughts,
    neither are your ways my ways,'
                declares the LORD.
  'As the heavens are higher than the earth,
    so are my ways higher than your ways
    and my thoughts than your thoughts.'

[17] 'But who are you, O man, to talk back to God? "Shall what is formed say to him who formed it, 'Why did you make me like this?' " '

perhaps, at the new name God had given him, Jacob made a bold request:

> *Jacob said, 'Please tell me your name.'*
> *But he replied, 'Why do you ask my name?' Then he blessed him there* (29).

God did not tell Jacob his name. It may be that he knew his Jacob very well and was aware that he was still capable of manipulating situations to his own advantage. To have someone's name meant having a degree of control over him or her, and that God would not give to Jacob. He chose to keep his name to himself, to remain inscrutable and mysterious.[18] So, we might conclude, we have no right to seek an explanation for the presence of evil and suffering in our world; we should simply accept the mystery.

Adopting this sort of position may well be right in some situations. Indeed, it could be argued that this is the main message of the book of Job. In the central part of the book Job and his friends all wrestle with the issues, struggling to find possible reasons for the disasters that have afflicted him. But at the end of the book God rebukes them and effectively states that they should never have attempted to understand his ways. However, other parts of Scripture do wrestle with the issues, and appear to indicate that, provided we are prepared to do it humbly before God, it is acceptable for us to ask the question 'Why?' and to seek to find an answer, even if it involves a struggle.

5. Asking the questions

We have already seen examples of this from the book of Psalms in chapter 4,[19] where we noted that the answers the Bible provides tend not to be carefully argued intellectual theodicies, but rather an insight into the great purposes of God into which we can then fit our particular problematic situation. Much the same applies elsewhere; Habakkuk, for example, starts his book wrestling with two great issues or 'complaints'. The first is why God allows evil and sin among his people;[20] God's response is that he has his answer ready: he will use the 'Babylonians' to punish his people. That leads to Habakkuk's

---

[18] 'The stranger has maintained his inscrutable role. He is not forced to tell his name. But on the other hand, Jacob receives the blessing he so craved. God remains God, his hiddenness intact. But Jacob is no longer Jacob. Now he is Israel'; Brueggemann, *Genesis*, p. 269.

[19] Page 44.

[20] Hab. 1:2–4.

second issue: why should a holy God use an evil nation to accomplish his purposes?[21] To this he is determined to get an answer.

> I will stand at my watch
>   and station myself on the ramparts;
> I will look to see what he will say to me,
>   and what answer I am to give to this complaint.[22]

God's response is that, though he may choose to use an evil nation to accomplish his purposes, all sin, including the arrogant sin of the 'Babylonians', will eventually be punished; what matters is that God's people should continue to live in righteousness and faith.[23] The magnificent third chapter, like the final chapters of Job, pictures the greatness and glory and holiness of God, before which we tremble, but in which we can confidently trust.

> God came from Teman,
>   the Holy One from Mount Paran.
> His glory covered the heavens
>   and his praise filled the earth.
> His splendour was like the sunrise:
>   rays flashed from his hand,
>   where his power was hidden.
> Plague went before him;
>   pestilence followed his steps.
> He stood, and shook the earth;
>   he looked, and made the nations tremble . . .
> In wrath you strode through the earth
>   and in anger you threshed the nations.
> You came out to deliver your people,
>   to save your anointed one . . .
> I heard and my heart pounded,
>   my lips quivered at the sound;
> decay crept into my bones,
>   and my legs trembled.
> Yet I will wait patiently for the day of calamity
>   to come on the nation invading us.
> Though the fig-tree does not bud
>   and there are no grapes on the vines,
> though the olive crop fails
>   and the fields produce no food,

[21] Hab. 1:12–17.
[22] Hab. 2:1.
[23] Hab. 2:4.

> though there are no sheep in the pen
> and no cattle in the stalls,
> yet I will rejoice in the LORD,
> I will be joyful in God my Saviour.
> The Sovereign LORD is my strength;
> he makes my feet like the feet of a deer,
> he enables me to go on the heights.[24]

Out of his struggling and questioning Habakkuk found a new awareness of the greatness of his God, and a new confidence that, come what may, he is utterly to be trusted.

In the next few chapters we are going to be tackling the question 'Why?' and seeking an answer, not so much from philosophers and theologians as from the pages of the Bible itself.[25] We do so aware that the kinds of answers we might want or expect may not be available; the answers we find may well be, like Habakkuk's, a new awareness of God and his greatness, rather than a neatly formulated logical explanation of his actions.

---

[24] Hab. 3:3–6, 12–14, 16–19.

[25] Many scholars state that the Bible does not give us a straightforward answer to the problem of evil and suffering (e.g. D. Simundson, *Faith under Fire* [Augsburg, 1980], p. 15). Acknowledged by many as an expert in the field of Old Testament theodicy, James Crenshaw concluded his magnum opus on the subject by saying that 'the problem of theodicy cannot be resolved' (J. L. Crenshaw, *Defending God: Biblical Responses to the Problem of Evil* [Oxford University Press, 2005], p. 195) – though it needs to be noted that his study virtually ignores the teaching of the New Testament. In this, however, the Bible is simply being consistent: it does not give us a straightforward answer to the issues of Christology or Trinity or divine sovereignty. The fact is, of course, that our Enlightenment demand for clear-cut explanations and 'answers' is quite alien to the spirit of the biblical writers. Truth, for them, like God, is far too big to be reduced to a neat formula. 'Answers' are much broader than logical explanations. The Bible's concern is to teach us how to live in an evil world, not to satisfy our intellectual curiosity. Wink writes of 'the New Testament's refusal to become preoccupied with evil as a theological problem. Its concern is instead practical. It wishes to overcome evil, not explain it'; W. Wink, *Engaging the Powers* (Fortress Press, 1992), p. 317. But to concede that the Bible does not provide the kind of answer that our contemporary culture might expect is not to say that it gives no answer. On the contrary, its response to evil and suffering is rich and varied.

Romans 8:17–27
14. From suffering to glory

If we had the opportunity to ask the New Testament writers, 'Why suffering?', we might well get the answer, 'Glory.' Prefigured in the Servant Song of Isaiah 52:13 – 53:12,[1] the two concepts go together all through the New Testament. Jesus' own summary of his life was, 'Did not the Christ have to suffer these things and then enter his glory?'[2] Peter speaks of 'the sufferings of Christ and the glories that would follow', and tells his readers to rejoice that they share in the sufferings of Christ, so that they may be 'overjoyed when his glory is revealed'.[3] The writer to the Hebrews wrote of Christ being made 'perfect through suffering' in bringing 'many sons to glory'.[4] In Paul's mind there was a very close link between the two. 'Our light and momentary troubles', he wrote, 'are achieving for us an eternal glory that far outweighs them all';[5] and in Romans 8:17 he stated, *We share in the sufferings of Christ in order that we may also share in his glory.*[6] Commenting on this verse, F. F. Bruce wrote, 'It is not merely that the glory is a compensation for the suffering; it actually grows out of the suffering. There is an organic relation between the two for the believer as surely as there was for his Lord.'[7] In similar vein Sanday and Headlam commented, 'It is nothing short of an

[1] The NIV aptly heads the section Isa. 52:13 – 53:12 as 'The Suffering and Glory of the Servant'.

[2] Luke 24:26.

[3] 1 Pet. 1:11, 4:13. Peter also links the two concepts in his appeal to the elders and in his penultimate benediction (5:1, 10).

[4] Heb. 2:10.

[5] 2 Cor. 4:17.

[6] 'We share in the sufferings' (*sympaschomen*) is a present indicating that 'the process of sharing in Christ's sufferings and death is a lifelong one'; J. D. G. Dunn, *Romans 1 – 8* (Word, 1988), p. 456. For other examples of the link between suffering and glory in Paul see Rom. 5:2–3; Eph. 3:13; 2 Tim. 3:8–13.

[7] F. F. Bruce, *The Epistle of Paul to the Romans* (IVP, 1985), p. 168.

universal law that suffering marks the road to glory',[8] and Dunn writes, 'Suffering with Christ is not an optional extra or a decline or lapse from the saving purpose of God. On the contrary, it is a necessary and indispensable part of that purpose. Without it future glory would not be attained.'[9] Moo states, 'What Paul is doing is setting forth an unbreakable "law of the kingdom" according to which glory can come only by way of suffering. For the glory of the kingdom of God is attained only through participation in Christ, and belonging to Christ cannot but bring participation in the sufferings of Christ,'[10] and John Stott writes, 'The sufferings and the glory are married; they cannot be divorced. They are welded; they cannot be broken apart.'[11]

1. The three groans (8:22–23, 26)

The mention in Romans 8:17 of the link between suffering and glory in the experience of Christians leads Paul on to a fascinating section where he extends the concept to the world around us. We shall start our study of it with three groans.

The created world, he says, *has been groaning as in the pains of childbirth right up to the present time* (Rom. 8:22). There is joy in the created order, a hymn of praise to its Creator;[12] but there is also sorrow and pain, pain as sharp as labour pains. Something is wrong; the 'very good' world that God made is suffering and struggling and groaning.

We, as Christians, of course, have our citizenship in heaven,[13] so in a sense we do not belong to this created order. Even so, says Paul, we also *groan* (23). As yet, even though we *have the firstfruits of the Spirit* (23),[14] we still suffer the pain of being human, and of living in this world. As a result, we groan.

But there is a third groan, alongside the groan of the created order and of the people of God. It is the groan of the Holy Spirit, of God

---

[8] W. Sanday and A. C. Headlam, *The Epistle to the Romans*, 5th edn (T. & T. Clark, 1902), p. 206.

[9] Dunn, *Romans 1 – 8*, p. 456.

[10] D. J. Moo, *The Epistle to the Romans* (Eerdmans, 1996), p. 506.

[11] J. Stott, *The Message of Romans* (IVP, 1994), p. 237.

[12] Ps. 65:12–13.

[13] Phil. 3:20.

[14] Moo prefers to interpret verse 23 as saying that we groan 'because' we possess the Spirit, not 'even though' we possess the Spirit: 'It is because we possess the Spirit as the first instalment and pledge of our complete salvation that we groan, yearning for the fulfilment of that salvation to take place'; Moo, *The Epistle to the Romans*, p. 520. His point is a valid one, but it is perfectly possible to read Paul's words as including both interpretations.

himself (26). Many translators and commentators have found the concept of God groaning hard to accept and have tried to evade the force of Paul's words by making the groaning refer to us and not to the Holy Spirit, or by translating it as 'speaking in tongues' or something similar. But the straight meaning of the Greek is as the NIV translates it, and it seems very unlikely that Paul would expect us to understand the word he has just used twice to mean painful groaning[15] in some radically different sense. Here again is our suffering God, this time specifically the third person of the Trinity. 'The Holy Spirit identifies with our groans, with the pain of the world and the church, and shares in the longing for the final freedom of both. We and he groan together.'[16]

2. The created order (8:19–22)

There are three things, says Paul, that cause the created order to groan: *frustration* (20), *bondage to decay* (21) and *the pains of childbirth* (22). 'Frustration' (*mataiotēs*) speaks of futility and purposelessness; it takes us back to Ecclesiastes 1:2: ' "Meaningless! Meaningless!" says the Teacher. "Utterly meaningless! Everything is meaningless." ' 'Bondage to decay' (*tēs douleias tēs phthoras*) could refer to the fact that animal and plant life (though not the rest of the created order) is locked into a repeated process of birth, life, aging, death and decay. But *phthora* has a strong feeling of 'destruction' about it, and it would seem more likely that Paul is referring to the fact that the world will not last for ever; the created order as we know it is not eternal; it is not immortal (*aphthartos*); it is destined for 'destruction'.[17]

But this, says Paul, is *not by its own choice* (20: *ouch hekousa*, 'not willingly'); we could almost say that frustration and decay are not inherent in creation itself; these are things that have been imposed upon it by God. God has decided that the world as we know it should not last for ever, that it should not make perfect sense, that we should not feel completely at home here, that it should not ultimately satisfy. For all its beauty, for all the way it reflects the glory of its Creator, it is not everlasting; it is not an end in itself; it is destined to give way to something even more glorious. Commentators debate the exact place of the words 'in hope' in the construction of the sentence in verses 20 and 21, but when he wrote them Paul was not concerned with the niceties of grammar. It does

[15] *Systenazei* (22), *stenazomen* (23), *stenagmois* (26).
[16] J. Stott, *The Message of Romans*, p. 245. The same verb (*estenazen*) is used of Jesus in Mark 7:34.
[17] 2 Pet. 3:7.

not matter exactly how they fit in; what matters is that over the whole sentence, indeed over the whole section, are stamped the two words 'in hope'. The frustration, the decay, the groaning of the created order all point forward, away from themselves, away from the world, to something amazing that God has in store.

This brings us to the third thing that causes the created order to groan, *the pains of childbirth* (22). The NIV translation, 'the whole creation has been groaning as in the pains of childbirth', is in danger of missing the force of Paul's words. He does not say that the creation is groaning as though it were a woman in labour; rather, he specifically says it *is* in labour, it is groaning together and it is going through the pain of giving birth together.[18] The repetition of 'together' may stress that all aspects of the created order are groaning and travailing, or, more likely in the context, that the created order is groaning and travailing together with the people of God and with God himself. The groaning and the pain, the frustration and the condemnation to destruction, are all leading up to a birth, a new creation, a new heaven and a new earth.[19]

Jesus, in his teaching on the Mount of Olives, spoke of deception, wars, earthquakes and famines as 'the beginning of birth-pains'.[20] They are the pain and the suffering that have to be gone through before the joy of a new birth. But it is not the pain that is the key element; it is the joy.[21] And that brings us to the main thread that runs all through this section. The created order does suffer; it is subject to frustration; it is destined for 'destruction'; but all that is but the prelude to the glorious future that God has in store for it, for which it waits *in eager expectation* (19), 'like spectators straining forward over the ropes to catch the first glimpse of some triumphal pageant'.[22] Paul's answer to the question 'Why suffering?' in the created order is, 'Glory.'

3. The people of God (8:23–27)

We listed in chapter 12 some of the evil and suffering that Paul personally went through. Although, as a leading apostle, he suffered more than most, the expectation of the New Testament was that all the people of God would suffer, both because as yet we live in this world, and because we walk the way of our Lord Jesus. Such suffering cannot, says Peter, prevent us from being 'filled with an

[18] *Pasa hē ktisis systenazei kai synōdinei.*
[19] Rev. 21:1.
[20] Mark 13:5–8.
[21] John 16:21.
[22] Sanday and Headlam, *The Epistle to the Romans*, p. 205.

inexpressible and glorious joy',[23] but nevertheless it causes pain so that we *groan inwardly* (23),[24] even though we have *the firstfruits of the Spirit*, the presence of God in our lives, the evidence of the work of the Holy Spirit in us, and the guarantee of much more to come.[25] Paul mentions here three things that cause us to groan, though there are many others besides: 'the incompleteness of our salvation',[26] our *bodies* (23) and our *weakness* (26).

Our salvation, of course, is complete. Christ's saving work is done;[27] we are redeemed, our sins are forgiven;[28] we are children of God;[29] nothing can separate us from his love.[30] But as yet, here on earth, we do not experience the completeness of our salvation (23). We are redeemed and forgiven, yet we still sin. We are the children of God, yet the world and the flesh and the devil still seem to have a hold on us. Nothing can separate us from the love of God, yet we so often feel alone. Because of this we groan and long for the day when what we now hold by faith will be clearly and totally ours, the full experience of being children of God.

Our body also causes us to groan (23). Paul is referring here to our physical body (*sōma*), with its aches and pains, not to mention its suffering through being stoned, shipwrecked, flogged and imprisoned, and that 'thorn in the flesh' that tormented him. Little wonder he groaned. Few Christians escape bodily illness and pain; some suffer horrifically; we *wait eagerly* for that day when our bodies will be made new, and 'there will be no more death or mourning or crying or pain'.[31]

We also groan in our *weakness* (26). The weakness that characterizes life this side of glory can take many forms; the one Paul highlights here is our weakness in prayer, but he could have mentioned weakness in faith, weakness in the face of temptation, weakness in our grasp of God's truth, and many other weaknesses with which we struggle.

---

[23] 1 Pet. 1:6, 8.

[24] The force of 'inwardly' may be that though our groaning is entirely appropriate and legitimate, it is not to be given the priority in our outward behaviour; our lives are to be marked by joy, not groaning; the right balance is to be 'sorrowful, yet always rejoicing' (2 Cor. 6:10).

[25] Eph. 1:14. Writing of 'believers' involvement in the eschatological travail of creation', Dunn stresses that 'the Spirit does not free from such tension, but actually creates or at least heightens that tension and brings it to more anguished expression'; Dunn, *Romans 1 – 8*, p. 474.

[26] Stott, *The Message of Romans*, p. 242.

[27] Heb. 1:3.

[28] Eph. 1:7.

[29] 1 John 3:2.

[30] Rom. 8:39.

[31] Rev. 21:4.

Those of us who are the people of God, then, like the created order, are not yet what God intended us to be. We have not yet arrived; the journey is still tough, and it causes us to groan. But it is a journey, and it has a great goal. Paul's word for the goal is 'glory'.

4. The glory (8:17–21)

If Paul's answer to 'Why suffering?' is 'Glory', what is this glory that so outweighs everything we go through? And how does it help us cope with the presence of evil and suffering in our world? In this passage Paul tells us four things about the glory.

a. It is Christ's glory (17)

If we are children, then we are heirs – heirs of God and co-heirs with Christ, if indeed we share in his sufferings in order that we may also share in his glory. Christ is God, so his glory is nothing less than God's glory; indeed, he specifically stated that this is so in Matthew 16:27, 'The Son of Man is going to come in his Father's glory.' The glory of God in biblical thought is something very big; indeed, the Hebrew word *kābôd* has a feeling of weight or heaviness about it; it is the opposite of trivial or transient or insignificant. It is weighty; it presses down on us; it forces us to our knees, down flat on our face. The glory of God is something very big. In Isaiah God had promised that he would show his glory to his people and through them to the whole world;[32] John and Paul declared that he has done this in the life and ministry of Jesus,[33] but we still await the full revelation of his glory, 'the surpassing glory'[34] the full outshining of his majesty and holiness and beauty and all that he is.

b. It is glory that outweighs our sufferings (18)

I consider[35] that our present sufferings are not worth comparing with the glory that will be revealed in us. When we see it, and not till then, we shall realize how beautiful and wonderful the glory is. When the savage lash cut into his flesh for the twentieth, fiftieth, hundredth time, or when he cried out in vain to God for release from the anguish of the thorn in his flesh, did Paul begin to feel that nothing could compensate for the suffering he had gone through?

[32] Isa. 60:1–3.
[33] John 1:14; 2 Cor. 4:6.
[34] 2 Cor. 3:10.
[35] *Logizomai*, 'I am firmly of the opinion that', 'It is my settled conviction that'; Dunn. *Romans 1 – 8*, p. 468.

When innocent Christians were flung to the lions for public amusement and burnt alive as human torches at Nero's festivities,[36] did the people of God decide that nothing could ever make up for such horrible torment? Amazingly, no, except perhaps in their weaker moments; for they were convinced that what God had in store for them was so wonderful that their present sufferings were not worth comparing with it. In a sermon on 1 John 3:2, 'We shall see him as he is', C. H. Spurgeon said, 'One short glimpse, one transitory vision of his glory, one brief glance at his marred, but now exalted and beaming countenance, would repay almost a world of trouble.'[37]

c. It is glory that will be revealed both to the people of God and in the people of God (18)

The strict translation of the preposition Paul uses (*eis*) would indicate that the glory is to be revealed 'to us', but the NIV is justified in interpreting it as 'in us', since when we see the glory of Christ we shall be filled with it.[38] We shall see the glory; we shall be 'glorified' (30); the glory will radiate from every part our being. From us it will flow out to the created order; we shall be a 'revelation' (19).[39] In us the world will see the glory of God, the amazing transformation that God's grace and salvation have produced, cleansing from sin, healing from brokenness, the transformation of our 'lowly bodies',[40] restoration, reconciliation, sanctification, glorification – the amazing miracle of a sinful humanity remade in the beauty of Christ and radiant with the glory of God. What it sees in us will spread by God's power to the world in its brokenness and pain, bringing restoration and healing so that to a new humanity God adds 'a new heaven and a new earth'.[41]

d. It is glory that brings freedom (21)

The NIV's *glorious freedom of the children of God* is more accurately 'the freedom of the glory of the children of God' (*tēn eleutherian tēs*

---

[36] Tacitus, *Annals* 15:44.
[37] C. H. Spurgeon, Sermon 61, 'The Beatific Vision', *New Park Street Pulpit*, 20 January 1856.
[38] Col. 3:4; 1 John 3:2.
[39] Paul uses the same word for the glory 'revealed' (*apokalyphthēnai*) to us (18) and our 'revelation' (*apokalypsin*) to the created order (19).
[40] Phil. 3:21.
[41] Rev. 21:1.

doxēs tōn teknōn tou theou). The key element is glory:[42] God's primary purpose is his glory for his people and his world. But out of glory comes freedom, liberation from everything that has held us and the world in bondage, the final breaking of the hold of the powers of darkness, the final removal of every form of bondage to sin and 'frustration' and 'decay' and weakness and suffering and pain and death and everything else that has sought to usurp the lordship of God over his creation.

5. The hope and the help (8:24–27)

In this hope we were saved (24). In the New Testament, of course, hope is not the vague and uncertain thing it often is in our thinking. It is a confident expectation. Paul was certain that God's glory awaits his people and his world. But as yet we do not experience it; *we wait for it patiently* (25). We might be tempted to contrast 'patiently' with the 'eager' waiting of verses 19 and 23, but in Paul's mind there was no contrast; of course we are eager, excited at what God is going to do, longing for it to be soon, and doing what we can to 'speed its coming';[43] and it is because of this that we can face the pressures and suffering of day-by-day living 'with patient endurance' (*di' hypomonēs*). We can cope with the present because we are eagerly confident of the future.

Or perhaps we cannot. Maybe as you read that last sentence you felt that this is just the point where the New Testament and our experience today part company. Paul and his Roman readers may well have gone through horrific suffering with steadfast endurance, strengthened by the vision of the glory that was to come, but today's Christians seem very different. The reality of present sufferings looms far larger than our expectation of glory to come; all too often for us it is the sufferings that outweigh the glory. We even hear Christians from time to time saying, 'My (or someone else's) suffering is so great that I cannot believe that anything in the future can ever compensate for it.' Very probably our inability to see things the way the New Testament sees them is because we are so influenced by our present culture. We think that God is there, like some great cosmic welfare agency, to solve all our problems and take away all our pains, and we expect him to keep the shortest of waiting lists. We are imbued with attitudes such as 'I want it now' and 'I demand my rights'; 'endurance' and 'patience' are

[42] *'Doxa*, "the glorified state", is the leading fact, not a subordinate fact, and *eleutheria* is its characteristic'; Sanday and Headlam, *The Epistle to the Romans*, p. 208.
[43] 2 Pet. 3:12.

rarely seen as virtues. As a result, we pervert those tremendous words of Paul at the end of 2 Corinthians 4: we lose heart; we fix our eyes on what is seen, not on what is unseen; what we suffer is the real and the eternal; what God has in store for us is the unreal and the ephemeral.

So we need help. And God knows that. He is well aware of our struggles. So he comes to our rescue; *the Spirit helps us in our weakness* (26). Again, he does this in many ways; the 'fruit' he produces in us includes 'patience', as well as joy and peace; he takes the teaching of Jesus and the promises of God and makes them real to us;[44] he sets us free from anything that would form a barrier between us and God, he shows us the glory of God, and he transforms us into the likeness of Jesus.[45] In particular, says Paul, he *intercedes for us with groans that words cannot express* (26).

Here is a godly man struggling with evil and suffering. His wife has cancer; he has recently been unfairly passed over for promotion; his teenage daughter has just announced that she is pregnant; a dear friend is struggling with alcoholism. In his bewilderment and pain he does not know how to pray; indeed, he hardly can pray. Should be pray for healing for his wife, or a quick end to her sufferings? Should he pray for justice in his job situation? Would it be right to pray for a miscarriage for his daughter, or that his friend should hit rock bottom? Should he fight against the suffering in his life? Or should he patiently accept it as part of the purposes of God? Bewildered and struggling, he cannot see an answer to the pain and suffering; at best he can only struggle in prayer. But God knows where he is at, says Paul (27), and, amazingly, through his Spirit, shares in his pain and groaning. But instead of being defeated by them the Spirit transforms them. All our weakness in prayer, every prayer where we do not get things quite right, where we ask for something that is not in the perfect will of God, is taken up and transformed by the Holy Spirit into a beautiful intercession that God will work for good according to his glorious purposes (28).[46] Here, as in every area of our lives, God joins his strength to our weakness, and guarantees grace that will bring good out of evil.[47]

Little wonder that Paul follows this great passage in the middle

---

[44] John 14:26; Eph. 6:17.

[45] 2 Cor. 4:16–18.

[46] 'Our failure to know God's will and consequent inability to petition God specifically and assuredly is met by God's Spirit, who himself expresses to God those intercessory petitions that perfectly match the will of God'; Moo, *The Epistle to the Romans*, p. 526.

[47] 2 Cor. 12:9–10.

163

of Romans 8 with the magnificent peroration of verses 28–39, climaxing in verses 35–39:

> ... trouble or hardship or persecution or famine or nakedness or sword ... in all these things we are more than conquerors through him who loved us. For am convinced that neither death nor life, neither angels nor demons, neither the present nor the future, nor any powers, neither height nor depth, nor anything else in all creation, will be able to separate us from the love of God that is in Christ Jesus our Lord.

In our own strength we stand little chance of coping with the evil and suffering life inevitably brings. But with the help of the Spirit the impossible becomes possible. His presence and his life in us carry us through the darkest experiences to the glory that he has guaranteed we shall one day enjoy.

Philippians 1:29–30
15. The gift of suffering

There was once a king of Phrygia called Midas, who, so the story goes, was given the power by Dionysos, the Greek god of wine and ecstasy, to turn anything he touched to gold. Our God is a lot wiser than Dionysos and would never let us loose with such dangerous power. But he is the God of transformation, and one of the things he transforms is suffering. His touch has the power to turn it to gold.

1. Grace

At the heart of the teaching of the New Testament is the concept of grace. Though it is expressed in a variety of ways,[1] the key term is *charis*, which, in its various forms, appears nearly two hundred times in the New Testament, the large majority of them rich with insights into the profound truth of a God who gives abundantly and gloriously to those who deserve nothing. Typically, Paul tells us that 'where sin increased, grace increased all the more ... to bring eternal life through Jesus Christ our Lord';[2] 'It is by grace you have been saved, through faith – and this not from yourselves, it is the gift of God';[3] 'by the grace of God I am what I am'.[4]

When God works in grace in our lives and bestows specific grace and gifts, the term Paul uses is *charisma*. He uses it in Romans 6:23 to refer to the gracious gift of eternal life, but its commonest use is to describe the gifts of the Holy Spirit such as those listed in Romans 12:6–8 and 1 Corinthians 12:1–31. In grace God gives us

---

[1] *Charis* in the sense of 'grace' does not appear among the recorded words of Jesus, yet his life and teaching are full of expressions and illustrations of it.
[2] Rom. 5:20–21.
[3] Eph. 2:8.
[4] 1 Cor. 15:10.

not just salvation and eternal life but everything we need to live as his people and serve him as Lord.

The verb that comes from *charis* is *charizomai*. It comes twenty-three times in the New Testament, most frequently in the writings of Paul. Its central meaning is to 'express grace', to 'give graciously'; this is seen in Romans 8:32, where Paul asks, 'He who did not spare his own Son, but gave him up for us all – how will he not also, along with him, graciously give [*charisetai*] us all things?' A derived meaning emphasizes that grace is expressed in forgiveness, as in the command, 'Be kind and compassionate to one another, forgiving [*charizomenoi*] each other, just as in Christ God forgave [*echarisato*] you.'[5]

2. The gracious gift of suffering (1:29)

All this rich heritage of the concept of the grace of God at work in our lives lies behind Paul's striking statement in Philippians 1:29, that suffering is a gracious gift (*echaristhē ... paschein*).[6] The NIV's *It has been granted to you ... to suffer* is hardly adequate; other translations make a better attempt at bringing out the meaning by saying that we have been granted or given 'the privilege' of suffering (NEB, Phillips, GNB, NLT), but even that misses the key link with grace. Suffering is more than something granted, more even than a privilege. It is a 'grace', as much an expression of God's outpoured love and goodness as forgiveness itself, as much a *charisma* as speaking in tongues or the ability to do miracles. Paul readily brackets it here with faith (*pisteuein*, to believe), which, Ephesians 2:8 makes clear, is a 'gift' 'by grace'. So to savour its full meaning we need to translate Philippians 1:29, 'It has been graciously given to you ... to suffer', or 'In grace the privilege has been granted to you ... to suffer.' The gift of suffering is no unwelcome imposition; it is as much an expression of God's love and goodness as any other of his gifts of grace.

Paul wrote to the Philippians 'in chains'.[7] He was facing the possibility of being killed.[8] Around him were so-called Christians who were seeking to 'stir up trouble' for him.[9] When he referred in

[5] Eph. 4:32.
[6] 'This magnificent statement is offered as a theodicy to help the Philippians to understand their sufferings at least in part. The passive voice *has been granted* is Paul's way of ascribing the activity to the will of God. The "divine passive" ... is an OT manner of speech to emphasize that God is in control of all events'; R. P. Martin, *Philippians* (Oliphants, 1976), p. 84.
[7] Phil. 1:13.
[8] Phil. 1:20.
[9] Phil. 1:17.

verse 12 to what had happened to him, he was, very probably, referring to the events described in Acts 21 – 28, which Alec Motyer summarizes as 'an entirely false accusation', a near-lynching, a narrow escape from a flogging, imprisonment, 'unjust and un-provoked insult and shame', 'malicious misrepresentation', 'deadly plot', 'deceit and malpractice and vilification', 'the prolonged trial of the storm at sea', and the arrival at Rome 'in the company of the condemned, bound by a chain, and destined to drag out at least two years under arrest awaiting the uncertain decision of an earthly king'.[10] Paul's summary is much briefer, but just as graphic; it is the one word *struggle* (*agōna*, 30),[11] which, he said, characterized his time at Philippi[12] and was continuing to characterize his life; and not his life only, but the life of God's people at Philippi and of all God's people (30).[13] From start to finish it was a battle, a fight, a struggle. It is against that background that he calls suffering a gracious gift, bracketing it together with the high calling to defend and establish the gospel, gifts and callings shared by both himself and his Philippian readers (29).[14]

3. Suffering and Christ (1:29)

Twice in verse 29 Paul uses the Greek preposition *hyper* with the genitive case to speak of the link between suffering and Christ (*hyper Christou … hyper autou*, translated by the NIV as *on behalf of Christ … for him*). The repetition is ignored by some translations (e.g. NEB, NLT), and some interpreters suggest that it could be accidental. But it seems more likely that Paul repeated himself because he was saying something particularly significant. Suffering is a gift because of its link with Christ. Without this link it would be meaningless; but given this link it is filled not just with meaning but with blessing.

What, then, is the special significance of suffering *hyper Christou*? There has been much debate over the meaning of *hyper* with the genitive in the context of atonement. It is used, for instance, in 2 Corinthians 5:14, 'one died for all'; scholars debate whether this

[10] A. Motyer, *The Message of Philippians* (IVP, 1984), p. 64.

[11] 'The word … originally signified a contest in the arena, whether gladiatorial or athletic, and that sense of the word would seem to be in the Apostle's mind here … The Christians are pictured as standing in the arena, pitted against deadly foes'; J. H. Michael, *The Epistle of Paul to the Philippians* (Hodder and Stoughton, 1928), p. 73.

[12] Paul uses the same word of his time at Philippi in 1 Thess. 2:2, where the NIV's 'in spite of strong opposition' (*en pollō agōni*) is rendered by the NEB, 'A hard struggle it was.'

[13] 2 Tim. 3:10–12.

[14] Phil. 1:7.

means that Christ died on behalf of all, as their representative, or in the place of all, as their substitute. Most commentators agree that the use of *hyper* with the genitive can indicate substitution, and there seems no doubt that any theory of the atonement must include the element of substitution, of Christ dying in our place. A positive outcome of the debate would seem to be that *hyper* with the genitive, rather than indicating either representation or substitution, generally suggests both; the article on *hyper* in the *New International Dictionary of New Testament Theology* concludes that 'a substitute represents and a representative may be a substitute'.[15]

This conclusion greatly enriches our understanding of Philippians 1:29. Twice Paul states that Christians suffer not just 'for Christ' in the sense of 'because they are Christians', but rather 'as the representatives and even substitutes of Christ'.[16] The first recorded words of Jesus to Paul were, 'Saul, Saul, why do you persecute me?'[17] Though his crusade was ultimately against Jesus, Saul was in fact persecuting the Christians, and they were suffering as Christ's representatives and substitutes. Once he became a Christian, Paul was conscious that the same thing was happening to him: 'The sufferings of Christ flow over into our lives,' he said;[18] 'I fill up in my flesh what is still lacking in regard to Christ's afflictions.'[19] This is not suggesting, of course, that there is any lack in the work of Christ on the cross; that is undoubtedly complete. But Christ yet suffers, not least in the 'birth pains' of the kingdom, and specifically in the people who are his representatives and in a sense substitutes in a hostile world. Not only does he share in our sufferings; we share in his.[20] As we live in him and he lives in us, as his life becomes our life and our life becomes his life, so our sufferings are his suffering and his sufferings are ours.

Perhaps this gives us two clues why Paul saw suffering as such a gracious gift. The first is that it is a means of 'fellowship'[21] with

---

[15] M. J. Harris, in *New International Dictionary of New Testament Theology* (Paternoster, 1988), 3, p. 1197.

Silva is reluctant to concede a substitutionary meaning here: 'The simplest and contextually most natural idea is that of suffering out of devotion for, on account of our identification with Christ ... Yet it must be acknowledged that the relationship in view is one of union with Christ, so that in this very letter Paul can speak about sharing in Christ's sufferings (3:10)'; M. Silva, *Philippians* (Moody Press, 1988), p. 97.

[16] Clearly, the element of substitution must not be pressed too far; our sufferings, for instance, are not redemptive. A helpful image is Simon of Cyrene carrying Jesus' cross (Luke 23:26).

[17] Acts 9:4.
[18] 2 Cor. 1:5.
[19] Col. 1:24.
[20] Phil. 3:10; 1 Pet. 4:13.
[21] Phil. 3:10.

168

Christ, of drawing very close to him, of experiencing him drawing close to us. The second is that it is a way of responding to what he has done for us. Christ has done everything for me, says Paul. He has loved me, poured out his life for me, saved me, forgiven me, called me, empowered me. Now I want to live for him; everything I do I want to do for him (*hyper Christou*). I will live for him, work for him, preach for him – and I will suffer for him. If he gives me a task, I will thank him for it because it gives me an opportunity to show how much I love him, and I will do it to his glory. If he gives me suffering, then I will thank him for it and I will suffer for his glory, because it gives me an opportunity to show how much I love him.

We may ask whether this teaching refers to all suffering or just to suffering that is clearly the result of being a Christian. I may, say, be passed over for promotion because I am a Christian, and I may damage my back falling downstairs. In the one case it seems easy to see that I am suffering because I am Christ's and thus that I am suffering as his representative and sharing his sufferings; but in the other I seem to be suffering just as any other person, and the fact that I am a Christian is irrelevant. But the fascinating truth is that, according to the Bible, the fact that we are Christians is never irrelevant to anything. Paul got stoned because he was preaching the gospel, and he also got shipwrecked because of bad weather and bad navigation; but he does not contrast the two. Once I am a Christian, a child of God, part of the people of God, everything that happens to me happens to me as a child of God; nothing is by chance; nothing is meaningless. If, say, my falling downstairs is the work of the devil, then the devil is attacking me because I am a child of God. If it is because I am doing too much and God has decided I need to spend a week lying flat on my back, then he is giving me a week's rest because I am his child. The sufferings of Christ in his people include shipwrecks as well as floggings, illness and pain as well as persecution.[22]

---

[22] Commenting on Rom. 8:18, 'our present sufferings', Moo states: 'These "sufferings of the present time" are not only those "trials" that are endured directly because of confession of Christ – for instance, persecution – but encompass the whole gamut of suffering, including such things as illness, bereavement, hunger, financial reverses, and death itself ... There is a sense in which all the suffering of Christians is "with Christ," inasmuch as Christ was himself subject, by virtue of his coming "in the form of sinful flesh," to the manifold sufferings of this world in rebellion against God'; D. J. Moo, *The Epistle to the Romans* (Eerdmans, 1996), p. 506. Silva comments, 'It surely would be impossible to think that believers who enjoy freedom of religion and so suffer no physical persecution or religious discrimination are thereby deprived of an essential element in their sanctification'; Silva, *Philippians*, p. 98. Fee, however, disagrees: 'What Paul is not doing is offering to believers

But what if I fall downstairs not because I am the target of Satan's malice or because God has some purpose he wishes to bring about, but as a result of my own stupidity or even sin? My wife warned me that the carpet on the top step was loose, but I took no notice; or I fell because I was dead drunk. If I am to blame for what I suffer, surely I can hardly talk of such suffering as sharing in the sufferings of Christ? I guess in practice I would not do so; but I am still convinced that, biblically speaking, because I am a child of God, the suffering I go through, even as the result of my own folly or sin, is still part of the suffering of Christ. After all, in the last analysis, all the sufferings of Christ, and in particular his sufferings on the cross, are the result of folly and sin. He suffers because I sin, and he suffers because I suffer as a result of my sin. In a beautiful passage in Isaiah 63, the prophet tells of 'the kindnesses of the LORD ... the many good things he has done for the house of Israel, according to his compassion and many kindnesses'. Central to them comes this: 'In all their distress he too was distressed', or 'In all their suffering he also suffered' (NLT).[23] The Hebrew word translated 'distress' is ṣārâ, a general word for 'trouble', 'anguish', 'calamity', 'distress'. Here again is our suffering God, suffering not just because of the oppression of his people under the Egyptians but through all their troubles, many if not most of them caused by their own folly and sin.

4. The perfection of fellowship (1:29)

We have a God who suffers. The evil and the sin of the world break his heart. The suffering and the hurt we go through cause him sorrow and pain. In love and grace and infinite goodness he has chosen to bear our sin and carry our sorrows, to draw close to us in our pain and our darkness. Confronted with such a profound truth, we can respond to our own suffering, whatever form it may take, in one of two ways. We can ignore God's involvement in it; we can face it alone, perhaps with stoic courage or perhaps by giving way to doubt, self-pity, anger and the like. Alternatively, we can accept God's involvement. We can acknowledge that he comes to us in our suffering; we can choose to be drawn near to him through it. With

---

encouragement about suffering in general ... He is speaking specifically of their living for Christ in a world that is openly hostile to God and resistant to his love lavished on them in Christ'; G. D. Fee, *Paul's Letter to the Philippians* (Eerdmans, 1995), pp. 171–172. However, we can accept that Paul had persecution specifically in mind and at the same time broaden the underlying theological truth to all forms of Christian suffering.

[23] Isa. 63:7, 9.

Paul we can say that we are willing to suffer anything in order to get closer to Christ, to know him and 'the fellowship of sharing in his sufferings, becoming like him in his death'.[24] As Barth puts it in his commentary on Philippians 1:29: 'The grace of being permitted to *believe* in Christ is surpassed by the grace of being permitted to *suffer* for him, of being permitted to walk the way of Christ himself to the perfection of fellowship with him.'[25]

'The perfection of fellowship' by 'being permitted to walk the way of Christ himself.' Here is something that confounds our naive logic that tries to argue that, if God loves us, he will never let us suffer, that all he will ever give us is wine and ecstasy and gold. For far more glorious than any of these is God himself, the one who came as 'a man of sorrows and familiar with suffering',[26] whom we can know in the fellowship of sharing his sufferings.

I have watched a friend die slowly of cancer. The suffering was intense, both for him and for his family and friends. For months he and we struggled; when he died many still cried, 'Why?' But one thing I know for sure: in those final months of suffering God drew near to him and he drew near to God as he had never done before; in the pain and darkness the beauty of Christ shone out and every one of us could see it. I know it does not always happen that way. Illness can turn us away from God; persecution can cause us to deny our Lord. But we are back to Paul's thorn. In our suffering and weakness he speaks grace to us; it is ours to choose whether we refuse that grace and walk the road alone, or take it and find it sufficient. For in the gift of suffering there is also the gift of the suffering one, and there can be no greater gift than that.

'Not that way,' we say. 'Any other way; the way of committed service, the way of holy living, the way of deep study of the Scriptures, the way of meditation and prayer. But not the way of suffering.' True, there are many ways of drawing close to our God, and he uses them all. But the choice of which ones he offers us has to be his. And of this we can be sure: our heavenly Father will give only good gifts to his children.

[24] Phil. 3:10.
[25] K. Barth, *The Epistle to the Philippians* (SCM, 1962), p. 49.
[26] Isa. 53:3.

Romans 8:28
16. Good out of evil

Long ago Aristotle pointed out that any question 'Why?' can be answered in a variety ways, all of which are equally valid. You meet your neighbour running down the street. You say to her, 'Why are you running?' She might answer, 'Because the doctor told me to get more exercise.' Or, 'Because I enjoy it.' Or, 'Because I'm going at ten miles an hour.' Or, 'To keep fit and live longer.' Or, 'Because the muscles of my legs are making them propel me forward at speed.' All her answers are true and valid; no one of them contradicts the others; but each of them is dealing with the question 'Why?' in a different way. Similarly, if we had asked Paul why he was in chains, he might have replied, 'Because that's the way the Romans stop their prisoners escaping.' Or, 'Because of the plots of the Jews.' Or, 'For Christ.' Or, 'To evangelize the palace guard.' Or, 'To share in the suffering of Jesus.'

In the same way there are many valid ways of answering the question, 'Why evil and suffering?' We can answer it in general terms of how evil and suffering originated, or why they are present in our world now. We can personalize it and deal with it very specifically, as in 'Why is my back hurting now?' We can approach it in terms of purpose: 'What is the meaning of suffering? Why does God allow this?' Even here, in the area of purpose, it is possible to have a number of different answers, all of which are valid and which we can hold together. Paul could, for example, have listed several valid purposes in his imprisonment: besides sharing in the suffering of Jesus and witnessing to the guard, he could have mentioned encouraging the Christians to speak 'more courageously and fearlessly',[1] as a 'sign' to unbelievers,[2] as a mark

[1] Phil. 1:14.
[2] Phil. 1:28.

of solidarity with the Philippians[3] and as an opportunity for growth in character.[4]

1. The purposes of God (8:28)

In this chapter we are going to be exploring a number of possible purposes in evil and suffering, looking at ways in which good may come from them. Of all the problems evil and suffering raise, the most awful is that of meaningless evil and suffering. Those who believe in a universe that is ruled by chance, in which nothing has any ultimate meaning or purpose, may be able simply to shrug their shoulders and ignore the question. But we do not believe in a purposeless universe. We are convinced that God is the Creator and Ruler of all, that he is wise and good, and that nothing is ultimately beyond his control. So we are convinced that behind every event, small and large, there is meaning, there are the purposes of God, and they are good.

That is not, of course, to say that we are able to know what the purpose of God is in any specific event or situation. Indeed, when we are in the thick of evil and suffering it is generally very hard to trace any meaning or any way in which God could be at work. Most of us fall far short of the experience, maturity and faith of Paul. At best we may speculate as to what God's purposes might be; most times we have to hang on in the darkness, confessing that we have no idea what God is up to, but trusting that he is still in charge and that he will work out his gracious purposes in due course. Indeed, that was something that even Paul, for all his experience and maturity, was familiar with; he called it 'hope', that confident expectation that God would fulfil his purposes. 'But hope that is seen', he says, 'is no hope at all';[5] if we can see what God is up to, we do not need to exercise that level of trust or hope, nor do we need the same degree of help from the Spirit.[6] But when all is dark, we can reach out to him in the simplest and profoundest faith and find that he is there.

That brings us to one of the best-known verses in Paul, Romans 8:28. God has great purposes, Paul has been saying, for his people and for his world. Despite our groans and our weaknesses, we can trust and hope with confidence in him. Indeed, *we know that in all things God works for the good of those who love him, who have*

---

[3] Phil. 1:30.
[4] Rom. 5:3.
[5] Rom. 8:24.
[6] Rom. 8:26–27.

been called according to his purpose.[7] This is the basis of our hope, our trust and confidence in God that enable us to face evil and suffering, however dark they may be. 'In all things',[8] whether we can see it or not, God is at work, and he is always working for good for those who love him, who have been called according to his purpose.

2. For whose good? (8:28)

Before we turn to some biblical examples of the great truth given us in Romans 8:28, we need to face an issue of interpretation which in its turn will lead us into a digression on one of the major questions that arise in the area of evil and suffering. The issue is the application of the words 'for the good', and the question is: 'When it says that God works for good in the lives of those who love him, does that mean he does not work for good in the lives of those who do not love him?'

Although the central thrust of verse 28 is clear, the words Paul wrote are open to a number of valid translations, particularly in two areas. The first ambiguity arises over the subject of the verb which the NIV translates 'works' (*synergei*). Paul's word order would make 'all things' the obvious subject (*panta synergei*), as in the AV's 'all things work together for good', a translation followed by Phillips and the NEB margin. Alternatively, the subject of *synergei* could be an undefined 'he', which could mean 'the Holy Spirit' (27) or God, taken from the phrase 'those who love God'. Indeed, a small group of manuscripts actually adds 'God' after *synergei* to make this clear. This is the approach taken by the NIV and several other recent translations. But this approach raises a further question, whether *panta* should be taken as the object of *synergei*, 'works all things together', or as an adverbial accusative, to be translated as in the NIV as 'in all things'. The differences between the possible translations are small, but they can be significant. In particular the NIV approach leads the translators to ignore the force of *synergei*, which means not simply 'works' but 'works with' or 'works together'.

---

[7] Despite the NIV's new section, verse 28 is linked closely with verses 18–27. The NEB does not even start a new sentence at verse 28, but makes the Spirit (27) the subject of 'works' ('co-operates') 'for good' (the Greek is simply 'he works', *synergei*, not 'God works'. Sanday and Headlam helpfully paraphrase: 'Yet another ground of confidence. The Christian knows that all things (including his sufferings) can have but one result, and that a good one, for those who love God and respond to the call in the pursuance of His purpose He addresses to them'; W. Sanday and A. C. Headlam, *The Epistle to the Romans*, 5th edn (T. & T. Clark, 1902), p. 214.

[8] 'The scope should probably not be restricted. Anything that is a part of this life – even our sins – can, by God's grace, contribute toward "good"'; D. J. Moo, *The Epistle to the Romans* (Eerdmans, 1996), p. 529.

The second area of interpretation open to debate is the phrase translated 'of those who love him' in the NIV. There is no 'of' in the Greek; 'those who love him' is in the dative, not the genitive; the literal translation is 'For (or "And") we know that with (or "for") those who love God everything works together to good (or "he works all things together for good").' My own feeling is that if Paul had wanted to say 'for the good of those who love God' he would have done so, using the genitive and making his meaning plain by the word order: *eis agathon tōn agapontōn ton theon*. His use of the dative would most readily be explained by the *syn* in *synergei*: 'he (or 'everything') works together with those who love God for good'. This avoids ignoring the force of *synergei*, and it broadens the application of 'good'. Rather than suggesting that 'good' is enjoyed just by 'those who love him' it allows us to understand that in all things God, together with his people, is working 'to good'. This approach is followed by several translations: 'God works for good with those who love him' (RSV, GNB), 'he co-operates for good with those who love God' (NEB), 'God works with those who love him ... to bring about what is good' (Goodspeed).

This brings us to the issue of God's work in the lives of those who do not love him. Verses 18–27 have spoken of two groups, the people of God and the created order, that are groaning and awaiting in hope the great purposes of God. Verses 28 onwards unpack the implications of God's purposes of good for his people. But no mention is made of those who are not his people. Are we to take verse 28 as specifically excluding from God's good purposes those who do not love him? Stott would seem to suggest that this is so, stating that 'for the good of those who love him' is a 'necessary limitation'. I would certainly agree with the statement with which he continues: 'Paul is not expressing a general, superficial optimism that everything tends to everybody's good in the end,'[9] but that is not the only alternative. I would suggest that the 'good' Paul has in mind here is not limited to the good of those who love him, nor is it 'everybody's good in the end'; rather, it is something much bigger than either, the only thing that, in the end, can be called totally good, and that is the fulfilment of the great purposes of the God of grace and love and goodness.[10]

[9] J. Stott, *The Message of Romans* (IVP, 1994), p. 247.

[10] For Christians this is principally seen in the great process described in verses 29–30, through which we are 'conformed to the likeness of his Son', even as we go through 'trouble' and 'hardship' and 'persecution' and the like (35). For 'the creation' it is liberation from bondage into 'the glorious freedom of the children of God' (21). But even where the powers of evil and their human representatives continue to rebel against him, our great God is committed to work for good, using even their rebellion to bring about his good and glorious purposes, as exemplified in Acts 4:27–28 and Rev. 17:16–17.

This in no way detracts from the personal comfort we as individual believers can draw from this verse when we go through difficult times. We have all learnt from experience that our idea of what is good for us and God's knowledge of what is good for us do not necessarily tally. Equally, we are well aware that what is good for us may be bad for others, and that what we see as our immediate good may be bad for us or for others in the long run. So, unless we are particularly self-centred or immature, even if we interpret Romans 8:28 as saying that God works everything for our personal good, we always add the rider that our personal good may not be what seems good to us, or it may not be our immediate good, or that the 'good' thing may be for us to forgo God's specific blessing so that someone else can have it. God certainly worked for good through Paul's struggles and sufferings, but most of the 'good' was experienced by the people who found salvation through his ministry; God brought plenty of good out of Stephen's martyrdom, but Stephen himself did not experience it. None of us in our right mind wants to insist that God's workings must be limited to what we see as our immediate good; our 'good' must always be submitted to his 'good'. It is the privilege of believers to follow their Master and choose God's perfect will, even if it involves suffering, rather than their imperfect will.[11] So the comfort drawn from this verse in fact increases as we broaden our understanding of 'good'; it is not my small and narrow good that God promises, but something much richer and deeper. We can have peace and confident hope because we know that on the broadest scale our gracious and wise God is working everything for good; even when we do not immediately see or experience it, whatever happens to us personally or in the world around, God is working out his purposes of good.

Does God, then, work everything 'for good' in the lives of those who do not love him? In that I am confident that God cannot do anything other than what is 'for good', I believe we can say that he does, though, of course, we need to qualify that statement in a number of ways.

1. The good for which God is working is the true good, that is, the fulfilment of his perfect purposes, 'to bring all things in heaven and on earth together under one head, even Christ'.[12]

2. His ultimate purpose, therefore, for each individual unbeliever is that he or she should come under the headship of Christ – that 'every knee should bow ... and every tongue confess that Jesus Christ is Lord, to the glory of the God the Father'.[13]

[11] Luke 22:42.
[12] Eph. 1:10.
[13] Phil. 2:10–11.

3. So the 'good' for which God is working in the lives of unbelievers is the end of their rebellion against him. To bring this about God freely offers salvation in Christ. His cry to the ends of the earth is, 'Turn to me and be saved.'[14] 'He wants all men to be saved and to come to a knowledge of the truth.'[15] This is the basis for the mission that God has given his people, the declaring of the good news of Jesus to everyone, offering them the greatest 'good' that anyone could ever find.

4. Where that offer is persistently refused, God has to continue to work 'for good'. He cannot, say, give up trying to turn unbelievers back to him as a bad job and decide to side with them in their rebellion against him. So their rebellion has to be brought to an end; it has to be judged and condemned and destroyed. This is the inevitable implication of his commitment to bring all things together under Christ. Where individuals refuse to do this willingly, it will still be done; God cannot allow rebellion and sin and evil to continue unchecked for ever. The Bible sees no contradiction at all between God's goodness and his destruction of evil and of those who insist on clinging to evil; indeed, God would not be good if he failed to destroy evil. So, for example, in the hymns of worship recorded for us in the book of Psalms, we frequently get statements of God's goodness and his destruction of those who are evil side by side:

> The LORD is gracious and compassionate,
>   slow to anger and rich in love.
> The LORD is good to all;
>   he has compassion on all he has made...
> The LORD is righteous in all his ways
>   and loving towards all he has made.
> The LORD is near to all who call upon him,
>   to all who call on him in truth...
> The LORD watches over all who love him,
>   but all the wicked he will destroy.[16]

The Psalmist has no doubt about God's compassion and love and goodness towards all he has made, but, equally, he has no doubt about his commitment to destroy the wicked. But passages like this make it absolutely clear that he is not some kind of vindictive deity who enjoys condemning people to hell. When Luke records Jesus' warning about the words he will have to say to some on judgment

[14] Isa. 45:22.
[15] 1 Tim. 2:3.
[16] Ps. 145:8–9, 17–18, 20.

day, 'Away from me, all you evildoers',[17] he goes on immediately to record Jesus' cry of sorrow over the city that rejected him.[18] The one who speaks of judgment is the one who wept over the city he judged. God carries the pain of hell, of men and women made in his image who, despite all he has done in Christ, are lost eternally because they have chosen darkness and evil and death rather than light and life.[19]

5. While believers should be able to recognize that all things in their lives are 'for good', we cannot expect unbelievers to do so. Believers and unbelievers respond to God's work in very different ways. Believers accept the lordship of God in their lives and submit their 'good' to his 'good'. So believers can be confident, whatever happens to them, that all things ultimately are for the greatest possible good, and, since they desire the greatest possible good, they happily accept it as their personal 'good'. Unbelievers cannot see this; though they may exhibit a degree of altruism and be willing to sacrifice their immediate good for the good of others or for some good long-term goal, the fact that they refuse the lordship of God in their lives means that they cannot have that total confidence in the good purposes of a sovereign God; so there will always be some things that they are unable to fit into the overall picture, some things that do not make sense, and so cannot in their understanding be for ultimate good.

6. The 'good' for which God is working in the lives of unbelievers may include their immediate good, as we have seen in the way God worked through Joseph to save the Egyptians from famine, and it may include the doing of deeds that are 'for good', as happened when God used the pagan king Cyrus to bring about the restoration of Jerusalem,[20] or the opposition of the Jewish leaders to bring about the great good of the cross,[21] or the plots of the Jews to get Paul to Rome.[22]

7. Though the contrast between believers and unbelievers is always clearly marked in God's eyes, it may not always be seen in practice. There will be elements of unbelief in many if not all believers, particularly when things are tough and we cannot see what good God is working in our situation or the world around us. We too refuse from time to time to let God work in our lives for good; when suffering comes, instead of radiating the beauty of Christ through it,

[17] Luke 13:27.
[18] Luke 13:34–35.
[19] John 3:16–21.
[20] Isa. 44:28.
[21] Acts 4:28.
[22] Phil. 1:12; Acts 21 – 28.

we turn grumpy and sour. But, amazingly, so great is God's grace towards his children that he can work even our weakness and failure into his purposes so that even they somehow become part of the 'all things' that he fits into his purposes of ultimate good.

8. There is a final point we need to bear in mind. All of us who are Christians can look back and see clear ways in which God was working for good in our lives well before we came to love him or heard his call. However we may formulate our theology of election, since we can never know who eventually is going to become a Christian we can never look at another human being and deny that God is working for good in his or her life. So, at the very least, we must allow for the possibility that God in his grace and wisdom is working for good in and through the lives of those around us, whether believers or unbelievers.

This consideration of the phrase 'all things for good' has reminded us that our understanding of what God is doing and how he is doing it is inevitably limited. But that does not have to mean that we have to admit defeat in our questioning. Our understanding of how the human body works, or how the universe operates, is inevitably limited, but that does not stop us living in the world and seeking to understand its mysteries. The call is not to understand the world first and then to choose to live, but rather to choose to live first and then to seek to understand. In the same way the call is not to understand the ways of God first and then to choose to trust and follow them, but rather to choose to trust first and then to begin to understand.

Perhaps we should end our digression on the way that God works 'for good' in the case of those who refuse to believe in him with Paul's great words at the end of Romans 11. Immediately after the powerful statements in Romans 8 of confident hope and trust in God's great purposes, he spends three chapters wrestling with the issue of the fate of his fellow Jews. Despite the heartbreaking tragedy of their rejection of Christ and all the profound mysteries of God's purposes, Paul is totally confident that even here God is working out great and glorious purposes of grace that are wholly and perfectly good, so much so that he ends his discussion with one of the greatest hymns of praise in the whole Bible:

> Oh, the depth of the riches of the wisdom
>   and knowledge of God!
> How unsearchable his judgments,
>   and his paths beyond tracing out!
> 'Who has known the mind of the Lord?
> Or who has been his counsellor?'

> 'Who has ever given to God,
>   that God should repay him?'
> For from him and through him and to him
>   are all things.
> To him be the glory for ever! Amen.[23]

From him and through him and to him – all things. All things for good. Of that we can be certain.

3. Good things out of evil

Quite apart from its teaching on the way God uses evil and suffering, the Bible gives us many examples of God working for good in and through both those who loved him and those who were fighting against him. We have already noted some in chapter 12, such as the story of Joseph, with its amazing climax, 'You intended to harm me, but God intended it for good to accomplish what is now being done, the saving of many lives';[24] the hardness of Pharaoh's heart, which resulted in the demonstration of the power and glory of God; and the incident of Ananias and Sapphira, through which God taught his church a profound lesson, and which was followed by a demonstration of spiritual power and many becoming Christians.

In the rest of this chapter we shall look at some further examples and teaching that the Bible provides for us in order to draw up a list of good outcomes that God brings about from evil and suffering. It is by no means a complete list; doubtless we could all add to it from our own experience or the experience of those we know. But it does illustrate the richness of the wisdom and power of God as he uses even what is evil to bring about what is good.

The coming of the king

The line of David and so of Christ was preserved as a result of famine and tragic bereavement. Famine drove Naomi with her husband Elimelech and their two sons from Bethlehem to Moab; within ten years her husband and sons were all dead.[25] Her daughter-in-law, Ruth, who was a Moabitess and so not part of the people of Israel, insisted on returning to Bethlehem with her; there, through the goodness of Boaz, a relative of Elimelech, Ruth is accepted into the community of God's people, and becomes the great-grandmother of David.[26]

[23] Rom. 11:33–36.
[24] Gen. 50:20.
[25] Ruth 1:1–5.
[26] Ruth 4:13–17.

Healing and conversion

Incursions by Syrian forces into Israel, and the capture of a girl who was then taken away as a slave, led to a high officer in the Syrian army being cured of leprosy and acknowledging the God of Israel as the only true God.[27] It would appear from 2 Kings 5:17 and Luke 4:27 that Naaman became a true worshipper of the God of Israel, even though his position dictated a degree of compromise with the Syrian religion.

Miracles and testimony

Persecution and suffering of God's people resulted in God's miraculous intervention and a clear demonstration of his power to those who did not believe in him. The book of Daniel gives us two examples of this in the stories of Shadrach, Meshach and Abednego and the furnace, and of Daniel and the lions. In each case the result was both deliverance and prosperity for God's servants and a declaration by a pagan king of the greatness of their God.[28]

'Worldwide' acknowledgment of God

A period of insanity for a pagan king resulted in his acknowledgment of God.[29] Warned by God in a dream, Nebuchadnezzar, one of the great kings of the ancient world, suffered a severe psychological breakdown, presumably for seven months ('seven times'), but then returned to full health, as a result of which he praised God and publicly declared 'to the peoples, nations and men of every language, who live in the world', that 'the Most High God', the God of Daniel, is 'sovereign over the kingdoms of men'; 'his dominion is an eternal dominion; his kingdom endures from generation to generation'.[30]

Correction

'Before I was afflicted I went astray,' said the Psalmist; 'but now I obey your word ... It was good for me to be afflicted so that I might learn your decrees.'[31] In an often quoted passage, C. S. Lewis states, 'God whispers to us in our pleasures, speaks in our conscience, but shouts in our pains: it is His megaphone to rouse a deaf world.'[32] On the Psalmist's words, Spurgeon commented, 'Often our trials act as a thorn hedge to keep us in the good pastures, but our prosperity is a

---

[27] 2 Kgs 5:1–18.
[28] Dan. 3:1–30; 6:1–28.
[29] Dan. 4:1–37.
[30] Dan. 4:1, 2, 25, 34.
[31] Ps. 119:67, 71.
[32] C. S. Lewis, *The Problem of Pain* (Geoffrey Bles, 1940), p. 81.

gap through which we go astray ... A thousand benefits have come to us through our pains and griefs, and among the rest is this – that we have thus been schooled in the law.'[33]

Revelation of Jesus

Jesus' power over nature was demonstrated in an incident arising out of a near-fatal storm at sea.[34] The danger was very real; the boat was 'being swamped' and death by drowning was staring the disciples in the face. Even greater than the danger was the calm authority of Jesus, who could command the winds and the water, 'and they obey him'.

Joy and courage

Prison, persecution and flogging for the apostles resulted in joy 'because they had been counted worthy of suffering disgrace for the Name' and in a fresh burst of courageous witnessing and preaching.[35] There was no holding these men down. Anything their enemies did to them was turned by God's grace and power into something positive for them and the kingdom.

Growth of the kingdom

The gospel spread rapidly among Samaritans and Gentiles as well as among Jews as a result of the death of Stephen and the 'great persecution' that arose against the church. All the Christians, except the apostles, 'were scattered throughout Judea and Samaria', and wherever they went they 'preached the word'. Some went 'as far as Phoenicia, Cyprus and Antioch', and before long they were telling 'the good news about the Lord Jesus' to non-Jews as well as Jews. 'The Lord's hand was with them, and a great number of people believed and turned to the Lord.'[36]

Christian growth for ourselves

Rich jewels of Christ-likeness arise out of sufferings. 'Perseverance', the ability to keep going; 'character', maturity, both emotional and spiritual; 'hope', that confident trust in God that knows he is working out great purposes of good; and, over them all, joy ('we rejoice in our sufferings') at the way God is bringing such good out of evil and suffering.[37]

---

[33] C. H. Spurgeon, *The Treasury of David* (Passmore and Alabaster, 1882), 6, pp. 163, 166.
[34] Luke 8:22–25.
[35] Acts 5:17–42.
[36] Acts 8:1, 4; 11:19–21.
[37] Rom. 5:3–4. See also Jas 1:2–3.

Resurrection life

Danger and death lead to resurrection life. 'We endanger ourselves every day,' says Paul; 'I die every day – I mean that, brothers.' But death's 'victory' and 'sting' have been taken away by the victory of our Lord Jesus Christ.[38]

> Jesus lives! Henceforth is death
> but the gate of life immortal.[39]

The ability to help others

In our 'troubles' 'the Father of compassion and the God of all comfort' 'comforts us', 'so that we can comfort those in any trouble with the comfort we ourselves have received from God'.[40] Many of us besides Paul have found that the experience of going through suffering equips us in a way nothing else could to help others who are going through parallel experiences.

A demonstration of the power of God

His glory is revealed in our weakness. We have the treasure of the gospel, said Paul, 'in jars of clay to show that this all-surpassing power is from God and not from us'.[41] Paul was grateful for his sufferings[42] because they gave God plenty of opportunity to show his supernatural power. When he first went to Corinth he was glad that he was not possessed of 'eloquence or superior wisdom', since that might have meant that he preached the message of Jesus in his own strength and won converts through his own personality; he was very happy to be weak and fearful and trembling, so that his hearers' faith 'might not rest on men's wisdom, but on God's power'.[43]

Maturity and Christ-likeness for others

'Struggling' brings believers to maturity and godly living.[44] Twice in two verses Paul uses the word *agōn*[45] to stress that, like the preaching of the gospel, the teaching and building up of the Christians were a question of conflict, a battle, a struggle. But out of it come maturity in Christ and encouragement and unity and a deep knowledge of Christ.

---

[38] 1 Cor. 15:31, 55–57.
[39] From the hymn 'Jesus lives!' by Christian Gellert.
[40] 2 Cor. 1:3–4.
[41] 2 Cor. 4:7.
[42] 2 Cor. 4:8–10.
[43] 1 Cor. 2:1–5.
[44] Col. 1:28 – 2:5.
[45] *Agōnizomenos* (1:29), *agōna* (2:1).

Holiness, righteousness and peace

Discipline makes us like our Father. The writer to the Hebrews was concerned lest his readers were growing weary and slack in their commitment to Jesus Christ. After his great chapter on the heroes of faith, he called his readers to 'run with perseverance the race marked out for us', fixing their eyes on Jesus, 'who endured such opposition from sinful men'. God was allowing them, he said, to go through 'struggle' and 'hardship' for a good purpose: he was treating them as his 'sons', shaping them through 'discipline' in order that they might become like him. In particular, God would use the discipline of suffering 'for our good, that we may share in his holiness', that is, become holy as he is holy, and experience a 'harvest of right-eousness and peace'.[46]

Confirmation of genuine conversion

Faith is 'proved genuine' by the way God's people 'suffer grief in all kinds of trials'.[47] This was a common theme in the early church:[48] the test of whether a person's profession of faith was a true and deep work of the Spirit or just a passing fad was whether that profession stood up to suffering and trials. The pressure was such that only those who were genuine children of God and had the power of the Holy Spirit in them would survive; the others would deny their faith or fall away. So trials were to be welcomed as a source of confirmation of salvation and so of personal assurance.[49]

Glory

'Praise, glory and honour when Jesus Christ is revealed' are the outcome of suffering 'grief in all kinds of trials'.[50] This too was a major theme of the New Testament writers, going back undoubt-edly to the words of Jesus in the Sermon on the Mount, 'Blessed are you when people insult you, persecute you and falsely say all kinds of evil against you because of me. Rejoice and be glad, because great is your reward in heaven.'.[51] Paul looked forward to 'eternal glory' that would far outweigh his 'light and momentary troubles'.[52] Peter does not say specifically that the 'praise, glory and honour' will be

[46] Heb. 12:1–11.

[47] 1 Pet. 1:6–7.

[48] See, for example, 2 Thess. 1:4–5, and the way that Paul uses the catalogues of his sufferings in 1 and 2 Corinthians to argue the genuineness of his apostleship and ministry. The concept also underlies Paul's confidence expressed in Rom. 8:28–39.

[49] Jas 1:2.

[50] 1 Pet. 1:6–7.

[51] Matt. 5:11–12. Again, the concept is amply illustrated in Rom. 8:17–39.

[52] 2 Cor. 4:17. For other examples of the close link between suffering and glory see pp. 155–156.

heaped on us, and we might feel that only Jesus is the worthy recipient of praise, glory and honour at his appearing. But Paul specifically adds the words 'for us', and Jesus is quite specific that the reward is ours.[53] When Christ appears the whole creation will heap praise and glory and honour upon him, and he, and all creation with him, in turn will heap praise and glory and honour on those who have walked the way of suffering with him and remained faithful.

A new perspective and new values

Suffering makes us stop and think. We all know people, both Christians and non-Christians, who have been brought up short when forced to go through suffering of some sort. Faced, say, with cancer, or the sudden death of a friend, they realize how shallow their lives are or how trivial the things they have been living for; they are forced to reassess what really matters. 'He who has suffered in his body', says Peter, 'is done with sin. As a result, he does not live the rest of his earthly life for evil human desires, but rather for the will of God.'[54]

God is committed to bringing his gracious and beautiful 'good' out of 'all things'. This survey of good things he brought out of evil and suffering in the Bible accounts is by no means complete, but it does illustrate two things: that God in his wisdom and power can bring good out of any situation, and that there is a huge variety in the good he does bring. Rarely is it possible to predict beforehand what good purpose or purposes he has in mind when he allows evil and suffering to come our way; rarely shall we know if it will be immediate or delayed, whether we shall be the ones to enjoy it or whether someone else will benefit. But of this we can be sure, that when we have the whole picture, when we can look back and trace the hand of God in all the dark and difficult times we have gone through, we shall be amazed at the wise and beautiful way he has worked together all things for good, good that beyond a shadow of a doubt makes all the suffering worthwhile.

[53] 2 Cor. 4:17; Matt. 5:12.
[54] 1 Pet. 4:1–2.

1 Peter 3:15–16
17. Giving reasons

The Christians to whom Peter was writing were well aware that they were likely to 'suffer for doing good', and that in so doing they were following in the steps of Jesus himself.[1] But while there would be many situations in which they should follow Jesus' example and suffer silently, there was one situation where they should do the opposite: if anyone asked them the reason for their confident trust and *hope* in God,[2] they must be ready to state it and defend it. The Greek for *Always be prepared to give an answer* (15) is *hetoimoi aei pros apologian*, 'ready always as regards an apologetic', always ready to express and explain and defend the 'reason' (*logon*) that underlies their belief.[3]

Peter added two further instructions, both of them vital to an effective Christian apologetic. The first is, *in your hearts set apart Christ as Lord* (15). Peter is here referring back to Isaiah 8:12–14, a passage he has already quoted from in 1 Peter 2:8. Do not be afraid of the things other people fear, he says, but hallow[4] or sanctify Jesus in your hearts as Lord; worship and obey him as the holy Lord of your life, with all its problems and sufferings, 'and he will be a sanctuary',[5] a safe and holy place; he will deal with the opposition and bring you through. Our defence of our trust in God and his purposes of ultimate good is not to be made in our own strength, according to specious arguments or eloquent

---

[1] 1 Pet. 3:17–18; 2:20–23; 4:12–19.

[2] Peter 'here summarizes the content of the Christian profession as "hope"'; F. W. Beare, *The First Epistle of Peter* (Blackwell, 1970), p. 165.

[3] Selwyn states, 'Our author is using a good classical Greek phrase here', and translates it 'a rational account'; E. G. Selwyn, *The First Epistle of St Peter* (Macmillan, 1955), p. 193.

[4] *Hagiasate*, from *hagios*, 'holy', the same verb as is used in the Lord's Prayer, 'hallowed be your name' (Matt. 6:9).

[5] Isa. 8:14.

presentation. Rather, it should be in humble dependence on the Holy Spirit, in the full knowledge that only he can finally persuade anyone of the truth.

The second instruction is that the stating and defending of the case for our hope should be *with gentleness and respect, keeping a clear conscience, so that those who speak maliciously against your behaviour in Christ may be ashamed of their slander* (15–16). 'Be as shrewd as snakes and as innocent as doves', was the way Jesus put it.[6] In no way must anything in our approach put our hearers off our message.

The problem of evil and suffering is a major issue for every one of us as we seek to defend the gospel before those around us. Perhaps more than any other single issue, it has become a significant emotional and intellectual barrier, preventing people from accepting belief in God, or even destroying what belief they had, when, say, they watch a friend die of cancer or see horrific pictures on their television screens of the devastation caused by a tsunami or a hurricane. When such things happen the cry of 'Why?' is often an expression of anger or helplessness, rather than a request for a carefully reasoned explanation; but we who believe there are answers both emotional and intellectual should always be ready to give what is appropriate. Often the response needed will not be arguments but Jesus, the one whom we have hallowed in our hearts as Lord, whose grace and love and compassion flow out from us to those who are hurting and perplexed. But at other times a reasoned answer will be needed, and in this chapter we shall be looking at some of the questions people may ask and suggesting possible ways we could answer.

Though the answers we give will always be faithful to the revelation of his truth that God has given us in the Bible, the way we present that truth will vary considerably according to the starting point of the person we are talking with. The approach we take with someone who cries an agonized 'Why?' at the sudden death of her husband will be very different from the one we take in a university debating society. In some situations, those we are speaking with will accept the authority of Scripture, and that will mean we can present our case using the appropriate Bible passages. But others will not accept the Bible, and we need to find a way of presenting the biblical answer that they will be able to accept. Again, our approach, say, to someone who accepts the Muslim concept of God will be very different from our approach to the person who believes that God's main task is to keep each one of us

---

[6] Matt. 10:16.

happy all the time. Some will be honestly seeking for an answer to their questions, longing to find a way out of their intellectual problems; others will be asking questions as a way of attacking Christianity, and however much we answer they will only attack more. So before we respond we need the wisdom and guidance of the Holy Spirit; no two situations are the same; there are no set answers.

Indeed, though the NIV uses the word 'answer', it may be wisest not to look on what we are doing as 'providing answers' in any final sense. Certainly we can suggest some ways of seeing things that may help people in their perplexity, but when the questions are so big it may be best not to claim that we have something that we can call the answer, except in the sense that God himself and all that he has done in Christ are the answer. All the other things we say, however true they may be and however well argued, can be nothing more than pointers to him. On occasion, after preaching, John Wesley would sum up what he had been doing with the words, 'I offered them Christ.' Doubtless he had carefully explained the doctrines of the Christian faith; doubtless, too, he had argued his case persuasively – he was, after all, an Oxford don who had lectured in logic and philosophy and had strong confidence in reason. But his main task, to which everything else was subsidiary, was to enable people to see Jesus, whether they saw him in what he said, or in the way he said it, or in who he was.

We shall work through a range of the questions people ask about evil and suffering by following a dialogue. Any of the responses given could be expanded considerably; so, too, doubtless, could the questions.

Why didn't God make a world where nothing bad ever happens?

There are a number of possible reasons. One is that he wanted to make a world where people were free. Without freedom we would just be robots, programmed machines. He wanted us to be real personal beings, like him, who could love freely, and make free, creative choices. But having freedom means that we can choose to do bad as well as to do good; tragically, that is what has happened; so the world contains hatred and cruelty and injustice and selfishness and vice and so on because we are free to do evil. It is not God who has put these things into the world; we have. Another possible reason is that the nature of our world is such that you cannot have good things happening without the possibility of bad things happening as well. Our eyes, say, are wonderfully sensitive, giving us the amazing ability to see. But because they are so sensitive we can easily damage them; if we look directly at the sun, for instance, we will feel pain. We have the joy and privilege of loving someone, but along with that goes the pain we feel when we are separated from her or him. Water is great when we drink it or sail a boat on it; but we can also drown in it. A third reason is that only in a world where bad things happen could we grow and mature as persons. Imagine a world where there is nothing the slightest bit evil or unpleasant; everything is always easy; nothing takes effort; nothing ever goes wrong. There would be nothing to stretch or challenge us, nothing to develop our personalities. Without any dangers we would never learn courage; without risks and problems we would not learn to trust; without people wronging us we would not learn grace or forgiveness or mercy or love of enemies. To develop the full potential of human personhood we need to live in a world where bad things happen.

But why is it all so unfair? Why do bad things happen to good people and not just to bad people?

One answer would be that not even the best among us can claim to be so good that we deserve no evil at all. Another might be that even good people still need to face tough situations in order to give them further opportunities to grow and express things like trust and forgiveness and love of enemies. But there are at least two further answers. The first is that we all, 'good' and 'bad', live in a world where bad things happen and so we all experience the evil in it. The bodies of good people are susceptible to disease or will get smashed up if they are in a car crash just as much as those of bad people. Our goodness does not prevent toothache or the pain we feel when a loved one dies. Setbacks and suffering are the common lot of all humanity. The second point is one that people might find hard to take, but it is one that the Bible states quite strongly. God in Jesus chose to share in the suffering of the world, chose to go through it all in order to overcome it. That is amazing grace; he so loved the world, he identified himself so closely with it, he willingly shared in all its hurts. The Christians of the first century saw this as the model they were to follow. It was not a matter of thinking, 'We're good people, and so we shouldn't suffer'; rather, it was that 'God in his love and grace has willingly shared in the suffering of the world; therefore we'll follow his example and do the same. We'll look on suffering, not as something unwelcome, but as a trust from God that enables us to walk the way of Christ.'

*Why doesn't God do something about the evil and suffering
in the world? Is he just standing idly by, helpless, or doesn't
he care?*

He does care, tremendously, and in no way does he stand helplessly
by. Already he has done tons – enough to deal with all the evil and
suffering in the world, and there is lots more that he is still doing.
Amazingly, he has done the exact opposite of standing idly by; he
has got totally involved. He has allowed all the evil and suffering in
the world to be piled on him; he has suffered it all in Jesus Christ,
all the sin, all the evil, all the suffering, all the sorrow, all the pain.
He did not have to do so, but he chose to do so, by coming and
living on planet Earth and dying on the cross, carrying the evil
and curse and pain of a fallen world. But, even more amazingly,
after he allowed evil to crush and kill him he rose again from the
dead, demonstrating once and for all that good is victorious over
evil; he broke the power of evil to destroy; he made it possible for
anyone to escape its clutches, offering his resurrection power to
anyone willing to experience it.

*But how can what God did two thousand years ago make
any difference to the evil and suffering we have to face
today?*

Because his presence and power through the Holy Spirit are able to
transform any situation of evil and suffering. He does not take us
out of the tough situations, but he gives us what we need to get
through them and come out on top. If our problem is sin, he gives us
forgiveness and freedom and a new start. If our problem is suffering,
he gives us the strength and faith and endurance and courage we
need. What's more, he always finds some way of using our
experiences of tough situations to bring about something good, for
us or for others, that would not otherwise have occurred, so that
when we look back we shall be able to say that it was all infinitely
worthwhile. Of course, it is up to us whether we let him work in
this kind of way in our lives; we do not have to accept his
forgiveness or his strength; we can refuse to let him work things
out for good in our lives; instead, say, of letting the experience of
losing our job teach us how to depend on God when we have no
money, or give us a real compassion for the poor or the long-term
unemployed, we can choose to become bitter and angry and full of
self-pity, so letting one evil breed several others. But it does not
have to be like that; God offers us an alternative, to transform evil
into good.

But what about those who get a really raw deal: children who are routinely abused; those who lose their homes and families in times of war; those who struggle for years with pain or disability, or those who die young?

I think we can say that the greater the pain and suffering the greater the compassion of God for that person, and the greater his offer of grace and help and his transforming power. Again, that is not to say that the person has to take it. Jesus made a point of going to the people with the greatest need; he offered 'rest' to all those who were 'weary and burdened';[7] but not everyone accepted his offer.

Maybe I need to spend a moment on those who die young. Because it has no real concept of life after death, our culture tends to see death as the ultimate evil, and early death as particularly awful. But that is very different from the way the Bible sees things. There, people accepted that God has the right to decide how long each of us should live and so when we should die. The attitude of our culture tends to be, 'It's my life; I have a right to live as long as I choose, and if I don't get to eighty I've been cheated.' The Bible's attitude is that we are created by God; life is his gift; we belong to him; the choice whether we live to twenty or to eighty is his, and he makes it in wisdom and love. Since earthly death, for the Christian, means 'to depart and be with Christ, which is better by far', even an early death is not the kind of disaster we tend to feel it is.

OK, so what you're saying is that God has done everything necessary to break the power of evil and bring good things out of any bad things we might experience. But that applies only to those who know about him. What about those who have never heard the gospel?

Of course we have a huge responsibility to tell everyone the good news of what God has done in Jesus, but I am not at all sure that what I have said applies only to those who have actually heard the gospel. God most certainly reveals at least something of himself to everyone whether they have heard the gospel or not, and everyone has an opportunity to respond to him.[8] The Bible gives us examples where God worked for good in the lives of those who did not belong to his people; after all, he is the Lord of all the earth, and his power and love are not limited to those who have heard the gospel.

[7] Matt. 11:28.
[8] Rom. 1:19–20.

That brings us to the issue of hell. Even if everyone has an opportunity to respond to God, you have to accept that some choose to reject him and so in effect choose hell rather than heaven. But that then means that since hell is evil, and it goes on for ever and ever, then evil goes on for ever and ever.

These are big issues, and I am not sure that it is wise to be too dogmatic about them. I am not even sure that it is fair to say that hell is evil. Hell is where evil is condemned and destroyed, and surely the condemning and destruction of evil is good. You might say that those in hell go on rebelling against God and that that is an evil. But even that is questionable. They still cling on to evil, gnawing at the shattered hopes of pushing God off the throne of the universe, but their rebellion is in fact at an end; they can no longer refuse to acknowledge God as God. Those verses about every knee bowing and every tongue confessing Jesus Christ as Lord must apply to those in hell as well as to those who gladly welcome Jesus as Lord.[9] There is a lot about hell that we have to admit we do not understand; but then that is true of heaven as well. But we can be sure there is nothing unjust or ultimately wrong about hell; however evil may have started, hell is as much under the lordship of our wise and gracious and just God as is heaven. We can trust him to make sure that, when the time comes for his final purposes to be fulfilled and good to triumph over evil, that will include even hell.[10]

You have talked about good coming out of evil, and I think I can accept that, if my suffering has a good result, then the goodness can outweigh the evil. But surely lots of suffering does not produce good results. Think of the Holocaust or a tsunami or an earthquake. The suffering there is huge and it is very difficult to think of any resulting good that would be big enough to outweigh that.

I agree. But the fact that it is very difficult for us to see any resulting good does not mean that it is past the wisdom and power of God to produce it. But you need to remember that God does not force people to respond positively to their suffering. There is no doubt that much good did come out of the Holocaust, and may yet come from it, if we are capable of learning from the past. Let me give you just one example: Viktor Frankl suffered horribly in Auschwitz, but instead of allowing it to break him he used his experiences to

[9] Phil. 2:10–11.
[10] For a fuller exposition of the Bible's teaching on hell see B. Milne, *The Message of Heaven and Hell* (IVP 2002).

develop a new counselling therapy (called 'logotherapy') that has greatly helped hundred of thousands, if not millions, of people since. One thing we need to remember is that we only ever get a very limited view of any event we live through, so it impossible for us to decide whether or not it ultimately brings about a justifying good. It is easier when we can look back to events in the past; back in the 1950s and 1960s, for example, the triumph of communism in China and the resulting savage persecution of Christians seemed to observers then totally disastrous. The church appeared to be virtually wiped out. But now, looking back, we can see how God used the persecution to purify the Chinese church and as a catalyst for amazing growth. I do not think anybody forty or fifty years ago could have imagined that he could do it, and yet God worked through all that evil and suffering to build a church that is one of the strongest in the world and that may now number fifty million believers.[11]

But surely it's the scale of the suffering that makes it so hard to accept that good can come out of one of these big tragedies. Six million deaths in the Holocaust, and 230,000 in a tsunami and 25,000 in an earthquake: how can good come out of anything as big as that?

I agree that when you quote numbers like that they sound horrific. Perhaps it might help a bit to set them in context. With six billion people in the world, death is a common event, and, except for those of us who live in wealthy nations, it is generally what we would call early and potentially preventable death; the average person in Sierra Leone dies at under forty. Terrible though the 2004 tsunami was, its death toll was less than the number of people who normally die every day. Now, the thought of all those deaths, with the suffering that goes with them, is more than we can bear. But we need to remember that no human person suffered all those deaths. Each person suffers only one death, or, if you include the death of close friends and family, a strictly limited number of deaths. No-one, except for God himself, suffers the pain of 230,000 deaths. C. S. Lewis puts it this way:

> We must never make the problem of pain worse than it is by vague talk about the 'unimaginable sum of human misery'. Suppose that I have a toothache of intensity x: and suppose that

[11] Statistic given in *East Asia's Billions*, the magazine of OMF International (April–June 2006), p. 6.

you, who are seated beside me, also begin to have a toothache of intensity x. You may, if you choose, say that the total amount of pain in the room is now $2x$. But you must remember that no one is suffering $2x$: search all time and all space and you will not find that composite pain in anyone's consciousness. There is no such thing as a sum of suffering, for no one suffers it. When we have reached the maximum that a single person can suffer, we have, no doubt, reached something very horrible, but we have reached all the suffering there ever can be in the universe. The addition of a million fellow-sufferers adds no more pain.[12]

What about the people who say that these disasters are God punishing the world for its sin?

The first thing I would do is to suggest they read Luke 13:1–5, where Jesus states very clearly that it is wrong to conclude that those who suffer a disaster do so because they are 'worse sinners' than the people who escape the disaster. I would not want to deny that God does at times punish people for their sins; he made it very clear to his people in the Old Testament that if they turned away from him he would punish them by letting their enemies overrun them. Of course, his punishment always had the aim of turning his people from their sin and bringing them back to him; read, say, Leviticus 26, where, after warning his people with a long list of the ways in which he will punish them if they refuse to follow him, he goes on to say that if they turn back to him and confess their sins he will restore his covenant relationship with them. But the important thing is that to say that God may sometimes punish a person for his or her sins does not entitle us to conclude that anyone who suffers a disaster is being punished by God. So, unless God has manifestly chosen and equipped us to be his prophets and has given us a clear revelation of his purposes, we should never take it upon ourselves to declare that any specific suffering is God's punishment. If we come across people who look upon their suffering as punishment from God (and some, maybe because of their psychological background, are more disposed to see things that way than others), we shall probably need to stress that God's main concern is to bring them into a right relationship with himself; once that happens, there is no need for them to feel guilty, because all the penalty for their sin has been borne by the Lord Jesus.

But, having said all that, it is still true that disasters, even if they are not a direct punishment for sin, are one of the ways God speaks

---

[12] C. S. Lewis, *The Problem of Pain* (Geoffrey Bles, 1940), pp. 103–104.

to us and warns us that not all is right with our world, and so one of the ways he calls us back to himself. Again, people have the choice which way they respond to disasters. They can realize how fragile life is, how trivial many of their values are, how deep are their needs for comfort and love, and so on, and turn to God as a result. Or they can shake their fist at God and curse him for their suffering and continue in their rebellion against him.

You say that in the Old Testament God warned his people that he would punish them if they sinned against him, and they did and he did. But what about the other places in the Old Testament where God tells his people to destroy other nations? Was that a punishment for their sins? And wasn't God's command to drive the nations out of the promised land a bit over the top? Couldn't the various nations have lived satisfactorily side by side?

That is a big question. It is an especially sensitive one for us today when we have seen the horrors of 'ethnic cleansing' and the struggles between Israel and the Arabs for possession of the land. The issue of the 'ban' (*ḥērem*) by which the cities they conquered were 'devoted' to the Lord[13] has caused a lot of discussion, and I can list only a few points that I personally find helpful.[14]

1. Though the issue is a big one for us today, it would not have been a problem in Bible days. The things we find difficult to cope with were actually standard practice in ancient warfare. Every nation consulted its gods before going to war and followed their instructions; wars were seen as battles between the various deities; just as it had been God versus the gods of the Egyptians back at the exodus, now it was God versus the gods of the Canaanites; the Canaanites would have accepted that just as much as the Israelites.[15] They would also have accepted that the winners would destroy the losers.[16] Indeed, what God commanded his people, to 'devote' everything and everyone to him, was considerably preferable to what normally happened in the pillage and rape of a defeated city.

2. Yes, it was a punishment for their sins. This is specifically stated in Deuteronomy 9 as the people prepared to enter the land.

---

[13] See, for example, Josh. 6:21.
[14] For more detailed discussions see C. J. H. Wright, *Old Testament Ethics* (IVP, 2004); A. Kirk (ed.), *Handling Problems of Peace and War* (Marshall Pickering, 1988); and S. Gundry (ed.), *Show Them No Mercy: Four Views on God and Canaanite Genocide* (Zondervan, 2003).
[15] See, for example, Josh. 2:8–11.
[16] Josh. 2:12–13.

Hear, O Israel. You are now about to cross the Jordan to go in and dispossess nations greater and stronger than you ... After the LORD your God has driven them out before you, do not say to yourself, 'The LORD has brought me here to take possession of this land because of my righteousness.' No, it is on account of the wickedness of these nations that the LORD is going to drive them out before you.[17]

3. There is a close parallel between what happened to Israel at the exile and what happened to the Canaanite nations at the conquest; God equally punishes his people and the pagan nations for their sins. In Leviticus, after warning his people against various sins, ending with child sacrifice and sexual perversions, God said:

'Do not defile yourself in any of these ways, because this is how the nations that I am going to drive out before you became defiled. Even the land was defiled; so I punished it for its sin, and the land vomited out its inhabitants. But you must keep my decrees and my laws. The native-born and the aliens living among you must not do any of these detestable things, for all these things were done by the people who lived in the land before you, and the land became defiled. And if you defile the land, it will vomit you out as it vomited out the nations that were before you.'[18]

God did not discriminate; the nations and his people suffered the same punishment for the same sins.

4. There was, of course, an additional factor that the Bible accounts mention several times. Though peaceful coexistence sounds a good option to us, it was vital that Israel became a distinctive nation, God's covenant 'holy' people, different from all the other nations, a clear expression of his nature and truth. So compromise was forbidden lest the people of the land should corrupt God's people by their evil practices.[19] In the event, of course, the Israelites did compromise, with disastrous results.

5. One thing of which I am absolutely certain is that these passages must never be used to justify warfare today; they were specific instructions for a specific situation which will never be repeated. The Christian approach to war must be based on the teaching of the whole Bible, culminating, of course, in the teaching and life of Christ.

[17] Deut. 9:1, 4–5.
[18] Lev. 18:24–28.
[19] Exod. 34:12–16.

OK. But what about other forms of suffering, like injustice, oppression, and poverty? Why does God let them happen?

Much of what I have already said applies there too. But it is hardly fair to put all the blame for injustice, oppression and poverty on God. Surely we ought to accept that most of the evils of the world are our fault, not his. God did not cause the Holocaust; the Nazis did. God does not keep the poor nations poor; our current world system does. To put things in perspective, on average something like a hundred times as many people die of hunger each year as die from natural disasters. Something like twenty-two million die every year from hunger, and that is a painful way to die. We may not be able to prevent earthquakes and hurricanes (though we could do much more than we do at present to avoid major loss of life), but there is plenty we can do to prevent twenty-two million people starving to death every year. Part of God's answer to injustice and poverty and so many of the other evils that are around us in the world is us: his love and compassion and provision flowing out through us to those who are hurting.

Interlude
Why on earth? Reasons for evil and suffering

We have seen that the question 'Why evil and suffering?' can be answered in several different ways, all of which are valid. If I ask why my tooth is aching at the moment, I could answer, 'Because I ate too many sweets as a boy', or 'Because my tooth is decayed', or 'Because I've put off going to the dentist', or 'As a warning that there is something wrong', or 'To get me to the dentist as soon as possible', or 'Because suffering is part of being human', or 'To give me an opportunity of suffering pain without complaining', or 'To enable me to empathize with those who suffer', or, 'To draw me nearer to Christ.'

Broadly, reasons for evil and suffering fall into two categories, which we could call causative and purposive. The causative reasons look back and answer the questions, 'Where did this evil or suffering come from?', 'What caused it?' The purposive reasons look forward, asking, 'What is it for?', 'What is the purpose behind it?', 'Where is it leading?' Perhaps our scientifically minded age encourages us to focus on the first group; the Bible would seem to encourage us to be much more interested in the second. Since God is God, our concern must be to work with him rather than against him in his purposes of good,[1] and to do this we need a Spirit-inspired awareness of what those purposes are, in broad terms if not in details.[2] Such an awareness, according to the Bible, is not just a matter of satisfying our curiosity and answering our question 'Why?' It is so that we can 'work together' with God and his purposes, using every situation, evil and well as good, painful as well as pleasant, to further the coming of his kingdom.

[1] Rom. 8:28.
[2] Eph. 1:17–18.

Perhaps our wrestling with God over the problems also falls into two categories. There is the wrestling that is an attack, an angry protest, in effect arraigning God for making such a mess of things. Or there is the struggling with a situation where we long to find the God of goodness and grace but cannot, where we are willing to accept his wisdom and purposes but simply do not know how to cope with the situation we face. God's compassion reaches out to us whichever category we may be in; but the danger with the first is that it can be an expression of rebellion against him and an insistence that our way of seeing things is right. The hope for the second is in the words of Jesus, 'Seek and you will find.'[3] If our desire is to trace the hand of God in the situation, and to identify ourselves with his purposes, however costly that may be, then we can be confident that in the end he will show himself to us, even though we have to hang on for a long time in faith.[4] Both Jacob and Habakkuk wrestled with God, Jacob over personal issues, Habakkuk over great issues of justice and international affairs. Perhaps neither of them found the full intellectual answer to their questionings, but what mattered was that they both found God, a new experience of him and a new awareness of who he was and what he was doing, and, above all, a new relationship with him.

For Paul, all other considerations faded into the background when he thought about the glory that was to come. Everything, he was confident, was ultimately under God's control; his purposes were wise and perfect; he was working everything 'for good'; and the climax of his purposes was 'glory'. Glory is nothing less than God himself, the glory of the triune God revealed, the veil finally removed, his beauty and goodness at last seen in their fullness; love and joy and peace and light and truth and majesty poured out upon us; the wonder of his presence, glorious beyond our wildest dreams.[5] And when God's glory shines out, it will fill those who belong to him; not only shall we see it, we shall 'be glorified',[6] we shall shine with the light of all that he is; through us, redeemed humanity radiant with the glory of the Redeemer Christ, all creation will be transformed; the new age will begin.

The path of suffering leads to glory. But even before we get there, God in his wisdom and grace uses evil and suffering to bring about good. It may be immediate or it may be long-term. It may be that the one who suffers the evil benefits, or it may be that the benefit is enjoyed by others. The good may be obvious, or it may be difficult

[3] Matt. 7:7.
[4] Hab. 2:2–4.
[5] 1 Cor. 2:9.
[6] Rom. 8:30.

to trace. The biblical examples show a wide variety, and each of us could supplement them with experiences of our own or in the lives of those we know.

Then, over and above these ways in which good comes from suffering, the Christian finds something else, nothing less than a foretaste of the glory that is to come. For the road of suffering is the way Christ walked, and as we walk it we find we are walking with him. Perhaps for most of us it is an Emmaus-road experience, when our sorrow and sadness dim our eyes and we are not able to realize who it is who walks with us. But, by the grace of God and with the eye of faith, we can let our pain draw us close to him, so that we 'know Christ ... and the fellowship of sharing in his sufferings'[7] and grow towards 'the perfection of fellowship with him'.[8] Then we can begin to realize that suffering is not a curse but a blessing, a gift of grace from a God of love.

[7] Phil. 3:10.
[8] Barth; see above, p. 171.

Part 5
How on earth? Living with evil and suffering

Matthew 10:16–39
18. The suffering people of a suffering God

'Come, follow me,' said Jesus, 'and I will make you fishers of men.'[1] Those who left their nets in response to his call hardly knew what a tough time they were letting themselves in for. But they soon began to learn. The first way they learnt was by watching Jesus and the opposition and suffering he faced. The second was through his explicit teaching.

1. Following the Master (10:24–25)

It is generally held that, although Matthew set each of his five great blocks of Jesus' teaching in a historical context, he felt at liberty to incorporate into them teaching given on other occasions. Thus, in chapter 10, the second of the blocks of teaching, which is set in the context of the sending out of the Twelve on mission, we find material which Luke records in his account of the sending out of the seventy-two,[2] and material which Mark includes in his Olivet discourse.[3] It is very likely, of course, that Jesus, like any good teacher, repeated his teaching on a number of occasions. But, however the body of teaching came together in Matthew 10, we can safely take it that its application, and particularly the application of verses 16–39, is wider than the specific mission of the Twelve. If that were not so, Matthew would not have included it in his Gospel at all. Inasmuch as Jesus intended his church to be a missionary church, this is teaching which Jesus intended for all his followers.

[1] Matt. 4:19.
[2] Luke 10:3–12.
[3] Mark 13:9, 11–13.

At the heart of the passage lies Jesus' statement:

*'A student is not above his teacher, nor a servant above his master.
It is enough for the student to be like his teacher, and the servant
like his master. If the head of the house has been called Beelzebub,
how much more the members of his household!'* (24–25).

Jesus used the image of his followers as students and servants in a
number of different ways. In John 13:16, for example, after washing
his disciples' feet, he stressed that his servants must follow their
Master's example in gracious and loving behaviour. In Matthew
24:45–51 the focus is on the need for servants to be 'faithful and
wise'. In Matthew 10 and in John 15:20 the message is that students
and servants will suffer as their Master suffers. We are called to
follow Jesus, and that means following him in every aspect of his
life, his teaching, his living, his example, his suffering, his death and
his resurrection. This is discipleship; this is identification, the shared
life, oneness with him.

Those who walk the way of Christ, according to the New
Testament, will walk the way of suffering. We are to expect nothing
less than he experienced. The clear anticipation in Matthew 10 is
that the followers of Jesus would suffer persecution, an expectation
shared by the rest of the New Testament and stated explicitly by
Paul: 'Everyone who wants to live a godly life in Christ Jesus will be
persecuted.'[4] Such an expectation comes as a challenge to those of us
who find ourselves living relatively persecution-free lives. Is this
because we have lost our distinctiveness and are no longer a threat to
those who belong to the world around us? Or is it because, for us in
our culture, opposition to the life and witness of the people of God
that underlies open persecution takes other, often more subtle
forms? Certainly the New Testament would teach us that if we
have no suffering at all to undergo then we are underprivileged,
deprived of God-given opportunities to follow our Master and
Teacher and walk with Christ on the road he trod.

2. Sheep and wolves (10:16–22)

It is good to feel that we, the people of God, are the salt of the earth
and the light of the world.[5] It is rather less encouraging to find that
he expects us to be *sheep* (or even lambs[6]) among a pack of *wolves*
(16). Granted, Spurgeon managed to find something in this image to

[4] 2 Tim. 3:12.
[5] Matt. 5:13, 14.
[6] Luke 10:3.

be cheerful about: 'The mission of sheep to wolves is a hopeful one, since we see in the natural world that the sheep, though so feeble, by far outnumber the wolves who are so fierce. The day will come when persecutors will be as scarce as wolves, and saints as numerous as sheep.'[7]

May that be so; but I doubt very much if that was the main thought in the minds of those who first heard these words, especially when Jesus went on to speak of floggings and imprisonment and execution and persecution and being hated by *all men* because of him (17–19, 21–22). The expectation of Jesus for his people is that they would be innocent victims in a cruel world. What is more, it is he who sends us into danger and suffering (16). It is not his wish that we stay cocooned and sheltered; as the Father sent him, he sends us,[8] and those who are sent will get hurt.

Two gleams of light cheer this gloomy picture. Being forewarned (*Be on your guard*, 17) and being *as shrewd as snakes and as innocent as doves* will help us survive (16); and the one whom Jesus calls *the Spirit of your Father* will be with us, not to rescue us out of danger, but to enable us to maintain a good witness, come what may (20). One of the responsibilities of church leaders in these days must surely be to prepare people for suffering and to teach them how to cope with it and how to allow it to be a means which the Holy Spirit can use to point others to Christ.

3. Divided families (10:21, 35–37)

Among the many things that Jesus suffered were misunderstanding, rejection and opposition from his own family.[9] Among the ways he expected his followers to suffer was through divided families (21, 35–37). Though in our culture, unlike in some places in today's world, the prospect of being betrayed to death by our brother or parent or child is remote, very many Christian believers struggle with the pressures and pains that arise when a family is split between those who follow the Lord Jesus and those who reject him. Jesus was very aware that his message would bring division and hurt in families;[10]

---

[7] C. H. Spurgeon, *The Gospel of the Kingdom* (Passmore and Alabaster, 1893), p. 70.

[8] John 20:21.

[9] Mark 3:21, 31–35; John 7:5.

[10] Verse 35 is not to be understood as 'I have come in order to turn a man against his father...', but rather, 'The outcome of my coming is that a man is turned against his father...' 'The *effects* produced by the preaching are given as the *purpose* for which Christ came. This is in accord with a Semitic manner of speaking, and indeed thinking, about God'; F. W. Beare, *The Gospel according to Matthew* (Blackwell, 1981), p. 249.

in the culture of his day, where strong family ties were an essential foundation for life, the prospect of such divisions was horrific.[11] But it was the cost of discipleship that Jesus expected his followers to be willing to pay.

Again, a gleam of light can be shed on this prospect by the words of Jesus when his own family rejected him:

> Then Jesus' mother and brothers arrived. Standing outside, they sent someone in to call him...
>
> 'Who are my mother and my brothers?' he asked.
>
> Then he looked at those seated in a circle around him and said, 'Here are my mother and my brothers! Whoever does God's will is my brother and sister and mother'.[12]

All believers who suffer in their family as a result of their commitment to Christ can take comfort, not just from the fact that they are walking the way Jesus walked, but from the replacement family that God gives; if we lose our natural family, God puts in its place something even more beautiful, the family of those who belong to him and do his will, our brothers and sisters in the Lord Jesus.

> 'No-one who has left home or brothers or sisters or mother or father or children or fields for me and the gospel will fail to receive a hundred times as much in this present age (homes, brothers, sisters, mothers, children and fields – and with them, persecutions) and in the age to come, eternal life.'[13]

4. 'You're the devil' (10:25)

'If the head of the house has been called Beelzebub, how much more the members of his household!' (25). To call the Son of God the devil

---

[11] 'When the son or daughter of a devout family became a Christian while the father or mother did not (or vice versa), it caused the bitterest hostility within the family. This came about in Gentile families perhaps even more acutely than in Jewish; for all the members of the family had a part to play in the domestic cult which was carried on every day, as well as in the ceremonies of the public cult. A son or a daughter converted to Christianity could not so much as pour a libation to the household gods, or walk in procession to the temple, or to Eleusis, say. Such an attitude could not fail to infuriate the parents. It could also happen that the children would rebel when the parents were converted. For many, this alienation would be harder to bear than the danger of arrest, or flogging, or death'; Beare, *The Gospel according to Matthew*, p. 249.

[12] Mark 3:31, 33–35.

[13] Mark 10:29–30.

is horrific; I guess the pain that Jesus felt when it happened was horrific, too. Many times the hurt we feel from the words or attitudes of others is as deep if not deeper than physical pain. Lies, slander, criticism and the like can cause a great deal of suffering. Christians may escape physical persecution in our culture, but we are still fair game for verbal attacks, mockery, misrepresentation, ridicule, caricature and the like. Tragically, such attacks come not only from those who are opposed to the gospel; we have all known situations where fellow Christians who disagree with us on some point of doctrine or practice have hurt us deeply by the things they have said or the way they have said them.

They did it to me, says Jesus, and they will do it to you. Indeed, he goes a stage further: if they did it to me they will do it even more to you. So do not be surprised when it happens.

'If the world hates you, keep in mind that it hated me first ... Remember the words I spoke to you: "No servant is greater than his master." If they persecuted me, they will persecute you also ... They will treat you this way because of my name.'[14]

5. Fear and faithfulness (10:26–33)

Three times in verses 26–33 Jesus says, *'Do not be afraid'* (26, 28, 31).[15] Twice he is specifically referring to being afraid of those who oppose and attack us and have the power to kill us; the third time he is much more general: 'Don't be afraid of anything.'

Once in this passage Jesus tells us to be afraid; the one thing, or rather person, we are to fear is God himself. He is the one before whom we shall stand. He, in Christ, will pass judgment on our lives; he has the power to destroy us *both body and soul in hell* (28). Tremble before him; be afraid lest you reject him or disown him (33); let acknowledging him and pleasing him and doing his will be the motivating power that drives you; take heart from the reassurance that if you give him his rightful place in your life you can know that this fearsome one is *your Father* (29) who cares passionately about you, who watches over you, who has promised to protect you and bring you safely through all the opposition and suffering you may meet (28–31).

Fear him, ye saints, and you will then
have nothing else to fear;

[14] John 15:18, 20–21.
[15] In Luke's parallel to verse 28 Jesus adds, 'my friends'.

> make but his service your delight;
> your wants shall be his care.[16]

'Do not be afraid' appears to be a phrase that was frequently on the lips of Jesus, often in circumstances where fear was the most natural human reaction. He said it when Jairus was confronted with the death of his daughter,[17] when the disciples saw a 'ghost' walking on the sea,[18] when the wolves were beginning to gather around the 'little flock' ready for the kill,[19] and when the disciples were trembling on the eve of the crucifixion.[20] We can safely say that in every situation we may have to face, of danger, opposition, persecution, illness, death, pain or suffering of any sort, he speaks to us, 'Do not be afraid.' 'In this world you will have trouble. But take heart! I have overcome the world.'[21] Ensure that God is in the central place in your life; remain faithful to him whatever evils may come your way, however great the pressure to give up, to turn away, to deny him. For his power to bring us safely through is greater than the power of any of these things to destroy us.

6. Not much chance of a peaceful life (10:34)

Peace is a great biblical theme. It is the gift of God to his people, whether in the great words of the Aaronic blessing, 'The LORD turn his face towards you and give you peace',[22] or in the words of Jesus in the upper room, 'Peace I leave with you; my peace I give to you.'[23] But, as Jesus adds, the peace that God gives is not 'as the world gives'; it is not a problem-free and trouble-free life. When the kingdom of God comes to a world in rebellion it will inevitably stir up conflict. The very nature of God's people as they live God's goodness and glory, not to mention the message they proclaim, will challenge the emptiness and evil of the world and stir up its opposition.[24] If we want what the world calls peace, an easy time with no hassles, then maybe we need to join the world's side. If we

---

[16] From the hymn 'Through all the changing scenes of life', an adaptation of Ps. 34:9–10 by Nahum Tate and Nicholas Brady.
[17] Luke 8:50.
[18] Mark 4:50.
[19] Luke 12:32.
[20] John 14:27.
[21] John 16:33.
[22] Num. 6:26.
[23] John 14:27.
[24] 'As long as some men refuse the lordship of God, to follow the Prince of peace will always be a way of conflict'; R. T. France, *The Gospel according to Matthew* (IVP, 1985), p. 188.

are on the Lord's side we need to accept that in this world he offers us *not peace but a sword* (34).

7. The people of the cross (10:34)

The climax of this passage comes in verse 38: *Anyone who does not take his cross and follow me is not worthy of me.* This is the first mention of the cross in the gospels; though less explicit than subsequent prophecies by Jesus about his death, it effectively says, 'I am going to be crucified, and I expect my followers to accept crucifixion too.' For the Jews of those days no more humiliating and terrifying fate could be imagined than crucifixion; there was nothing more awful: public disgrace; hours, even days, of excruciating pain; and the even deeper agony of being forsaken by God.[25] Yet that was the way Jesus was ready to go, and the way he called his disciples to follow. Though for most of us the call will be to less extreme forms of suffering, there is little comfort here for those who expect following Jesus to guarantee a problem-free and a pain-free life. That is not the way Jesus went, and it is not the way he calls his people to follow.

Seven New Testament reasons for rejoicing in suffering

Before we close this chapter, it is worth seeking to summarize the reasons why the New Testament sees walking the road of suffering with Christ as such a positive and desirable thing.

a. Identification

The basic one is identification. God in grace has chosen the way of identifying with us. Instead of remaining apart, 'he made himself nothing', taking the 'very nature' of a slave (*doulou*), coming in human form, 'humbling himself', even to 'death on a cross';[26] he chose to be poor, rejected, criticized, misunderstood, hungry, weary, forsaken, abused, maltreated, to suffer physically and mentally and emotional and spiritually, to be tempted, to suffer injustice, to know darkness and Godforsakenness. This is his identification with us in our humanity and our suffering. And it was so real and so powerful that those who followed him could think of nothing better than becoming like him in his life and sufferings and death.[27] Who would opt for a life of riches who had seen the beauty of Christ's poverty? Who would walk the road of

---

[25] Gal. 3:13.
[26] Phil. 2:6–8.
[27] Phil. 3:10.

ease and comfort when their Lord had 'nowhere to lay his head'?[28] Who would ask for popularity or a trouble-free life when he was 'despised and rejected by men, a man of sorrows, and familiar with suffering'?[29] To stand with him as he has stood with us; to suffer with him as he has suffered with us; to 'follow' him in all that he went through for us – there can be no greater privilege, no more worthwhile way of living our lives.

b. Deepening our relationship with Jesus

Closely related to this is the element of growing in our knowledge of him and our relationship with him. Our suffering is much more than an imitation or replay of the life and sufferings of Christ. When Paul talks about the 'fellowship of sharing in his sufferings' it is in the context of his longing to 'know Christ', to draw as close as possible to his heart, to go deep into a personal relationship with him. He is the God who suffers; to know him deeply we too need to know suffering. The path of suffering was the path to the heart of God, to the incalculable privilege of knowing the Lord of glory.

c. Showing Jesus

Thirdly, the way of suffering gives opportunity to express key aspects of the character of Jesus. This is Peter's point when he writes about undeserved suffering.[30] Only as we experience unfair suffering can we follow the grace and courage and endurance and mercy that Jesus showed when he suffered. It is then that a special 'Spirit of glory and of God' rests on us;[31] the way we respond to suffering allows the glory of God through the Holy Spirit to anoint and shine out from us; just as John the Baptist recognized Jesus as God's Son by the anointing of the Spirit on him,[32] so we show that we are truly God's children through this special anointing of the glory of God through his Spirit.

d. Developing our character

Linked to this is the point made several times in the New Testament that suffering shapes our character for good. James

---

[28] Luke 9:58.
[29] Isa. 53:3.
[30] 1 Pet. 2:18–24; 3:13–18; 4:12–19.
[31] 1 Pet. 4:14; literally 'the of the glory and the of God Spirit' (*to tēs doxēs kai to tou theou pneuma*).
[32] John 1:32–34.

starts his letter: 'Consider it pure joy, my brothers, whenever you face trials of many kinds, because you know that the testing of your faith develops perseverance. Perseverance must finish its work so that you may be mature and complete, not lacking anything.'[33]

e. Achieving eternal glory

A fifth reason why the New Testament writers see suffering so positively is that for them there is a correlation between our suffering and the glory that is to come. Paul states this explicitly in 2 Corinthians 4:17: 'Our light and momentary troubles are achieving for us an eternal glory that far outweighs them all.' It is not, of course, that we earn glory by enduring suffering; rather, God in his grace is pleased to give us extra blessing in glory because we have gladly walked the way of suffering for Christ's sake. Hodge comments, 'Afflictions are the cause of eternal glory. Not the meritorious cause, but still the procuring cause. God has seen fit to reveal his purpose not only to reward with exceeding joy the afflictions of his people, but to make those afflictions the means of working out that joy.'[34]

f. Filling up the sum of suffering

It is possible that Paul's words in Colossians 1:24 give us a sixth reason why the New Testament has such a positive view of suffering. Though the interpretation of the verse is disputed, it would seem that Paul's phrase 'what is still lacking in regard to Christ's afflictions' would indicate that Christ continues to suffer and will continue to suffer until a sum of suffering has been 'filled up'. This cannot be referring to his atoning suffering on the cross, which the New Testament declares is complete;[35] so it would appear to mean the suffering that Christ continues to suffer in his body, the church, the birth pains of the coming of the kingdom. If there is a certain tally of sufferings that has to be undergone before the kingdom is finally established, then, Paul may be saying, I want to get on and do my part in suffering them so that the kingdom may come all the sooner. The word he uses for 'I fill up' (*antanaplērō*) can suggest that Paul felt that the more he suffered the less others

[33] Jas 1:2–4.
[34] C. Hodge, *1 and 2 Corinthians* (Banner of Truth Trust, 1974), p. 480.
[35] See, for example, Heb. 9:25 – 10:18.

would have to suffer, and, so like his Master was he, he rejoiced to be able to do this.[36]

g. Proclaiming the gospel

Finally, a major reason for rejoicing in sufferings was that it was the experience of the early church that the witness of a suffering people of God was hugely effective.[37] Perhaps it never even occurred to them that the gospel could be spread without suffering, that conversions could be gained without toil and danger and opposition, that the church could grow without the blood of the martyrs. Suffering was for them a key accompaniment of declaring the good news of the gospel. And not just an accompaniment; in a sense it was part of the message. How those early Christians would have coped with prosperous television evangelists using the preaching of the gospel to make money is hard to conceive; for them the declaration of the gospel was the proclaiming of Christ, and they did that not just by word but by who they were. As Christ loved, so they loved. As Christ was holy, so they were holy. And as Christ suffered, so they suffered. As they thus presented Christ, many saw him and responded to him and became his followers.

---

[36] Paul 'cannot mean that the redeeming work of Christ on the cross was incomplete and needed to be supplemented by the suffering of his followers. He believed that Christ had died once for all (Rom. 6:10), and the next paragraph of this letter is one of his most forceful statements of this theme ... He is thinking rather of what Christ continues to suffer in *his body, the church* (cp. Matt. 25:45; Acts 9:4). In this corporate sense of the word "Christ" (cp. 1 Cor. 1:13; 12:12; Phil. 2:1, 5) *Christ's afflictions* will not be complete until the final victory over evil is won. Someone must carry the burden, and the strong may take over the share of the weak (Gal. 6:2). It is almost as if he is thinking of a fixed quota of suffering to be endured, so that the more he can attract to himself the less will remain for others'; G. B. Caird, *Paul's Letters from Prison* (Oxford University Press, 1976), p. 184. 'This remarkable statement can best be understood if we bear in mind the oscillation in Hebrew thought between individual and corporate personality ... At the back of Paul's mind there may be the rabbinical concept of the messianic birth pangs which were to be endured in the last days – from Paul's new Christian perspective, in the period leading up to the *parousia*. Jesus, the Messiah, had suffered on the cross; now his people, the members of his body, had their quota of affliction to bear, and Paul was eager to absorb as much as possible of this in his own "flesh"'; F. F. Bruce, *The Epistles to the Colossians, to Philemon, and to the Ephesians* (Eerdmans, 1984), pp. 82–83.

[37] See, for example, 2 Cor. 4:10–15; Col. 1:24 – 2:1.

Job; 2 Corinthians 4:7 – 5:10
19. Living with suffering

There can be little doubt that the Bible is more concerned to answer the question 'How?' than the question 'Why?' It was written primarily to give us God's instructions on how to live before him, and only secondarily as a handbook on theology. To be just a hearer of its message is insufficient; we must be doers.[1] There is little profit in building a biblical theology of suffering if it does not change the way we live through suffering. No amount of philosophizing over the source and nature of evil will eradicate it from the world; only action in the power of the Holy Spirit. So it is essential that we now turn to the teaching of the Bible on how we are to react to evil and suffering. In this chapter we shall focus on living with suffering; in order to do so we shall draw from the story of Job and one of Paul's great passages on suffering. The experiences and responses of these two men are not given to us as a blueprint or pattern to follow rigidly; our situations will never be the same as theirs. But studying them can help us build up a picture of the way God calls us to respond when we walk the road of suffering.

1. Job

When we read the story of Job we start with the book's prologue and at once have a great advantage over him. For there we read two things: that God is totally committed to Job, and that in the account of Satan's challenge there is an adequate explanation for all that happens to him (1:6–12). Job knows nothing of the second and struggles to hold on to the first.

Here, then, is a man who is *blameless and upright*, wise and good, prosperous and great and deeply committed to God (1:1–6). At a

---

[1] Matt. 7:24–27; Jas 1:22.

stroke he loses everything except his wife and his health (1:13–19). By chapter 2, thanks to a second round of Satanic interference, his health has been taken and his wife is calling on him to curse God and die (2:1–10). How does he cope, and what can we learn from his story? His response, inevitably, is complex and very untidy; this is a man in anguish reacting to unbelievable disaster; we cannot expect him to be consistent or even comprehensible. But, for our purposes, it is possible to pick out a number of elements in his response which will help us as we explore how God's people should react to suffering.[2]

a. Trust

The most outstanding feature of Job's reaction is his trust in God. In an age when the faithfulness of God was measured by how much he prospered the righteous, Job insists on continuing to trust in God against all appearances. Inevitably, at times his faith wavers; but fundamentally it is there, from his initial affirmation that *the LORD gave and the LORD has taken away; may the name of the LORD be praised* (1:21), through his continual insistence that God will vindicate him, to his final presentation of his case before God in chapter 31. Job was a man who refused to let his suffering destroy his faith in God. Curse God, said his wife; turn your back on him; give up on him; stop being faithful to him.[3] But he would not. *Though he slay me, yet will I hope in him* (13:15). Here was a man who endured, who held on to trust in God through loss and pain and bewilderment and darkness and chaos.

Our culture's view of faith has debased it from the strong and beautiful thing it is in the Bible to something thin and tenuous, something we link with uncertainty: 'We can't be sure, but we still exercise faith.' Neither Jesus nor Paul nor the writer to the Hebrews would have accepted such a view. For them faith was not tenuous; the God in whom they trusted was so utterly trustworthy that faith could never be anything but confident assurance. At the end of Romans 8 Paul did not climax his discussion of suffering with a

---

[2] David Atkinson skilfully and perceptively traces the development of Job's response using the insights of contemporary psychotherapy and counselling into 'the stages of grief'. He traces 'seven phases of his grief': numbed shock, anger, despair, terror, hope, questioning, and resolution; D. Atkinson, *The Message of Job* (IVP, 1991), pp. 71–105. Though the concept of 'the stages of grief' is a useful tool in seeking to understand grieving, few people in real life follow the process as given in the textbooks; grieving is too complex an experience to be fitted into a strict process, and Job's bewilderment and inconsistencies and changes of mood illustrate this complexity.

[3] Job 2:9.

tenuous trust that God would see him through; his cry was, 'I am convinced.'[4] The writer to the Hebrews starts his great chapter on faith with the words, 'Faith is being sure ... and certain.'[5] Perhaps the great mistake we make with faith is that we root it in ourselves, just as in a subjective age we root truth in ourselves. That means we measure it by what we can see in ourselves. But that is not the Bible's way. What we can see in ourselves is not the criterion; it does not matter if it is as small as a mustard seed.[6] What matters is God and his faithfulness: his love and power and commitment to us on which we can totally depend. Our need, well before we have to face suffering, is to grasp the greatness and trustworthiness of our God, to broaden our awareness of his love and power and wisdom, to know the profound truths of passages like Romans 8. Then, though in the fires our faith may be shrivelled to the size of a seed, we shall have what it takes to see us through.

b. Anguish and protest

Grief, pain, bewilderment, helplessness, frustration, misery, distress, torment, perplexity – overwhelmed by it all, Job cried out:

> '*I will not keep silent;*
> *I will speak out in the anguish of my spirit,*
> *I will complain in the bitterness of my soul*' (7:11).

He was in anguish and he gave voice to his anguish; he was perplexed and he cried out, 'Why?' (7:1–21). He could not understand what God was doing, so he poured out his questions (10:1–9). He struggled with God's hiddenness and silence (13:24; 30:20). He longed to find an answer, to argue his case, to get things sorted out (13:3; 23:1–7). Helpful though it may have been to sit for a week in silence with his three friends, there was no way Job could keep all that he was suffering to himself. It had to come out, and it came out in cries of pain, in frustration at the easy answers of those around him, and in protest at what God was doing to him. His first cry of pain bursts out in chapter 3, where he curses the day of his birth. Again and again throughout his speeches he gives voice to his torment of body, mind and spirit.[7] But, more than anything, he wrestles with God. He had no doubt that God was sovereign and

---

[4] Rom. 8:38, *pepeismai*, which comes from the same root (*peith* or *pith*) as *pistis*, 'faith'.

[5] Heb. 11:1.

[6] Luke 17:6.

[7] See, for example, 3:24–26; 19:14–20; 30:16–19.

thus was in at least some sense responsible for his suffering.[8] But he was equally convinced that God was good and that the facile answer of his culture that he must be punishing him for his sins was wrong. So he cries out in protest at God's hiddenness and apparent unfairness:

> *'I loathe my very life;*
> *therefore I will give free reign to my complaint*
> *and speak out in the bitterness of my soul.*
> *I will say to God: Do not condemn me,*
> *but tell me what charges you have against me.*
> *Does it please you to oppress me,*
> *to spurn the work of your hands,*
> *while you smile on the schemes of the wicked? . . .*

> *'Your hands shaped me and made me,*
> *Will you now turn and destroy me?*
> *Remember that you moulded me like clay.*
> *Will you now turn me to dust again?'* (10:1–3, 8–9).

Brave man, thus to give voice to his questioning of the ways of God. But God is big enough to cope with our questions and protests. They do not force him into a corner; God felt under no obligation to give a detailed defence of his actions to Job. But it was still right for him to be honest before God, to express his anguish and bewilderment, and to cry to God for mercy and help. For the key factor was that Job was protesting from within his trust in God, not as a result of abandoning it.[9] Like the psalmist who cried, 'Why have you forsaken me?' to the one whom he could still call 'My God',[10] Job protests because he knows that his God is there to listen to his protest and to give it a fair hearing. At the end of the story God is going to make two comments on what Job has said. The second is that he has *spoken of me what is right* (42:7). The first is, *'Who is this that darkens my counsel with words without knowledge?'* (38:2).[11] God is quite blunt: Job has done a good job hanging on to a 'right' concept of God against all the odds, but that does not mean that

---

[8] See, for example, 16:7–14; 17:6; 19:8–13.

[9] 'What makes this protesting Job a model for other sufferers is that he directs himself constantly toward God, whom he regards as the one who is responsible, both immediately and ultimately, for his suffering'; D. J. A. Clines, *Job 1 – 20* (Word, 1989), p. xxxviii.

[10] Ps. 22:1.

[11] Some commentators, concerned at the note of disapproval in this verse, suggest that God is referring not to Job but to Elihu. That seems very unlikely, however, given the context of verse 1 and verse 3 and the way Job picks the question up in 42:3.

everything that he has said is right; much of it simply shows up his ignorance. But God does not mind that; he knows we are ignorant; he knew Job had not read chapter 1. In no way does he blame him for his anguish and his protest.

Suffering provokes a range of responses. Sometimes we can sit with Job and say those beautiful words of calm trust, *The* LORD *gave and the* LORD *has taken away; may the name of the* LORD *be praised* (1:21). At other times we can only scream aloud in our pain. For some the valley of the shadow is short; the pain and bewilderment soon give way to peace and a deep awareness of God and his grace; for others the darkness lasts much longer, or lifts only to return again. At some times our faith will be strong, shining all the more clearly as the darkness gets deeper; at other times the darkness will overwhelm us and appear to stifle our faith altogether, so that we can barely even cry for help. In all our anguish God knows where we are at; our struggles and fears and doubts do not take him by surprise. To him we can take each one. Before him we can be honest. On to his shoulders we can throw all that burdens us.[12]

c. Despair and hope

What had happened to Job was final. His sons and his daughters were dead. They could never be brought back to life. His possessions were gone, irretrievably destroyed. His body was rotting away; what short life was left to him could only be fearsome suffering. There was no future, no hope. When Job expressed his despair he was describing things as they were; an early death was the only way out:

> 'Oh, that I might have my request,
>   that God would grant me what I hope for,
>   that God would be willing to crush me,
>   to let loose his hand and cut me off!' (6:8–9).[13]

For a man to hold on to any hope at all in that situation would be amazing, and at times Job's hope seems to have been totally overwhelmed (7:6; 14:19; 17:15). Yet, at other times, a ray of hope does shine for a moment in the darkness, when Job looks not at his suffering and the hopelessness of his situation but at God. For all his hiddenness, for all the incomprehensibility of his ways, he still

---

[12] Matt. 11:28–29; 1 Pet. 5:7.
[13] See also, for example, 7:13–16; 10:18–22; 14:7–12.

was God, still sovereign, still wise, still good, and still utterly trustworthy.

> *'Though he slay me, yet will I hope in him;*
>   *I will surely defend my ways to his face . . .*
> *Now that I have prepared my case,*
>   *I know I will be vindicated . . .*
>
> *'Even now my witness is in heaven;*
>   *my advocate is on high . . .*
>
> *'I know that my Redeemer lives,*
>   *and that in the end he will stand upon the earth.*
> *And after my skin has been destroyed,*
>   *yet in my flesh I will see God;*
> *I myself will see him*
>   *with my own eyes – I, and not another.*
> *How my heart yearns within me! . . .*
>
> *'But he knows the way that I take;*
>   *when he has tested me, I shall come forth as gold'*
>   (13:15, 18; 16:19; 19:25–27; 23:10)

Many of us, as we have gone through the darkness, struggling with the hopelessness of despair, have found comfort and hope in these words of a man who suffered much more than we are called to go through, and yet who had a God who was big enough to give hope even in the most impossible situation. For his God is our God. Indeed, we have an even clearer knowledge of this God than Job had, for he knew nothing of the cross where God himself carried the evil and suffering of the world, nor of the resurrection where his righteousness and justice and victory were so dramatically demonstrated. If Job could hang on to hope even when so overwhelmed with hopeless despair, then so can we. But we can do it only if by God's grace we are able to turn from the darkness of our suffering and catch a glimpse of the greatness and wisdom and goodness of our God.

d. Hunger for God

'Curse God and die,' urged his wife (2:9). But Job would not do that. Not because he did not want to die – he longed for death – but because he would not sever the relationship he had with God. Never does he reach the revolutionary insight of the New Testament that

suffering can be the means of drawing us close to the heart of God, that through it we can know Christ, though perhaps after God had spoken in the final chapters Job would have reflected that without the suffering there would have been no theophany. But all his struggle was fuelled by a hunger for the God he had known, who had 'watched over' him, whose *lamp* had *shone* on him, in whose *light* he had *walked through darkness*, and whose *intimate friend-ship* had *blessed* his *house* (29:2–4). Among all his sufferings the loss of fellowship with his God was the most grievous.

Here, again, is a reminder that suffering, like many of life's situations, always presents us with a choice. We can choose to let it destroy us, to break our relationship with God, to harden and embitter us. Or, by the power of God's Holy Spirit, we can choose the opposite, to let it bring us closer to him, to open up new areas of trust and awareness and understanding, to find his heart and to walk close to our Saviour. As with Job, coming to such a place may take time; for some it may be years; for a few it may not happen this side of heaven. But the wait will not be in vain.

e. Submission before God

The great final chapters of the book of Job make it abundantly clear that, whatever our doubts and questions and protests, God is God and he remains God. His ways may be beyond our understanding, but they are undeniably his ways, and because of that they are glorious and good and utterly trustworthy. Faced with God's revelation, Job rightly draws back from his vehement protests:

> The LORD said to Job:
> *'Will the one who contends with the Almighty correct him?*
>   *Let him who accuses God answer him!'*
> Then Job answered the LORD:
> *'I am unworthy – how can I reply to you?*
>   *I put my hand over my mouth.*
> *I spoke once, but I have no answer –*
>   *twice, but I will say no more …*
>
> *'My ears had heard of you*
>   *but now my eyes have seen you.*
> *Therefore I despise myself*
>   *and repent in dust and ashes'* (40:1–5; 42:5–6).

This is not a crushed and broken Job, but it is a man before his Creator, acknowledging his smallness, his total lack of understanding

217

compared with the greatness and wisdom of his God. Here is right and good humility; here is fitting submission; here is true worship, the acknowledging that God is God, that we are not God, that we have no right ever to claim to be. Here is a final lesson from Job to help us face our suffering. Despite all our need to give voice to our anguish and to offload our protest on to a God who in grace always listens, our right place before him is not as his accusers or his judges, but as his children: little children, whose understanding is so limited, but who so trust the love and goodness of their Father that all through the storm they can snuggle into his arms and know that, come what may, they are safe. To those who were going through 'painful trial' Peter summed up his counsel: 'Humble yourselves, therefore, under God's mighty hand, that he may lift you up in due time. Cast all your anxiety on him because he cares for you.'[14]

Job suffered horrifically, yet in the end God restored his fortunes, and 'blessed the latter part of Job's life more than the first'.[15] In the second part of this chapter we turn to Paul, a man whose sufferings were continuous, right to the day of his execution.

2. Paul: 2 Corinthians 4:7 – 5:10

a. Groaning: the downside (4:7–12, 16–17; 5:2, 4)

Suffering hurts, whether it is sudden disaster and bereavement and agonizing sores,[16] or prison, floggings, shipwreck, danger, hunger, poverty[17] and all the other things Paul had to face. Though, as far as we know, Paul did not give vent to his feelings in as violent a way as Job did, he did not ignore or belittle the reality of his suffering.[18] He suffered and it hurt, physically, mentally, emotionally and spiritually. So, he says, *we groan and are burdened* (5:2, 4; *stenazomen baroumenoi*, 'we groan, being burdened'). The details of the interpretation of 2 Corinthians 5:2–4 are debated by the commentators, but the general meaning is clear; living in this body is a weight, a pressure, a burden; it makes us groan. Some of the things Paul groaned at are listed in 4:7–12, 16–17: he was *hard pressed, perplexed, persecuted, struck down*, experiencing *the death of Jesus* in his body, *always being given over to death*, knowing what it is to

---

[14] 1 Pet. 4:12; 5:6–7.
[15] Job 42:12.
[16] Job 1:13–19; 2:7.
[17] 2 Cor. 11:23–28.
[18] His phrase *our light and momentary troubles* is not minimizing their severity, but bringing out the greatness of the contrast between them, severe though they are, and *the eternal glory that far outweighs them all* (4:17).

have *death at work* in him, and outwardly *wasting away*. How he groaned and to whom he groaned he does not say, but he does say enough to remind us that he was no insensitive triumphalist; like the rest of us he was a clay pot; his sufferings were real and he struggled with them. We have a gospel that gives us victory over suffering, that takes its sting and brings blessing out of it. But it cannot do this by taking it away; that would be like expecting the Olympic runner to be given the gold medal without running the race. The suffering our gospel conquers and makes into a blessing is real, and we have to bear it.

b. God: the upside (4:7–17)

But all we have picked out from 2 Corinthians 4:7 – 5:10 so far is hopelessly one-sided. Paul does not speak just about suffering and groaning. Every phrase in the passage that expresses pain and suffering is counterbalanced by a phrase or phrases that speak of the grace and glory of God. Of course life is full of suffering, says Paul; we are followers of the Man of Sorrows. But life is far more than suffering, for we know not just the sorrows of Christ, but his presence and his love and his glory. Yes, we are *jars of clay*; but in those jars is a *treasure*, nothing less than *the light of the knowledge of the glory of God in the face of Christ* (4:6),[19] that is, the presence of the Lord Jesus himself. Radiating from the clay pot was the *all-surpassing power* of God (7). Who worries about the pot when that is what it holds?

To each of the phrases in the next few verses (8–17) that speaks of suffering, Paul adds another phrase that speaks of grace and blessing. *Hard pressed* and *perplexed*, yes; but, by the grace of God and through the presence of Christ *not crushed* and *not in despair*. *Persecuted* and *struck down*, often; but never *abandoned* and never *destroyed*. The upside of the continual carrying around in his body the suffering and dying of Jesus was a constant stream of resurrection life, sustaining him personally, and flowing out through him to others (11–15). Outwardly he was *wasting away*, but inwardly he was *being renewed day by day*; *troubles* there were in plenty, but

[19] Some, for example Calvin (*The Second Epistle of Paul the Apostle to the Corinthians*, trans. T. A. Smail [Oliver and Boyd, 1964]), p. 58, and R. H. Strachan (*The Second Epistle of Paul to the Corinthians* [Hodder and Stoughton, 1935], p. 93), take 'treasure' to refer back to 'this ministry' (4:1); contrast Hughes: 'The treasure in question is "the light of the knowledge of the glory of God" (v. 6).'; P. E. Hughes, *Paul's Second Epistle to the Corinthians* (Marshall, Morgan and Scott, 1962), p. 135. Calvin's and Strachan's interpretation is very possible, but it would not exclude reference to verse 6; Paul viewed his ministry as the ministering of Christ; he carried with him and shared with others not just a message but a person.

they were not worth comparing with the *glory* that would come through them (17).

We have already quoted verse 17 a number of times, but it is worth pausing to highlight the force of Paul's language here. What any normal person would call the crushing weight of his present (and so temporary) suffering he calls 'light'; and it is precisely that light suffering that is working through for us (*katergazetai hēmin*; the verb carries a feel of achievement by hard work[20]) an eternal weight of glory. But that is not all; in the middle of the verse Paul adds *kath' hyperbolēn eis hyperbolēn*, 'surpassingly and more surpassingly'. The weight of glory is heavier than the weight of suffering; it is far heavier; it is surpassingly heavier; it is surpassingly heavier and more surpassingly heavier. The upside outweighs the downside as the great eternal God himself outweighs the momentary and little events in the life of one of his creatures. But it is out of the downside that the upside comes; in the clay pot is the treasure, from the pain comes the glory.

c. Confident trust: the link (5:5–6, 8)

We are always confident, declares Paul, and to emphasize the fact he says it again (5:6, 8). The repetition balances the earlier repetition of *We do not lose heart;*[21] it also links back with 'we are very bold'.[22] The verb he uses for 'we do not lose heart' (*ouk enkakoumen*) is from the root *kakos*, 'evil' and originally meant to 'behave badly' in a situation. Although in the New Testament it has generally acquired the meaning of becoming tired and careless, it seems likely that some of the original meaning was in Paul's mind here', since he follows it by listing three or four bad ways of reacting to his situation.[23] The same verb is used in Ephesians 3, where Paul writes that, thanks to God's eternal purposes in Christ, we can approach him 'with freedom and confidence'; so he asks his readers 'not to be discouraged (*mē enkakein*) because of my sufferings for you, which are your glory'.[24] Sufferings, he is saying, whether our own or someone else's, can cause a negative reaction; we can respond in a bad way to them and let them cause us to 'lose heart' or 'be discouraged'; that is something we must not let happen.

---

[20] 'It is not simply that the *glory* is the compensation for the *affliction* ... rather the *glory* is the product of the *affliction*, produced in measure *beyond all comparison*'; F. F. Bruce, *1 and 2 Corinthians* (Oliphants, 1971), p. 199.

[21] 2 Cor. 4:1; 4:16.

[22] 2 Cor. 3:13.

[23] 2 Cor. 4:2.

[24] Eph. 3:11–13.

Here again is the clear choice that suffering sets before us. It can cause us to behave badly; we can let it get us down. But, equally, we can respond positively and creatively, 'with freedom and confidence',[25] even choosing to be *always confident* (5:6). Again, the ground of our confidence is most certainly not our circumstances or our own ability to win through. *We are always confident* is preceded by *Therefore*, which points us back to verse 5: *It is God who has made us for this very purpose* (eternal life with him) *and has given us the Spirit as a deposit, guaranteeing what is to come.* The key to confidence is the Holy Spirit.

> The presence of the Holy Spirit, Paul here asserts, is the source not only of his unshakeable confidence as he looks out on the future, but also of his sustained courage as he faces the present ... This courage never fails the Christian, however great the dangers that confront him. It is *always* possible for him to show it, because the Holy Spirit is always present with him. Despair is therefore an experience to which he does not submit; for to despair is to disown the Spirit, and to disown the Spirit is not to be a Christian at all.[26]

Strong words, we may feel, but they are an accurate expression of Paul's teaching, provided we recognize that neither Tasker nor Paul is stating that to submit on occasion to despair is to cease to be a Christian. Those of us who, like Job, go through times when the darkness seems absolute and 'confidence' drains right away are not disowning the Spirit. Just as God looks upon us as clothed in the righteousness of Christ, even when we fall into sin, so he accepts the foundational trust that is at the heart of our relationship with him even when in our immediate experience it is overwhelmed by despair.

d. Working with the Spirit (4:18; 5:6–10)

The presence and power of the Holy Spirit are the source of our confidence and the key to avoiding a 'bad' response to the suffering we have to face. But, as ever, we shall not get very far if we sit idly back and expect him to carry us through our sufferings without our doing anything at all. That certainly was not Paul's way. In at least half a dozen ways, he tells us, he works with the Spirit to ensure that his response is good and pleasing to God (5:9).

[25] Eph. 3:12.
[26] R. V. G. Tasker, *The Second Epistle of Paul to the Corinthians* (Tyndale Press, 1958), pp. 81–82.

i. Focus (4:18)

We fix our eyes not on what is seen, but on what is unseen (4:18).
When we are in pain or when something has upset us, it is hard to
avoid the pain or the upset filling our whole horizon. They clamour
for our attention; they are the real, the immediate, the pressing. But
Paul had learnt that, however much they may clamour, they are not
the ultimately real; they are in fact *light and momentary* (17); the
truly real are God and his glory. So the priority is to fix our eyes on
him and his truth: his love, his grace, his promises to keep us, his
purposes for and through us, his goodness, his power, his kingdom,
his glory. Our age, perhaps more than any other, is obsessed with
'what is seen', the physical, the material, the immediate, possessions, results, the here and now. But in a world where God is the
one true reality, nothing will ever fit if we focus on anything but
him. Indeed, to fix our eyes on anything else is idolatry; to use
anything other than him as the touchstone for what matters or is
real is setting up a rival god. To understand anything, to live in
God's world, to survive whatever evil and suffering may throw at
us, we must make sure that we fix our focus on the only thing that
ultimately matters, that is ultimately real, the eternal God and all
that he is.

ii. Perspective (4:18; 5:10)

As we focus on God, his reality and his truth, we learn to see things
the way he sees them, to get his perspective. This applies in all
areas, the purpose of our lives, the things that really matter, values,
relationships. To have God's perspective on our sufferings is a
tremendous help towards facing them constructively. Much of Job's
spiritual and emotional pain was caused by his ignorance of what
God was up to. But we are in a much stronger position. Though we
may not be able to read the mind of God to discover the details,
we have been given enough to know that no suffering that he may
allow into our lives is purposeless, that he is working for good in all
things. Whatever the pressure to view suffering from our perspective, seeing it as an unwanted and meaningless intrusion, ours is the
privilege to see it from God's perspective, as something that he is
going to use for his glory and our blessing. J. B. Phillips paraphrases
James 1:2: 'When all kinds of trials and temptations crowd into your
lives, my brothers, don't resent them as intruders, but welcome
them as friends.'

One specific perspective Paul mentions in these verses is that of
judgment day (5:10). The view from that point will doubtless be
very different from the way we are conditioned to see things now;
but it is the judgment-day perspective that is the one that matters.

Another perspective that was especially meaningful to Paul was the one he highlighted in 4:17; if we can only realize the weight of the eternal glory that our sufferings are achieving for us we would appreciate how small the price is that we are having to pay for so much. In return for a few hours or days or years of pain we will be given an eternity of glory – heaven itself, God himself, Jesus himself. What a bargain! What an incentive to face the suffering positively, to bear it willingly, perhaps even to rejoice in it.

iii. Trust (4:13–14, 5:6–8)
Trust radiates from all this passage, but it especially surfaces in 4:13–14 and 5:6–8:

> *It is written: 'I believed; therefore I have spoken.' With that same spirit of faith we also believe and therefore speak, because we know that the one who raised the Lord Jesus from the dead will also raise us up with Jesus and present us with you in his presence ... Therefore we are always confident and know that as long as we are at home in the body we are away from the Lord. We live by faith, not by sight. We are confident, I say, and would prefer to be away from the body and at home with the Lord.*

The psalmist in Psalm 116 knew what it was to suffer. The 'cords of death entangled' him, he was 'overcome by trouble and sorrow'. Then he 'called on the name of the LORD', and he delivered his 'soul from death', his 'eyes from tears', his 'feet from stumbling'.[27] He had a God whom he could trust, and so Paul, whose experience was exactly parallel, echoed his words, *'I believed; therefore I have spoken'*,[28] affirming both his confidence in God and declaring God's trustworthiness and truth to all who would hear. Trusting God in the darkness not only brings us through, it loosens our tongues to pray, to praise and to witness. Indeed, trust or faith is the necessary foundation for the whole of our life: *We live by faith* (5:17), literally, 'for we are walking around through faith' (*dia pisteōs gar peripatoumen*); our actions and reactions in every situation are not based on *sight*, that is, *what is seen* (4:18); they are based on the God on whom *we fix our eyes* and in whom we trust. Without this foundation of trust in God we can only take our sufferings at their face value: a disaster is a disaster pure and simple; a hopeless situation is hopeless; meaningless suffering is

---

[27] Ps. 116:3–4, 8.
[28] Ps. 116:10; 2 Cor. 4:13.

meaningless. But with the foundation of trust, all is transformed, even the final disaster of death (5:8).

iv. Pleasing God (5:9)

Come life, come death, says Paul, *we make it our goal to please him* (5:9). Maybe 'make it our goal' (*philotimoumetha*) is a touch weak as a translation. From its literal meaning, to 'love honour', the verb came to speak of ambition and commitment to an goal, and so of working eagerly to achieve something. The thing that drives us is the desire to see his smile, to know that he is pleased, to hear his 'Well done.' Here is a setback, a disappointment, loss, a frustration, a pain; I can choose to respond in all sorts of ways: with anger, resentment, bitterness, self-pity and the like; or with grace and patience and trust and love and the beauty of Jesus. The criterion is simple: what will please him?

v. Openness to anything (5:9)

'If you want to give it, Lord,' Paul might have said, 'I'm willing to receive it' – persecutions, pains, weakness, even death itself. God took him at his word, and gave him all of them. None of us knows the path God is going to call us to tread. But we all know, at least in theory, that we can do nothing better than follow him as our guide. But, all too often, when we come to the fork in the road we insist on choosing our way, or we complain if God makes what we think is the wrong choice. We are back to Job; happy the man or the woman who can say, 'The LORD gave and the LORD has taken away; may the name of the LORD be praised.'[29]

vi. Getting on with it (4:7–16)

This passage is not a reflection on suffering and death by a philosopher or a theologian; it is an account of the everyday experience of a man who did things. He was a man with a God-given task (4:1) and he was committed to getting on and doing it. Nothing, short of God himself, was going to stop him (4:8–15). Nothing would divert him, or make him go slow or give up (16). Fulfilling the task God had given him, including walking the path of suffering that he set before him, was possible because in him was *all-surpassing power* (4:7), not his – he would have been the first to admit he was no superhero – but God's. Confident that his great and powerful God would not fail him, he got on with living the life to which God had called him. There is a sense in which facing suffering is no different from facing every other experience God sets

---

[29] Job 1:20.

before us. We can respond well or badly to success and prosperity, just as we can respond well or badly to setbacks and suffering. But the basic call is to get on and live the life to which he calls us, to walk with him wherever he leads. His is the choice, whether to give us joys or sorrows, prosperity or adversity. It is ours to get on and follow.

Titus 2:11–14; Matthew 5:13–16; John 20:21–22
20. Living with evil

We have no choice but to live in an evil world. But we can choose how we live there. We can choose to withdraw, to protect ourselves, to stress that we do not belong, to keep apart. Or we can choose to be involved, to expose ourselves, to get our hands dirty, to engage with evil and seek to defeat it. Those opting for the first approach could use as their model the people of God in the Old Testament, who were called to remain separate, to avoid defilement through mixing with the evils of the nations around, to be holy to their God. For the second approach the model could be Jesus himself, who chose not to remain separate but got involved, becoming incarnate, experiencing evil, mixing with sinners, accepting the worst that a rebellious world could do to him. Though there are many elements of God's instructions to his people under the old covenant from which we can learn, we as Christians are the people of the new covenant; our primary model is Jesus. So in order to find teaching on how to live in an evil world we now turn to the New Testament, to three passages, two in the Gospels, but first one in Paul.

1. Titus 2:11–14

It would be fair to say that 'How to live in an evil world' is the central theme of the letter to Titus, as it is in the practical later sections of most of the New Testament letters. Titus had responsibility for the groups of Christians scattered throughout Crete, and Paul gives some instructions to him on how to help these groups to function as local churches. But most of his instruction is on the kinds of lives the Christians should be living, whether they are church leaders or slaves or ordinary Christians. The instructions are practical and down to earth; Paul readily accepts the judgment that all Cretans, including, presumably, the new Christians before they were converted, are 'liars, evil brutes, lazy gluttons'.[1] Significantly, he has to include the evils of drunkenness, violence and dishonesty as inappropriate in one who is going to be a church elder, and he sums up the pre-conversion Cretan character (graciously using 'we' rather than 'you') as 'foolish, disobedient, deceived and enslaved by all kinds of passions and pleasures. We lived in malice and envy, being hated and hating one another.'[2] In that setting the Cretan Christians were called to live as the people of God.

Our passage, 2:11–14, follows straight on from the instructions that Titus is to give to the slaves who often made up a substantial proportion of the early Christian congregations; they were to be subject to their masters in everything, honest and trustworthy, 'so that in every way they will make the teaching about God our Saviour attractive'.[3] The reason they should do this, indeed, the basis for all Christian behaviour, is that *the grace of God that brings salvation has appeared to all men* (11). Into an evil world has come a radical new power, the saving grace of God. We do not have to continue to behave as once we did. Society no longer has to be characterized by violence and dishonesty and hatred. The world does not have to continue to be dominated by evil. The light of the grace and salvation of God is shining in the darkness.[4] There is debate whether the phrase 'to all men' is to be attached to the verb 'has appeared' or to 'that brings salvation'.[5] Almost all versions (apart from the AV and NIV) follow the natural sense of the Greek and link 'all men' with 'salvation'. This does not have to imply universalism; *sōtērios* is a straight adjective from *sōtēr*, 'saviour', and can be understood as meaning 'offering salvation' rather than 'providing salvation'.[6]

This saving grace offered to all has a radical threefold effect on our relationship with *this present age*, the rebellious world order that is all around us (12). Its first effect is strongly negative:

---

[1] Titus 1:12. The quotation is generally taken as a line from Epimenides, a sixth-century Cretan philosopher.

[2] Titus 3:3.

[3] Titus 2:9–10.

[4] *Epephanē* is correctly translated 'has appeared', but in Luke 1:78–79 it is used of the rising sun shining: 'because of the tender mercy of our God, by which the rising sun will come to us from heaven to shine [*epiphanai*] on those living in darkness'. We are used to linking the word 'epiphany' with the coming of Christ, and Paul himself is about to do this in verse 13, so we can safely assume that 'the grace of God that brings salvation' is in effect an alternative way of referring to the Saviour, Jesus.

[5] The Greek places 'to all men' immediately after 'that brings salvation' (*sōtērios pasin anthrōpois*).

[6] Alternatively, 'all men' can be interpreted as 'all sorts of men', that is, including slaves and their masters.

It teaches us to say 'No' to ungodliness and worldly passions. Its second effect is very positive: *and to live self-controlled, upright and godly lives in this present age.* Its third effect is a wholly different perspective.

a. Repudiation (2:12)

The root evil from which all other evils spring is the rejection of God, the refusal to let him be God. The word the New Testament uses for this is *asebeia*, 'godlessness' or 'ungodliness', and it is the primary thing that God's people repudiate, or say 'No' to (12). The repudiation must be total; every form of ungodliness is to be rejected and combated, whether it is the initial refusal to accept God, or the sins and evils that result.

One of the most powerful expressions of *asebeia* in our culture today is the determined attempt to find a 'theory of everything' that excludes God, that indoctrinates our children with a totally secular worldview, an understanding of the world and science and life that is wholly naturalistic and has no place for God at all. Sadly, Christians have at times been willing to compromise with this kind of worldview, accepting, for example, that the godless, 'scientific' way of seeing things is the correct one and so banishing God from any action in the material world, with the result that God's role becomes limited to a personal subjective religious sphere. The Bible will allow no such compromise. Since God is God, everything else can be understood only with reference to him; the scientists may provide accurate descriptions and analyses of the mechanics of the universe, but any attempt on their part to declare the eradication of God from involvement in the world must be vigorously repudiated.[7] The call to the people of God today is to reject and combat godlessness wherever it is found; in the words of Isaiah 43:12 God still speaks to us: ' "You are my witnesses," declares the LORD, "that I am God." '

After *asebeia*, the rejection of God, the second thing we are to repudiate is *worldly passions* (*tas kosmikas epithymias*), 'all desires entirely centred in the present world system';[8] the *kosmos* in this context is the world that has rejected God and so rejects all that

---

[7] Very many scientists and scientific thinkers who work within this God-denying scientific approach are themselves committed to belief in God, but the overall approach remains anti-God. Significantly, Antony Flew, one of the leading atheistic philosophers of the second half of the twentieth century, has recently announced that he now believes in God (though not specifically the Christian God) as a result of examining the scientific evidence.

[8] D. Guthrie, *The Pastoral Epistles* (Tyndale Press, 1957), p. 198.

God's people represent.[9] We in turn are to discipline our thoughts and desires and say 'No' to anything that is based on the world's values and way of living.

b. Counter-culture (2:12, 14)

Repudiating godlessness and worldly passions may sound wholly negative and give the impression that we are to withdraw and be separate from the world. But the negative is there to provide a base for the positive. We are to reject the godlessness of the world around us so that we can demonstrate a radical alternative, one summed up in the three words which the NIV translates *self-controlled, upright and godly* (*sōphronōs, dikaiōs, eusebōs*) (12). The first of the three was traditionally translated 'soberly';[10] more recent translators tend to use 'self-control' and the like, but both these translations greatly limit a word that was rich with meaning in the ancient world. Perhaps the best clue in the New Testament to its meaning comes from its use in the story of the healing of the demon-possessed man known as Legion. When the demons had left him he was found sitting at the feet of Jesus *sōphronounta*, 'in his right mind'.[11] The root of the word is *sōs* (linking back with *sōtērios* in Titus 2:11), 'safe', 'sound', 'saved', and *phrēn*, 'mind'; it speaks of a mind or a disposition that gets things right, that has the right focus, the right perspective, supremely, the focus and perspective that come from 'saving grace', that have been redeemed and transformed by God.[12] Here is the root of our counter-culture: minds that see things God's way.

The second of the three words, *dikaiōs*, brings with it pro-found depths of meaning from the Old Testament and the New Testament. The noun behind it is *dikaiosynē*, normally translated 'righteousness', and the verb is *dikaioō*, the Bible's term for 'justify'. So Paul's use of *dikaiōs* here embraces all that the Bible teaches on the themes of righteousness and justification. In an evil world, our lives are to radiate righteousness and all that it means: a right relationship with God made possible because we are 'justified' by the work of Christ; right relationships with others – barriers

---

[9] John 15:18–19.

[10] So AV, RV, RSV. Calvin preferred 'temperate' to 'sober' and actually comments on Titus 2:2 (where NIV uses 'temperate') that Paul desires old men to be temperate 'because excessive drinking is a fault all too common in old age'; J. Calvin, *The Second Epistle of Paul the Apostle to the Corinthians and the Epistles to Timothy, Titus and Philemon*, trans. T. A. Smail (Oliver and Boyd, 1964), pp. 224, 369.

[11] Luke 8:35.

[12] Rom. 12:2; 1 Cor. 2:16.

removed, peace restored, the character of Christ expressed in our attitudes and actions; righteousness and salvation 'springing up' on the earth;[13] the offer of God's gift of righteousness through Christ to all – bringing cleansing and forgiveness and salvation. In an evil world we are called to be people who radiate the righteousness of God, showing it in our lives and spreading it on the earth.

The third word, *eusebōs*, is the direct opposite of *asebeia*. In a world characterized by the rejection of God, we are to be 'godly', filled with the living God, demonstrating his reality, living his life, expressing his truth and love and goodness. The answer to godlessness is God, and God's way of revealing himself to a godless world is through his people. With *sōphronōs* and *dikaiōs*, *eusebōs* calls us to confront the evil in the world with a true counter-culture, with lives that are radically different because our whole way of seeing things is radically different and because we are truly the people of God. That, after all, is why Christ came; he *gave himself for us to redeem us from all wickedness and to purify for himself a people that are his very own, eager to do what is good* (14). Some of the force of *zēlōtēn kalōn ergōn* ('eager to do what is good') is lost in translation. 'Zealots' were not just eager; they were dedicated to live and die for their cause. Calvin speaks of being 'consecrated to good works';[14] Phillips translates, 'our hearts set upon living a life that is good'.

c. Perspective (2:13)

Many contemporary sermons on living in an evil world would stop at this point, but Paul, typically, brings in an additional dimension: *while we wait for the blessed hope – the glorious appearing of our great God and Saviour, Jesus Christ* (13). In the New Testament the call to be the people of God in an evil world could never be divorced from God's ultimate purpose both for his people and for the world. Our living and our witnessing and our good works are firmly set in a context, the awareness that these are the end times, evil is having its final fling, Christ is soon to return, judgment day is near. 'This present age' (12) must always be seen in relation to the age to come; that is the perspective that will not only transform our attitude to suffering but also motivate and empower our repudiation of godlessness and our commitment to a right mind, righteousness and the Lord himself.

[13] Isa. 45:8.
[14] Calvin, *Corinthians, Timothy, Titus and Philemon*, p. 375.

2. Matthew 5:13–16

'So there's this guy, with a long beard and a long robe, sitting on a hillside with a dozen other guys, all about as scruffy as he is, and he's telling them that they're the answer to everything that's wrong with the world. They've got what it takes to stop the rot, to make the place what it ought to be; they're the salt of the earth, the light of the world. I'm telling you, it's hard to think of anything more crazy.'

But it happened. Not just on the hillside, but spreading out from there, to Jerusalem, Judea, Samaria, and to the ends of the earth. Today it is the same. To small groups of believers scattered all over the world, groups made up of ordinary people, often weak people, 'lowly' and 'despised' as Paul would call them,[15] God says, *You are the salt of the earth ... You are the light of the world* (Matt. 5:13–14). He may say it as well to powerful ecclesiastical structures, to well-organized and well-managed pressure groups, to those who are in high places and can influence the people that matter. But I have a feeling that ecclesiastical structures and influence in high places are not our God's primary answer to an evil world. Much more crucial to his purposes are ordinary Christian women and men, however 'foolish' and 'weak' and 'lowly' and 'despised'; it is them he has chosen; it is through them he plans to 'shame the 'wise' and the 'strong', and to 'nullify the things that are'.[16]

Salt had several uses in the ancient world, and it seems unlikely that we need to choose just one of them in order to interpret Jesus' words. It was used as a preservative in food and medicinally as an antiseptic. It was used for flavouring, and when scattered thinly it acted as a fertilizer. It was required in the Old Testament covenant rituals[17] and, to a Jew, would have spoken of purging and costly sacrifice;[18] it also symbolized friendship and wisdom. Light is rather more straightforward: it destroys darkness, and it illuminates. Using these images, we can draw out from this passage several insights into the way God expects ordinary Christians to react to the evil that is in the world.

a. The people of God have a crucial role to play in an evil world (5:13–14)

If the words had been spoken by anyone other than the Son of God, they would have been ridiculous. How could a handful of nobodies

[15] 1 Cor. 1:26–29.
[16] 1 Cor. 1:27–28.
[17] Lev. 2:13.
[18] Mark 9:49.

illuminate the whole world, or prevent the earth going rotten? What had they to offer where Zarathustra and Plato and Epicurus and many other great minds had failed? The answer was, of course, the coming of the kingdom, the power and presence of God himself. He is the true light;[19] he is the one who rescues from putrefaction. But he radiates his light and his salvation through his people; if we do not shine, the world remains in darkness; if we do not bring salvation, the earth is lost.[20] Both sayings start with an emphatic 'You are' (*Hymeis este*). If we are the people of God we are the one thing that can save the earth, the one thing that can deal with the darkness of the world. God has chosen to make us a key part of his answer to a fallen world. So we have no option; if we are faithful to our Lord we cannot be ineffective salt, we cannot withdraw and keep our light under a bowl (13, 15).

b. Our impact on the world is radical (5:13–16)

We stop it going rotten. We flood it with light. Again, humanly speaking, this seems impossibly optimistic. By the time of his death the impact that the ministry of Jesus himself had made upon the world as a whole was minuscule. As the first century wore on, the impact of his people increased, but even by AD 100, according to global standards, it was still tiny. Today there are many more Christians as a proportion of the world population,[21] but we still feel impotent in the face of the evils all around us. Perhaps we are right to do so, but we should not allow that to absolve us of our responsibility to fulfil our Lord's expectation and calling, that through us his impact on the world should indeed be radical. Again, we need to remember that his criteria for radical impact may not be the same as ours. We may feel that lobbying governments to remove trade tariffs that put poor countries at a disadvantage is the most effective way to have an impact. But it could be that in God's eyes, however worthwhile lobbying may be, much more is accomplished by the faithful, believing prayers of ordinary Christians. For him, perhaps, the breakthrough of the gospel in a South American country with tens of thousands of very ordinary people finding salvation in Christ is more significant than the toppling of a dictator. Paul would remind us that our battle is not against flesh and blood

[19] John 1:9; 8:12.
[20] These sayings are a warning to Jesus' hearers 'that their essential character and privilege as members of the kingdom of heaven is not for their own enjoyment but for the benefit of others, and for the glory of God the Father in heaven'; F. W. Beare, *The Gospel according to Matthew* (Blackwell, 1981), p. 136.
[21] About one-third of the population of the world claim to be Christians.

but against 'spiritual forces of evil in the heavenly realms'.[22] Victories over them and successful assaults on the 'gates of Hades'[23] do not always show up in the television news. Perhaps one day we shall discover that the underlying cause of the dramatic events of 1989 in Eastern Europe was not economics or politics but the faithfulness of the martyr people of God under communist regimes.

c. Our impact is hugely beneficial (5:13–16)

Almost all the images associated with salt are means of making life richer, of getting rid of corruption, improving flavour, making it more productive, adding wisdom and sparkle. Light, too, enriches in many ways, dissipating darkness, illuminating everything around, enabling growth, making life itself possible. God sees a world that is being destroyed by evil and darkness; in love and mercy he reaches out to bless it through his people. We are the expression of that love; through us, as we are truly his people, the world is hugely enriched.

d. Impacting the world is confrontational and costly (5:13)

Despite all the good that the salt and light of God's people undoubtedly do in the world, we should not be at all surprised to meet opposition. It is there in Matthew's context, with the preceding verses warning of persecution,[24] and in Mark's context, with the words, 'Everyone will be salted with fire.'[25] Salt may be antiseptic, but few people will thank you for rubbing it into their wounds;[26] darkness is hardly going to be enthusiastic about being banished by light. 'Light has come into the world,' says Jesus, 'but men loved darkness instead of light because their deeds were evil. Everyone who does evil hates the light, and will not come into the light for fear that his deeds will be exposed.'[27]

[22] Eph. 6:12.
[23] Matt. 16:18.
[24] Matt. 5:10–12.
[25] Mark 9:49. France comments that the reference to salt and fire here would make a Jew think immediately of the Temple sacrifices; it 'speaks of one who follows Jesus as totally dedicated to God's service, and warns that such dedication will inevitably be costly in terms of personal suffering'; R. T. France, *The Gospel of Mark* (Eerdmans, 2002), p. 394.
[26] 'It is a disadvantage to be salt ... If you get salt into a wound, it hurts, and when God's children are among those who are "raw" towards God, their presence hurts ... the "salt" causes excessive irritation which spells persecution for the saint'; Oswald Chambers, *Studies in the Sermon on the Mount* (Simpkin Marshall, n.d.), p. 19.
[27] John 3:19–20.

They tell us that sodium chloride, being a stable chemical compound, can never *lose its saltiness* (13). But the two types of salt that Jesus was referring to in this passage certainly can. The salt in common use in Palestine contained impurities which in time could cause it to become useless.[28] The people of God, for all their potential, can become insipid and make no impact on the world. We may feel that this is our present condition; if it is, we need to take seriously these words of Jesus. His expectation was that his people would decisively impact the world for good; if it was his expectation, we can safely assume that his resources are sufficient for the task. If we are failing, the responsibility for failure rests with us; we have ceased to be the people of God he has called us to be and we are *no longer good for anything but to be thrown out and trampled by men.*

3. John 20:21–22

These two verses speak so clearly they need very little unpacking. In an extended note,[29] Westcott pointed out the significance of the tense of *As the Father has sent me*, and of the use of two different words for 'send'. The tense is perfect (*apestalken*), not aorist;[30] the perfect tense 'describes a mission which continues in its present effects'.[31] On the change from *apostellō* for the Father's sending to *pempō* for Christ's sending, Westcott comments that *apostellō* has overtones of 'despatch', 'envoy', 'special commission' and 'delegated authority', while *pempō* 'marks nothing more than the immediate relation of the sender to the sent'. He concludes his discussion: 'The general result of the examination of these facts seems to be that in this charge the Lord presents His own Mission as the one abiding Mission of the Father; this he fulfils through His church. His disciples receive no new commission, but carry out His ... they are not (in this respect) His envoys, but in a secondary degree envoys of the Father.'

As the Father has sent me, I am sending you (21). The model for our mission to a world of evil and suffering is Jesus. The task he began, and which he made gloriously possible through his unique atoning death and resurrection, is ours to continue. We now are to be the means by which God brings in his kingdom; the ministry of Luke 4:18–19 is now ours; we are to be the light of the world as he is

[28] For examples of this see N. Hillyer, 'Salt', in C. Brown (ed.), *New International Dictionary of New Testament Theology* (Paternoster, 1975–8), 3, p. 446.
[29] B. F. Westcott, *The Gospel according to St John* (James Clarke, 1958), p. 298.
[30] *Apesteilen*, as at, for example, John 3:17.
[31] Cf. 1 John 4:14.

the light of the world.[32] The task that was his is now ours; or, more accurately, the task that is his is now ours because we are his, his body, his people. He continues his ministry in us. He is more than the model for our ministry; it is he who is ministering through us as we minister. This is the significance of verse 22: *And with that he breathed on them and said, 'Receive the Holy Spirit.'* The full anointing of the Spirit was to come at Pentecost, but already here Jesus is symbolically breathing his life-breath, his very being, into his disciples; he is now in them, as they are in him.[33] That alone equips them for ministry; without him they could do nothing.[34] But with him the most amazing things are not only possible, but to be expected.[35]

We can explore the implications of these two verses in several ways.

a. We are sent (20:21)

We can readily appreciate the awareness that Jesus had of being *sent;*[36] from the act of incarnation to commitment to the cross he was aware that his life had a purpose and a goal; his Father had sent him to do a task; everything he did was the fulfilling of a commission. Such a sense of being 'sent' seems largely limited in our day to 'missionaries' and those aware of God calling them to a specific vocation. But these verses state that each of us should have an awareness of being sent. The writer to the Hebrews applies Psalm 40:6–8 to Jesus as he came into the world, with its climax: 'Here I am – it is written about me in the scroll – I have come to do your will, O God.'[37] The words are not just appropriate for the Psalmist and for the Christ; they should have a central place in the hearts and on the lips of each one of God's people. Whether we are feeding the starving in Niger or managing the accounts in an office, we are (unless we are disobeying God's leading) in a place to which we have been sent, and we are sent there to do God's will. There is a pressing need for the recovery by every Christian of this sense of being sent, hand-picked by God and placed as his emissary in a specific situation to fulfil his purposes by doing his will.

[32] John 8:12.
[33] John 15:4.
[34] John 15:5.
[35] John 14:12.
[36] 'The thought that the Father has sent the Son is one of the master thoughts of his Gospel. It is repeated over and over again'; L. Morris, *The Gospel according to John* (Marshall, Morgan and Scott, 1971), p. 845.
[37] Heb. 10:7.

b. Empowered for ministry (20:22)

If we are hand-picked and sent, we are also equipped for the task to which he sends us. The Father did not send the Son without the anointing of the Spirit;[38] perhaps the awareness of that anointing was in his mind as he passed his mission and his Spirit on to his disciples (John 20:22). It is vital to remember that the anointing or empowering by the Holy Spirit is to enable us to do the task he has set before us. Too often we see the task and refuse to attempt it because we do not feel we have the power. But the empowering is not something he gives us which we then keep in reserve until we have an opportunity to use it. It is the supernatural anointing of the Holy Spirit on our lives or actions or words as we go forward in faith and obedience. God's call is to trust him and go ahead, to attempt the task, and as we do so he will demonstrate 'the Spirit's power'.[39]

c. The centrality of obedience (20:21)

The relationship of the Son to the Father who sent him was one of obedience;[40] the driving force behind our mission in an evil world must be obedience to the leading of God. If we accept that no situation and no event are beyond his redeeming power for good, and that we are called to be those through whom that good comes, then it is essential for us to respond to that situation or event according to his wisdom and purpose. This will involve both drawing underlying principles from the Bible, and hearing from the Spirit specific guidance on how we should apply those principles in a given situation. A Christian employee, for example, told by his boss to follow deceitful business practices, will accept the clear teaching of the Bible that he cannot do this; but he will need the Holy Spirit's guidance on what specific steps he should take, whether he should resign the job, or talk the issues through with his boss, or appeal to the human-resources department or a trade union, or whatever. If he accepts that God has put him into that firm in order to be salt and light, then he can also be confident that God will show him the most effective means that he must follow to fulfil that calling.

d. Bias to the 'sick' (20:21)

God sends each of us to a hand-picked situation where he calls us to be salt and light. For some this may well mean being called to serve

---

[38] Luke 4:18.
[39] 1 Cor. 2:4.
[40] John 4:34.

where life is comfortable, prosperous and easy. But if Jesus is the model, then it would seem likely that God will want most of his people serving him in places and situations that are not comfortable and prosperous and easy. Jesus seems to have focused especially on the hurting, the needy and 'sinners'. 'It is not the healthy who need a doctor, but the sick.'[41] Since comfort and prosperity can very readily cause us to lose sight of God's call to radical discipleship, we need to be constantly checking that we have got our calling right. 'Thank you, Lord, for a good wage, a nice house in suburbia, a wonderful local church to go to, and lots of green pastures and still waters; but if you ask me to sell all that I have and give it to the poor,[42] and leave my pleasant job and comfortable church fellowship to go and start a church in a remote part of Albania, I'll go.'

e. Tackling the evils (20:21)

Jesus did not set up leprosaria, but, confronted with a leper, he healed him. Paul did not work for the abolition of slavery, but he gave instructions on how slaves and their masters should treat each other. From the fourth century onwards Christians did a marvellous job at starting hospitals, schools, and a whole range of social-welfare organizations; more recently it was evangelical Christians who were at the forefront of movements to abolish slavery, improve working conditions in factories, care for children, and so on. Again, God calls each of us to specific tasks, and some, undoubtedly, are called to be contemporary Wilberforces and Barnardos. But even if that is not our calling, we are all most certainly called to tackle the individual evils that we meet in our daily lives. Among our neighbours there will be someone who is lonely, a teenager who is being drawn into the drug culture, someone struggling with unemployment or debt. Whether or not we campaign for better social services, tougher laws on drugs, and so on, we are undoubtedly called to tackle these individual evils.

f. Changing the people (20:21)

C. S. Lewis wrote a 'Meditation on the Third Commandment'. It faces the question of how Christians, as a minority in the country, should tackle the issues and evils of society. In it Lewis rejected calls to set up a Christian political party, and lent his weight instead to calls for Christians to use their democratic rights to influence the

[41] Matt. 9:12.
[42] Mark 10:21.

decision-makers by 'pestering M.P.s with letters'. Then, at the end of the essay, he adds: 'There is a third way – by becoming a majority. He who converts his neighbour has performed the most practical Christian-political act of all.'[43]

To campaign for better government provision for those who live alone is good; to befriend a lonely neighbour is even better; to introduce that neighbour to a living relationship with Jesus is best of all. In the words of Jesus' commission at the end of Matthew's Gospel, our primary task in an evil world is to 'make disciples of all nations'.

[43] C. S. Lewis, 'Meditation on the Third Commandment' (reprinted from *The Guardian*, 10 January 1941) in *Undeceptions* (Geoffrey Bles, 1971), p. 160.

Interlude
How on earth? Living with evil and suffering

The coming of the kingdom of God into a person's life transforms everything. The very act of entering the kingdom requires a revolution, a total turn-around; instead of rejecting God, living in rebellion against him, running from him or ignoring him, we receive him, accept him as Lord, crown him as King of our lives, and make him the centre of all that we are and do. Once we are in the kingdom, we find that its truths and values, the principles on which it operates, are radically different from anything in the world. And life in the kingdom, living in Christ and knowing the anointing and empowering of the Holy Spirit, is a wholly new experience.[1]

So the Bible says. So, too, we believe, even though, in these days of compromise and weak discipleship, many of us find our experience falling short of the biblical teaching. But the teaching is there, and we know it is right. If the Creator God, Lord and King over all, is our heavenly Father, then we have no need to be anxious about anything.[2] 'If God is for us, who can be against us?'[3] If 'our light and momentary troubles are achieving for us an eternal glory that far outweighs them all',[4] then we have the strongest of motivations to keep going, come what may. If we really are 'the light of the world' and 'the salt of the earth', then few things really matter compared with making sure that we radiate light into the darkness and do all the things our Lord expects his salt to do.

The Bible is not concerned to give instructions on how a compromising, weak disciple can cope with evil and suffering. Its

[1] 2 Cor. 5:17.
[2] Matt. 6:25–33.
[3] Rom. 8:31.
[4] 2 Cor. 4:17.

teaching is not directed at those who have only a vague belief in God and a tenuous relationship with him. Its foundational conviction is that, faced with an evil and hurting world, God has acted, 'the grace of God that brings salvation' has appeared.[5] In Christ he has come. As a result, we do not have to face evil and suffering on our own, as though there were no God, or as though God were absent. The broken and hurting world in which we live is now different because God has come. We can face its evil and suffering in a totally new way, God's way.

So the Bible's call is to a deep relationship and a full commitment, both to the truths of God's revelation and to God himself, and its teaching on living with evil and suffering is directed at those who have responded to that call. When it tells us not to be anxious, it presupposes that we have accepted God as our heavenly Father; when it speaks of the Spirit helping us in our weakness, it presupposes that we have opened our lives to the grace and power of the Holy Spirit. The key to joy and peace in the middle of adversity is the presence of Christ as Lord of our lives. To have him as Lord means that we have turned from looking at things our way to seeing things his way, from running our lives ourselves to following him. Living under his lordship means having his mind,[6] being close to his heart, responding to evil and suffering as he did. It means that we are taken up in his mission, bringing in his kingdom, expressing his compassion, being the means by which his goodness and love flow out into the world. It means sharing in his sufferings and accepting those sufferings as he accepted his. All this is revolutionary and may well be costly; without his grace and power it would be impossible. But it is to this that we are called.

Here is the secret of being 'more than conquerors' in all the pain and disasters of daily living.[7] We do not conquer by being spared the struggles and the suffering, any more than the athlete wins the gold medal by being excused the race. But we conquer because the evil and suffering which we go through do not break us or destroy us; by the grace of God we come out on top. And not just as conquerors; we are 'more than' conquerors, for the struggle and the suffering are transformed by the grace and power of our God into a thousand means of blessing. In his infinite wisdom and love God uses them for good, both in our lives and in his broader purposes for his kingdom in the world.

Here, too, is the key to making a real impact for good in our contemporary world. If we face it on our own, the task of sorting

---

[5] Titus 2:11.
[6] 1 Cor. 2:16.
[7] Rom. 8:35–39.

out the evils of our world will be far too great and we shall soon despair. But we face it with Christ. We face it not alone, but as his body, the people of God, weak indeed in ourselves, but 'strong in the Lord and in his mighty power'.[8] We face it not with 'the weapons of the world' but with weapons that have 'divine power to demolish strongholds'.[9]

One of the key 'weapons' God has given us is prayer. In our 'struggle ... against the rulers, against the authorities, against the powers of this dark world and against the spiritual forces of evil in the heavenly realms', we are to 'pray in the Spirit on all occasions with all kinds of prayers and requests'.[10] On our own we can make little headway against the evil and suffering of our world. Through prayer we can see mountains moved.[11] It is to prayer we turn in the final part of our study, to the prayer given to us by Jesus himself.

[8] Eph. 6:10.
[9] 2 Cor 10:4. Hughes comments, 'Only spiritual weapons are divinely powerful for the overthrow of the fortresses of evil. This constitutes an admonition to the Church and particularly to her leaders, for the temptation is ever present to meet the challenge of the world, which is under the sway of the evil one, with the carnal weapons of this world – with human wisdom and philosophy, with the attractions of secular entertainment, with the display of massive organization. Not only do such weapons fail to make an impression on the strongholds of Satan, but a secularized Church is a Church, which, having adopted the standards of the world, has ceased to fight and is herself overshadowed by the powers of darkness'; P. E. Hughes, *Paul's Second Epistle to the Corinthians* (Marshall, Morgan and Scott, 1962), p. 350.
[10] Eph. 6:12, 18.
[11] Mark 11:22–25.

Part 6
From the evil one to our Father

Matthew 6:9–13
21. The Lord's Prayer

The Lord's Prayer starts[1] with our Father and ends with the devil. Perhaps it is not surprising that the early church soon added the familiar doxology to make a more fitting closing for the prayer's use in public worship: *for yours is the kingdom and the power and the glory for ever. Amen.*[2] Since it would seem better to end our study with our Father than with the devil, we shall work through the phrases of the Lord's Prayer from the last to the first, using its familiar yet profound words to draw together many of the Bible's insights into evil and suffering that we have been studying.

1. Deliverance (6:13)

'Deliver us from the evil one' (13). *Tou ponērou*, from which we ask to be delivered or rescued, could be masculine or neuter, 'the evil one' or 'evil'. Most commentators opt for masculine; *ho ponēros* is used elsewhere in Matthew for the devil,[3] and the preposition used for 'from' (*apo*, not *ek*) favours the masculine. So Jesus is not so much teaching us to pray to be delivered from evil as to be rescued from the devil. The difference is significant. If God had said 'Yes' to Jesus' prayer in Gethsemane, 'Take this cup from me',[4] Jesus would have been delivered from the evil of the agony of the cross, but he would have played right into the hands of the evil one.[5] Job suffered

---

[1] In introducing the Lord's Prayer, Jesus emphasizes the radical difference between it and prayers of the 'hypocrites' and the 'babbling' of the 'pagans' (Matt. 10:5–9). The stress in *'This, then, is how you should pray'* is firmly on 'you' (*houtōs oun proseuchesthe hymeis*).

[2] Verse 13, margin. Though very early, the doxology does not seem to have been part of the prayer as Jesus taught it; manuscript support for it is patchy and varied. Three of the most significant manuscripts omit it; it is not in Luke's version.

[3] Matt. 5:17; 13:19, 38. It comes five times in 1 John, for example 3:12.

[4] Luke 22:42.

[5] Matt. 16:2–23.

a catalogue of evils, but God retained final authority over Satan; he allowed disaster and suffering, but kept him ultimately secure from the evil one.[6] The real disaster is not to suffer evil, but to be overwhelmed by the evil one, for Satan to break us and destroy us.

Our tendency when saying the Lord's Prayer is to apply its phrases personally: 'Don't lead me into temptation, but deliver me from the evil one.' That is legitimate as far as it goes, but Jesus' vision is much wider. Clearly, *'Give us today our daily bread'* does not entail 'Keep me well fed and let the hungry half of the world go without'. In the same way, *'Deliver us from the evil one'* means much more than 'Rescue me from Satan.' It must apply also to others and to the world; it is nothing less than a prayer for the shattering of the kingdom of darkness, for the breaking of the devil's hold, whether on our personal lives, or on the lives of all his captives, or on the structures of our world. It is the essential precursor to *'Your kingdom come'* (10): 'Father, throw the devil out and bring in the King.'

It is true, of course, that Satan's power is already broken through the work of Christ on the cross. But the task of carrying off 'the strong man's' possessions[7] is still far from complete. God's desire is that as much as is possible should be rescued from the shattered ruins of the kingdom of darkness. For this, says Jesus, we must pray, and, since prayer without action is dead, to this end we must work.

Here, then, in this phrase of the Lord's Prayer, is a five-fold vision.

a. The renouncing of the devil and all his works

In no way can we honestly pray 'Deliver us from the evil one' and at the same time deliberately choose to submit to him, either by allowing him to be the lord of some part of our life or by supporting some aspect of his cause in the world. Granted, all of us at times fall prey to his wiles, but our foundational commitment must be to God, and that necessarily entails repudiation of 'ungodliness and worldly passions'[8] and renunciation of the devil and all his works.

b. A commitment to rescue people from the kingdom of darkness

Again, to pray that the Lord should deliver us from the evil one, but to do nothing to rescue our neighbour or the unsaved millions of the world from his dominion, is clearly hypocritical. God's concern is

[6] Job 1:12; 2:6.
[7] Matt. 12:29.
[8] Titus 2:12.

the whole world; his offer of salvation is for all. The early church was fired with a vision to proclaim the good news; those who were scattered as a result of the persecution that arose after the killing of Stephen 'preached the word wherever they went';[9] their commission was to 'make disciples of all nations',[10] to rescue women and men 'from the dominion of darkness' and bring them 'into the kingdom' of the one 'in whom we have redemption, the forgiveness of sins'.[11] For all the effectiveness of church programmes and evangelistic methods, it is still indisputable that the most effective way of rescuing people from the dominion of darkness is by personal friendship and witness that introduce them to Jesus as he lives in us. There is hardly a person in our land who does not somehow have contact with at least one child of God; our Lord gives each of us our hand-picked mission field, and calls us to get to 'work' to bring in the 'plentiful' harvest.[12]

c. A commitment to 'destroy the devil's work'[13]

Despoiling the devil's possessions means undoing his work as well as releasing his captives. He is the 'father of lies';[14] ours is the task to challenge the false concepts and values with which he has indoctrinated our world, and to proclaim in their place the truth of God. He perverts and corrupts the good and beautiful things that God has given us, turning possessions into idols, twisting love and sexuality to lust and perversion, and corrupting our capacity for joy into an endless quest for self-indulgence. God has called us to demonstrate the true use of his gifts, a different way of living, so that those around us can see the beauty and loveliness of God's purposes and the tawdriness of the devil's alternative. Satan blinds eyes and enslaves minds; he delights in injustice and oppression; all his works are destructive. If we pray for deliverance from the evil one, then we must be committed to destroying his works wherever we find them.

d. A commitment to replacing the kingdom of Satan with the kingdom of God

There is a real sense in which we do not ultimately have to worry about destroying the devil's work. If we switch on the light in a dark

---

[9] Acts 8:4.
[10] Matt. 28:19.
[11] Col. 1:13–14.
[12] Matt. 9:37.
[13] 1 John 3:8.
[14] John 8:44.

room we do not additionally have to chase away the darkness; the light does that for us. Our responsibility is to be the means through which the kingdom of God comes; that is the key to the destruction of all the works of darkness.

e. A recognition that 'this kind can come out only by prayer'

The disciples knew all about exorcism; they had watched Jesus do it, and they had driven out many demons themselves.[15] But, confronted by a spirit-possessed boy, they were powerless. Not so Jesus, whose command set the boy free. 'Why couldn't we drive it out?' they asked. Jesus replied, 'This kind can come out only by prayer.'[16] France wisely observes that Jesus is not suggesting that the specific category of demon encountered on this occasion required prayer before exorcism could be successful, with the implication that other categories did not require prayer. Rather, 'this kind' 'denotes demons in general as a *genos* which can never be tackled in merely human strength'.[17] What is true of 'demons in general' is true of all the works of the devil. Jesus commanded us to pray for deliverance from the evil one, not just when practising exorcism, but when confronted with any of his works. Too often the people of God appear to tackle the evils of the world in ways that are indistinguishable from those of godless philanthropists and pressure groups. Not only does this neglect our greatest asset; it disobeys the explicit command of our God.

2. Testing (6:13)

'*Lead us not into temptation.*' However familiar this phrase, it poses a problem in that it seems to present an image of a God who is going to take us deliberately into situations where we shall be tempted to do evil, and the only way we can prevent this is to ask him not to do it. This hardly fits the picture of God we have from the rest of the New Testament; James specifically states that God 'cannot be tempted by evil, nor does he tempt anyone'.[18] So, before we apply this phrase to the issue of evil and suffering, we need to clarify the meaning of *temptation* in this phrase. The word used is *peirasmos*. It speaks of testing, rather than seeking to lead astray, and corresponds to *nāsâ* in the Old Testament. Significantly, where the AV translated *nāsâ* as 'tempt', the NIV always uses

---

[15] Mark 6:12.
[16] Mark 9:14–29.
[17] R. T. France, *The Gospel of Mark* (Eerdmans, 2002), p. 370.
[18] Jas 1:13.

'test'.[19] It is, perhaps, unfortunate that it does not follow this practice in the New Testament when translating *peirasmos*. For the nature of testing or 'temptation' throughout the Bible depends on who is doing the testing. Where it is Satan, it is with evil intent; but where it is God, the intent is good. So the NEB's translation, 'Do not put us to the test', is a more satisfactory one for Matthew 6:13.[20]

But if God's intention in putting us to the test is a good one, why does he teach us to pray that he will not do it? And how do we square this prayer with the teaching of the New Testament that God is using the suffering and evils we face to bring about good, or with passages like James 1:2–4, 'Consider it pure joy, my brothers, whenever you face trials (*peirasmois*) of many kinds, because you know that the testing of your faith develops perseverance ... so that you may be mature and complete'?

It is helpful to distinguish between two types of prayer: prayers where we can be sure the answer is 'Yes', and prayers where we add, 'Yet not my will but yours be done.'[21] In the Lord's Prayer, the prayer for forgiveness falls into the first category, while the prayer for daily bread is in the second. That is, God has committed himself to forgiving us if we sincerely ask him for forgiveness, so he will always give it. But he has not committed himself to provide food each day for all who ask, so some go hungry; those who pray this prayer have to say, 'Lord, I would love a good meal today, but if that's not in your purposes I'm willing to go hungry.' 'Lead us not into temptation' also falls into the second category; each time we pray it we are saying, 'Lord, spare me suffering, but if you have good reasons for putting me through it then I'm willing to trust you.'

This fits well with what we have already seen. Paul rightly prayed earnestly for the thorn in his flesh to be removed, that God would spare him that particular suffering. But he prayed knowing that God had the right to answer 'No'. And when he did, Paul was able to accept that he had good reason for doing so, and so he could even 'delight' in the suffering.[22] Jesus prayed in Gethsemane that he would be spared the agony of the cross, but he accepted his Father's 'No'. Paul's friends prayed that he would be kept from persecution and allowed freedom to preach the gospel, but when God had said

---

[19] For example, Gen. 22:1. At the time of the writing of the AV, 'tempt' meant simply 'test' and had no connotation of seeking to lead astray.

[20] Tasker suggests 'Give us the necessary strength so that life's trials do not become for us occasions of temptation'; R. V. G. Tasker, *The Gospel according to St Matthew* (Tyndale Press, 1961), p. 74.

[21] Luke 22:42.

[22] 2 Cor. 12:7–19.

'No' to their requests Paul was able to write from prison that the suffering and setbacks had 'served to advance the gospel'.[23]

In the upper room Jesus warned Peter that Satan 'has asked to sift you as wheat'. We might have expected Jesus to continue, 'But I told him to leave you alone.' Instead he made it clear that he was doing nothing to stop him. It was not his purpose to spare Peter the disaster and pain of denial, though it was his purpose to bring him through and use the experience for his glory.[24]

It was absolutely right that Paul prayed for the thorn to be removed, that Jesus prayed as he did in Gethsemane, and that Paul's friends prayed for a trouble-free ministry, even though all of them received the answer 'No'. In the same way it is absolutely right for us to pray to be spared times of testing, provided we acknowledge God's right to refuse our request and use the suffering for his glory.

Focusing on instances like Peter's denial and Paul's thorn, not to mention the story of Job, may give us the impression that God prefers to choose the hard road for us rather than the trouble-free one. If it does, this phrase in the Lord's Prayer is a useful corrective. It is he who tells us to pray it, and therefore he must delight to answer 'Yes'. When we get to glory we will be amazed to discover how many times he has in fact intervened to save us from disaster, to spare us suffering, and to rescue us from the assaults of the evil one.

This phrase also cautions us that we should not seek suffering. Perhaps it is unlikely that any of us would ever be inclined to do so, but there have been times in church history when people have been so taken with the promises of blessing for those who suffer for Christ that they have deliberately sought suffering and even martyrdom. This seems both unnecessary and unwise; we can safely take it that if God wants us to go through suffering for his glory or for our blessing, then he will bring it about without our having to manipulate it. Paul was able to delight in his sufferings because he knew that they were God's gracious gift, not something he had engineered.

3. Forgiveness (6:12)

a. 'As we also have forgiven our debtors'

The Aramaic word *hoba* meant both 'debt' and 'sin'; the Jews of Jesus' day looked on sin as a debt; when we sin we put ourselves

---

[23] Phil. 1:12.
[24] Luke 22:31–32.

under an obligation to make a payment in order to remove the sin. The use of debt as a picture of sin is seen in Jesus' parable of the unmerciful servant.[25] *'Forgive us our debts, as we also have forgiven our debtors'*, is referring not to finance but to sin and those who sin against us; Jesus makes this clear in his comments following the giving of the prayer: 'For if you forgive men when they sin against you, your heavenly Father will also forgive you. But if you do not forgive men their sins, your Father will not forgive your sins.'[26]

These were – and are – radical words, stressing the significance the second half of the petition. The Jews of Jesus' day emphasized the importance of seeking the forgiveness of those we have wronged before we ask God to forgive us. But Jesus goes far beyond that. He requires that we, the innocent party, should forgive those who wrong us, before we ask for God's forgiveness. We have done no wrong; we are under no obligation; we owe nothing; all the debt is on the other side. By rights, the other person should make the first step, should apologize, should ask our forgiveness. But instead, we take the initiative and write off the debt; whatever they have done, we forgive – everybody for everything. Only then can we turn to God and ask for his forgiveness.

Here is a profound insight into how God expects us to live in an evil world. Our lives must be characterized by forgiveness. When we are victimized, we forgive. When we are cheated or robbed or mocked or cold shouldered, we forgive. When we are persecuted and tortured and nailed on to a cross, we forgive. Resentment and anger and getting our own back are not in our vocabulary. We do not want justice;[27] we choose mercy. Instead of turning inward and giving way to indignation and self-pity, we reach out in grace and love to those who have wronged us.

We can broaden the application. Back in Genesis 9:13, God, who had responded with righteous anger to the evils of the world and sent the flood, took his bow from his shoulder and put it on the shelf, or, rather, in the sky, where we can all see it and know that while the earth remains he will show mercy instead of exacting justice. He is the God who is wronged by the rebellion and sin of the human race. He is the one who suffers at our hands. Yet in grace he takes the initiative, he makes the first move. He does not wait for

[25] Matt. 18:23–35.

[26] Matt. 6:14–15.

[27] We can draw a distinction between a vengeful desire for justice ('I won't rest until he suffers like he's made me suffer') and a spirit of forgiveness which nevertheless accepts that the law of the land should take its course. The Christian family of the murdered teenager Anthony Walker (see p. 102) expressed their forgiveness of the murderers, but rightly accepted that they should be imprisoned for their crime.

us to come to him with an apology; he loves, he reaches out, he sends a Saviour. To an evil world he shows amazing grace.

That is the pattern for us. Too many in the world around us see Christians as judgmental, condemning and rejecting. While it is undoubtedly right that we should take a firm stand for justice, honesty, chastity and the like, it is essential that we do it in such a way that we do not obscure the central truth that God's people are people who forgive, who show amazing grace. Nor must our grace and forgiveness be conditional. Jesus did not wait until those who nailed him to the cross had repented before he cried, 'Father, forgive.' The early Christians did not wait for an apology from their persecutors before they forgave them. We do not wait to offer grace and love and a forgiving spirit until the person who offends us by his sexual behaviour has turned from the error of his ways, or our colleague at work has apologized for spreading malicious gossip about us. Just as we are to love our enemies even when they continue to persecute us,[28] so we forgive even when our forgiveness is neither wanted nor accepted. If we fear that showing grace to sinners could be taken as condoning their sin, we need to draw closer to our Master and learn from him how to be a 'friend of sinners'[29] and at the same time live a life that is so transparently holy that there can be no doubt about what we think of sin.

b. 'Forgive us our debts'

Again, wonderful though these words are when we use them personally to seek God's mercy and pardon for our individual sins, they also speak of a much broader desire in the heart of God, that men and women everywhere should seek him and come to him for grace and forgiveness, that a world in rebellion against its Creator should turn from its sin and evil, should come back from the distant country to the Father's house, and find welcome and healing and cleansing and restoration. Here is the missionary vision at the heart of the Lord's Prayer. It is the missionary vision of the risen Lord Jesus; on that first Easter Sunday evening, when he spoke the words of commission, 'As the Father has sent me, I am sending you',[30] he also summarized the purpose of God: 'This is what is written: The Christ will suffer and rise from the dead on the third day, and repentance and forgiveness of sins will be preached in his name to all nations, beginning at Jerusalem. You are witnesses of these things.'[31]

[28] Matt. 5:44–45.
[29] Matt. 11:19.
[30] John 20:21.
[31] Luke 24:46–48.

The debt of sin has been paid on the cross of Calvary.[32] The foundational response of God's people to a world in rebellion against God is the offer of grace and forgiveness to all who will receive them.

4. Food for the hungry (6:11)

Every day we said the Lord's Prayer at school. If there was one phrase that seemed irrelevant to me it was the request *'Give us today our daily bread'* (11). I knew that my lunchtime sandwiches were already secure at the back of my desk; I knew that the cupboard at home, or the shop on the corner, was well stocked for our evening meal. God had already provided my daily bread; why bother to ask for it? Doubtless I needed daily protection from temptation and evil; doubtless I also needed daily forgiveness. But why trouble the Almighty over my daily bread?

Scholars debate the precise meaning of 'daily',[33] but that seems hardly important compared with the implications of this verse in a world where 60,000 die of hunger every day and 1.3 billion (getting on for a quarter of the total population) live in 'extreme poverty' on less than 60p a day. Perhaps, since the prayer for daily bread seemed so irrelevant for me, I should have revised it and prayed, 'Give my starving brother his daily bread.'

Why did Jesus put this phrase into his model prayer? To tell us that God is concerned with our everyday lives and needs, say some. To remind us that we depend daily on him for our food and so for our lives, say others.[34] To point out that Christianity is the most materialistic of religions, say others. Or to remind us of manna in the wilderness. Or to teach us that God wants us to be neither poor nor rich.[35] Doubtless true, all of them, but still its primary message to us in a world of such appalling unfairness is that our God cares for the hungry and he expects us to care for them too.

Martin suggests that 'we may legitimately take "bread" here to stand as a symbol for all bodily needs, food, clothing, shelter, employment, and the like. The body should be an effective instrument

---

[32] Col. 2:13–14.

[33] The word used, *epiousion*, is virtually unique, and several ways of interpreting it have been proposed, none which affects the overall impact of the verse.

[34] When Jesus spoke these words his hearers would have been only too aware of the ever-present threat of crop failure and famine, and so of their dependence on God for their daily bread.

[35] The phrase could be a quotation from Proverbs 30:8–9: 'Give me neither poverty nor riches, but give me only my daily bread. Otherwise I may have too much and disown you and say, "Who is the LORD?" Or I may become poor and steal, and so dishonour the name of my God.'

and "bread" is whatever is needed to make it that.'[36] If that is so, then this phrase is a call to be concerned about disease, Aids, illiteracy, the unavailability of education or of adequate medical care, homelessness, unemployment, and all the scourges from which so many throughout the world suffer. Those of us who are the salt and light of this world have no option but to express the compassion and love of our God towards all whose lives lack daily necessities.

5. Heaven on earth (6:10)

The phrase *on earth as it is in heaven* is almost certainly to be taken with all three preceding phrases;[37] in Greek the three are exactly balanced in construction, each ending with an emphatic 'of you' (*sou*):

> *Your* name be hallowed,
> *your* kingdom come,
> *your* will be done,
>   as in heaven also on earth.

'On earth as it is in heaven' can therefore serve us, as we work backwards through the prayer, as an introduction to those three great phrases.

a. God's purpose for earth is heaven

At present, for all its beauty and glory, planet Earth is not heaven. It is not the unshadowed presence of God. It is not holiness and pure joy and unspoilt beauty. But that is what God intends it to be. When Jesus uttered the Beatitudes, he said of the 'poor in spirit' that 'theirs in the kingdom of heaven', and then went on to promise that 'the meek ... will inherit the earth'.[38] These were no two contrasting ideas; they were different ways of expressing the same thing. When all things are united under the headship of Christ, then earth will be heaven. When the new heaven and the new earth are revealed, the two will be seen as one; the dwelling of God will be with men; the Holy City will be on earth; the 'throne of God and of the Lamb will be in the city'.[39]

---

[36] H. Martin, *The Lord's Prayer* (SCM, 1951), p. 80.
[37] Gundry, however, rejects this on the grounds that 'the kingdom does not "come" in heaven'; R. H. Gundry, *Matthew* (Eerdmans, 1982), p. 107.
[38] Matt. 5:3, 5.
[39] Rev. 21:1–3; 22:3.

b. The pattern for earth is heaven

The purpose of God is heaven on earth. Though this will not be fulfilled until Christ returns, our task, as we pray, is to do whatever we can to make our bit of earth as much like heaven as possible. We already have our citizenship in heaven,[40] we know its truths and values, and through the Holy Spirit we have its empowering that enables us to express its reality and nature in the way we live and by the way the Lord lives in us. In a sense we are the representatives or ambassadors of heaven here on earth. So the words 'as in heaven, so on earth', call us to pattern our living on earth on life in heaven, to seek to make life here a foretaste of heaven, to express the love and joy and truth and beauty and goodness of heaven in as many ways as possible, and so to give those around us a vision and awareness of the real thing.

c. From heaven to earth

God walked in the garden in the cool of the day;[41] but for most of the story of human life on planet Earth God has seemed absent. But in Christ he has come: the King of heaven has come to earth. And as the King comes the kingdom comes: the kingdom of heaven comes on earth. This phrase in the Lord's Prayer is part of what Beasley-Murray calls a 'movement':

> The basic notion of the sovereignty of God is a movement from heaven to earth, from God to man. In the context of this prayer, Jesus is seeking an act of God to produce a 'movement' that will be a part of the greater 'movement' God has already initiated in Jesus. Heaven has already invaded the earth in the mission of Jesus; here he is praying for a completion of what God has begun in him, for a securing of his purpose to unite heaven and earth.[42]

Heaven has already invaded the earth; we, then, as the people of the King, are the troops of the occupying power, the bridgehead through which the movement from heaven to earth continues and spreads.

---

[40] Phil. 3:20.
[41] Gen. 3:8.
[42] G. R. Beasley-Murray, *Jesus and the Kingdom of God* (Eerdmans, 1986), p. 152.

6. The will of God (6:10)

a. 'Your will be done': two problems

Both the Bible and Enlightenment rationalism have problems with the will of God. But they are not the same problem. The Bible's problem is practical: we do not yet see the will of God being worked out here on earth. Evil is still rampant; the wicked still prosper; his kingdom is slow in coming. The outcome of the Bible's problem is a heartfelt cry to God to come and reign on planet Earth, and a renewed commitment on the part of the people of God to put his will into operation through our lives.

The Enlightenment's problem is logical. It runs something like this:

> Either God's will is being done on earth or it is not being done on earth.
> Evil things happen on earth.
> If God's will is being done on earth and evil things happen, God must will evil things.
> This means that God is not good.
> But we know that God is good.
> Therefore he cannot will evil things.
> Therefore God's will is not being done on earth.

The outcome of the Enlightenment's problem is bewilderment and a sneaking suspicion that God is not in control of the world after all; he is standing helplessly by, unable to fulfil his purposes. As a result we, too, as the people of God, feel we are standing helplessly by, unable to do anything to overcome the powers of evil.

The answer to the Enlightenment's problem is Revelation 5:5. A contemporary elder might say to us, 'Don't be bewildered. See, the Wisdom of God,[43] the one "in whom are hidden all the treasures of wisdom and knowledge",[44] has triumphed. He is able to put into practice the will of God on the earth.' Yes, superficially, the will of God is not being done, since evil is rampant on the earth. But, because of what God in his glorious wisdom has done on the cross, we can in fact be confident that he is in control. He is taking the evil in the world, summed up in the nailing of Christ to the cross, and is working his will through it, breaking its power and using it for his purposes. He can do this because the victory of the cross is total;

---

[43] 1 Cor. 1:24, 28.
[44] Col. 2:3.

the price that was paid there by God himself was complete; there is no evil that he has not borne and cannot transform; there is nothing that in his wisdom he cannot turn to good.

b. Doing, not understanding

However confident we may be that God in his wisdom knows how he is working all things together for good, we have to rest content with much more limited knowledge. The prayer is 'Your will be done', not 'Your will be understood.' Our response to the will of God is to do it, even when we do not understand it. It is not the one who understands who 'will enter the kingdom of heaven, but only he who does the will of my Father who is in heaven'.[45] But to admit that we do not understand the ways of God is not, as some seem to conclude, to say that God's ways are in themselves illogical, or paradoxical, or 'in tension'. Just as the message of the cross itself is 'foolishness' to the 'scholar' and 'philosopher of this age' and yet is the most outstanding expression of the wisdom of God,[46] so to our earthbound minds the ways of God that are beyond our understanding will one day be seen as the most brilliant expressions of his wisdom and power.

c. Resignation or adventure

'Inshallah', says the Muslim, and often the feeling is one of help-lessness before the inexorable will of God. 'If God has his will,' says the philosopher, 'then there is no room for our free will; everything we do must be predetermined.' But our God is bigger than that. In his wisdom and grace his will is big enough to embrace whatever we do with our freedom; if we use it for good, then he uses that good to fulfil his purposes. If we use it for evil, then through the cross he triumphs over that evil and uses it for good. No wonder Paul exclaimed:

> Oh, the depth of the riches of the wisdom
>   and knowledge of God!
> How unsearchable his judgments,
>   and his paths beyond tracing out!
> 'Who has known the mind of the Lord?
>   Or who has been his counsellor?'
> 'Who has ever given to God,
>   that God should repay him?'

[45] Matt. 7:21.
[46] 1 Cor. 1:18–25.

> For from him and through him and
> to him are all things.
> To him be the glory for ever! Amen.[47]

One thing Paul would never have accepted was that praying for the will of God to be done on earth meant primarily patient submission to the evils and suffering God had decided he should go through. 'To say that God's will is that I should suffer', he would say, 'is to get things the wrong way round. God's will is that I should preach the gospel, that I should spend my life serving Jesus, that I should be at the forefront of the assault on the kingdom of darkness. That's his will, and that's what I'm doing. True, doing that inevitably means I'll suffer; if I preach the gospel I'll get stoned and flogged; if I travel I'll get robbed by bandits and shipwrecked; if I walk the way that Jesus walked I will suffer. But that's the spin-off; that's only secondary to the real thing, which is God's call to me to serve and follow my Master.'

So the will of God is not something we endure; it is something we gladly choose to do. Spurgeon commented. 'We desire for the supreme will *to be done in earth*, with a cheerful, constant, universal obedience like that of "heaven".'[48] Ours is the privilege of spending our lives in the adventure of furthering God's will with cheerful obedience.

7. The kingdom of God (6:10)

We are near the end of our study; it is hard to think of a better way of drawing together our thoughts on God and the evil and suffering we face in this world than by looking at the three phrases that are left to us in the Lord's Prayer: *your kingdom come*; *hallowed be your name*; and *Our Father in heaven*.

'Your kingdom come.' The theme of the kingdom of God has recurred again and again as we have worked through the Bible teaching. It is the vision and cry of the Old Testament. Its coming was the message of Jesus.[49] Its proclamation was the mission of the

---

[47] Rom. 11:33–36.

[48] C. H. Spurgeon, *The Gospel of the Kingdom* (Passmore and Alabaster, 1893), p. 34.

[49] T. W. Manson concluded his magisterial study of the teaching of Jesus, *The Sayings of Jesus* (SCM, 1949), by saying: 'It is probable that the key to the teaching and ministry of Jesus, and indeed to the whole New Testament, lies in a single phrase, which expresses, as perfectly as words can, the supreme interest of our Lord, that for which he lived and died, for which he endured hardship, loneliness, and obloquy, that to which he gave his whole undivided devotion – not "the Law and the Prophets," not "the Kingdom of our father David," but "the Kingdom of my Father"' (p. 345).

New Testament church. Its consummation is the goal of God's purposes. When we pray for it we are crying out to God for an end to all rebellion against him, the end of the refusal to let God be God, the destruction of evil, the springing up of righteousness, the healing of all hurts, the coming of the King. Then every knee shall bow, and every tongue confess that Jesus Christ is Lord, to the glory of God the Father.

a. The kingdom and evil

'Seek first', said Jesus, God's 'kingdom and his righteousness.' If we get that in its right place, then everything else will fit around it,[50] not least the issue of evil. For evil begins with the rejection of the reign of God, and it will not be removed until that reign is universally restored. But the King has never abdicated, and even in the Old Testament he still reigned supreme over the raging of the nations and the plotting of the evil powers. And the coming of the King in the Lord Jesus Christ has meant the establishing of the kingdom here on the earth, a kingdom which, like yeast, is working its way through the doughy mass of life in our world.[51]

b. The kingdom and righteousness

Seek the kingdom; for in the coming of the kingdom will come God's righteousness. Every attempt to bring justice and righteousness on the earth is to be applauded, but Christians know that merely treating the symptoms will be far less effective than dealing with the root cause. Only the coming of the kingdom can break the power of evil; only the King can forgive sin and change the human heart; only the atoning death of Christ can redeem and transform the brokenness and hurt that evil and sin leave in their wake. To Christians who were getting bogged down in matters of secondary importance, Paul incisively wrote, 'The kingdom of God is not a matter of eating and drinking, but of righteousness, peace and joy in the Holy Spirit.'[52] That was his experience, both on a personal level and as the kingdom spread through one community after another. When the kingdom comes, it brings with it the healing of relationships and the righting of

---

[50] Matt. 6:33.
[51] Matt. 13:33.
[52] Rom. 14:17.

wrongs; almost all times of revival have had profound social impact.[53]

c. The kingdom and power

Seek the kingdom, for in the kingdom is power. The doxology links the kingdom and the power; both are God's, and they go together. True, often the kingdom comes virtually unnoticed, hidden like a seed; but in the seed is the power of life, a power independent of the sower. 'Night and day, whether he sleeps or gets up, the seed sprouts and grows, though he does not know how'; even the smallest of seeds will grow into 'the largest of all garden plants',[54] for in the seed is the power of life. So in the kingdom is the power of the life of God. In each child of the kingdom is the power of the Spirit of God, the presence of the King, power to resist temptation, to thwart the purposes of the powers of evil, to turn evil to good, to proclaim kingdom truth and live kingdom values.

d. The kingdom and suffering

Seek the kingdom, for in the kingdom lies God's answer to suffering. Other philosophies and religions have offered their answers, denying the reality of suffering, or training us in endurance, or offering us compensation. But none of them has a God who has come down and taken suffering upon himself, and borne its agony, and broken its power to destroy, and lifted it up and transformed it and crowned it with glory. In the kingdom of this God, suffering is a gracious gift which draws us nearer to him, which he uses for good in the working out of his purposes for us as individuals and for the world at large. In the kingdom, since the King reigns, suffering ceases to be random and meaningless; it ceases even to be unwelcome and resented. For it comes from the nail-pierced hand of the King himself. Amazingly, even though most of us rarely manage it, those who belong to the kingdom can rejoice in suffering, allowing the awareness that God's hand is upon us and his good purposes are being fulfilled through the suffering to outweigh

---

[53] Of the 1904 revival in Wales, Eifion Evans writes: 'The social impact of the revival became proverbial. The pit-ponies could no longer understand the miners' instructions because of the absence of oaths and curses. The most notable effect of the revival was the precipitous decline in drunkenness.' He quotes a contemporary account: 'Old debts are paid; jealousy vanishes; church and family feuds are healed; great drunkards, prize-fighters, and gamblers pray in the services'; E. Evans, *The Welsh Revival of 1904* (Evangelical Press, 1969), pp. 161–162.

[54] Mark 4:26–32.

the pain and hurt. So the prayer for the coming of the kingdom, though it ultimately looks forward to the time when all suffering shall cease and every tear be wiped away, is not a prayer for an end to suffering for the people of God here and now. It is a prayer that the King will reign, using us in any way he may choose to extend his kingdom, ruling over our lives and the situations that we face and the experiences we go through, guaranteeing that nothing, not 'trouble or hardship or persecution or famine or nakedness or danger or sword ... nor anything else in all creation, will be able to separate us from the love of God that is in Christ Jesus our Lord.' Since that is so, by his strength we can face anything, all the suffering that comes to those who follow in the footsteps of Christ, and know what it is to be 'more than conquerors through him who loved us'.[55]

8. Let God be God (6:9)

'*Hallowed be your name.*' As with most of the phrases in the Lord's Prayer, scholars debate whether this request refers to life here and now on planet Earth, or to the final coming of the kingdom at the end of the age.[56] But, as we have seen again and again, the two cannot be separated; it would be folly to pray for the hallowing of God's name at the end of the age and care nothing about hallowing it in the meantime.[57]

'*Hallowed*' (*hagiasthētō*) can mean 'make holy' or 'treat as holy'; here it clearly means the second. In Jewish thought, to refer to the name of God was often to refer to God himself, especially in the context of what he has revealed of himself to the human race.[58] So, though this prayer doubtless includes a request that the name of God should be used reverently, its scope is far wider. It is nothing less than a cry that God should be treated as the holy and glorious being that he has shown himself to be, that he should be recognized and acknowledged truly as God.

---

[55] Rom. 8:35–39.

[56] Beare states that the first three petitions are concerned only with the future consummation; F. W. Beare, *The Gospel according to Matthew* (Blackwell, 1981), pp. 172–175.

[57] 'This clause may ... express both a desire to see God truly honoured as God in the world today, and an eschatological longing for the day when all men acknowledge God as the Lord'; R. T. France, *The Gospel according to Matthew* (IVP, 1985), p. 134.

[58] 'The "name" ... means all that is true of God, and all that has been revealed concerning God. It means God in all His attributes, God in all that He is in and of Himself, and God in all that He has done and all that He is doing'; D. M. Lloyd-Jones, *Studies in the Sermon on the Mount*, 2 (IVP, 1960), p. 59.

Here, again, Jesus points us to the key issue which underlies all the Bible's teaching on evil and suffering. Evil exists because the name of God is not hallowed; the world is polluted with sin and pain and meaningless suffering because God is not accepted and worshipped and obeyed as the holy and wise and glorious Creator and Lord over everything. Evil will cease to exist only when all rebellion is ended, when every tongue confesses the lordship of Christ, and every knee bows in submission to God.

As we have seen in all the phrases of the Lord's Prayer, the request here is primarily that God will act to bring about what we are asking for, with the added implication that he will empower us to work together with him to fulfil his purposes. So when we pray '*Hallowed be your name*', we are saying to God, 'Lord, show yourself to a broken and evil world, so that people will see your power and glory and goodness and love and truth, and will turn from evil and acknowledge you as God.' Beasley-Murray writes:

> The prayer for the sanctification of the divine name denotes a plea for God to act in such a manner that his name be acknowledged in all the world as 'holy and terrible' (Ps. 111:9 RSV). It is more than a prayer for mankind to confess that truth of God; it implies a desire for the sovereign God to unveil his glory in the judgment and salvation that initiate his kingdom in order that men may see who he is and give him the glory due to his name.[59]

It is worth noting how God-centred this petition is. It is possible that we could look on the phrases 'your kingdom come' and 'your will be done' as largely asking for things which will be for our benefit: 'Lord, bring in your kingdom to get rid of evil and suffering from our world'; 'May your will be done rather than the devil's will that brings us so much pain and hurt.' But, though the coming of the kingdom and the doing of God's will undoubtedly bring great benefit to humanity, we are not the centre of the universe; God is, and this request for the hallowing of his name reminds us of that. First and foremost, more essential than the need for evil and suffering to be removed from planet Earth, is the requirement that God be acknowledged as God, that he should be allowed his rightful place by all his creatures.

So the request '*Hallowed be your name*' is the most foundational prayer of all, that God should be the centre, the Lord, the Beginning and the End, Sovereign, All in all. Like the psalmists and the

---

[59] Beasley-Murray, *Jesus and the Kingdom of God*, p. 150.

prophets, we cry to God to show his power and his glory.[60] Since God's clearest revelation of himself is in Christ, it is also a prayer that God, through the Holy Spirit, would show the world Jesus. When he was facing the cross Jesus prayed, 'Father, glorify your name!' From heaven came a voice, 'I have glorified it, and will glorify it again.'[61] A little later, as he prayed his great prayer before Gethsemane, he said, 'Father, the time has come. Glorify your Son, that your Son may glorify you.'[62] When we cry to God to show the world his glory, the greatest revelation he can give is that of the cross. It was in the context of his prayer 'Father, glorify your name' that Jesus stated, 'I, when I am lifted up from the earth, will draw all men to myself.'[63]

So it is that by the preaching and the living of the cross we have our greatest opportunity to bring those around us to the point of hallowing the name of our God. We proclaim the cross as God's response to evil; we point to the Christ on the cross as the one hope of a broken world; we live the cross as the suffering people of a suffering God so that through suffering will come glory, not just for us, but for all the world, and, supremely, for God himself.

9. 'Our Father in heaven' (6:9)

a. The end of the rebellion

To say 'Our Father in heaven' is to acknowledge God as God. It is to turn from rebellion and the insistence that we have the right to be god in our own lives or in our own world, and to recognize that he alone is God. In the early church only Christians were permitted to speak the Lord's Prayer. Only God's people can declare God is their Father. Indeed, to say these words and mean them is to make a profession of faith; they are an acceptance that we come from him, that we depend on him, and that we acknowledge his lordship over our lives.

b. Paradise regained

The essence of evil is the refusal to let God be God, and the paradigm evil is the breaking of the relationship between us and God. To call God 'Our Father' not only acknowledges him as God, it expresses the glorious miracle of that broken relationship

---

[60] For example, Ps. 99:1–3; Isa. 64:1–3.
[61] John 12:28.
[62] John 17:1.
[63] John 12:32.

restored. Only Jesus could pray 'Abba',[64] and that was because there was perfect oneness between him and the Father. Yet here he teaches his disciples to pray it too. This is nothing other than Paradise Regained, the broken relationship gloriously restored.

c. The King on the throne

This Father is 'in heaven'. This is the God who is on the throne of the universe. This is the sovereign Lord, who is working out his purposes of grace and goodness according to his infinite wisdom and power. No weak Father this, no less-than-omnipotent God struggling with the problems and pains of the world. This God is big. Here is someone we can trust totally. Even though we do not understand all his ways, we can have full confidence in his love and wisdom and goodness. If he is both our Father and the Lord of the universe, what have we to fear? If this God is for us, who can be against us?

d. Children of God

If he is 'Our Father', then we are his children. At work in our lives is 'the Spirit of sonship' by whom we cry, '*Abba*, Father.' If we are children, then we are heirs, heirs of the kingdom and co-heirs with Christ, in whose sufferings we are graciously privileged to share so that one day we may share in his glory.[65] To be a child of this God is to be loved, to be treasured, to be kept through all the experiences that life can throw at us. It is to have all the resources of heaven available to enable us to live as his children before a watching world: to love with his love, to express his holiness, to live his truth. It is to be sent into a world of evil and suffering, as our Father sent Jesus, to proclaim good news that God has come in grace to redeem and transform. It is to be empowered, by the anointing of the Holy Spirit, to set free captives, to heal the broken and hurting, to deliver from evil, and to destroy the works of the devil, so that God is acknowledged as God, his kingdom comes, and his will is done, on earth as it is in heaven.

---

[64] Scholars debate the extent to which Jews of the first century referred to God as 'Father'. It is generally agreed that, though they spoke of him at times as 'Father of Israel', they would never use the personal form *abba*, 'my dad', which, all agree, was the word Jesus always used and the word that lies behind 'Our Father' in the Lord's Prayer.

[65] Rom. 8:15–17.

Study guide

The aim of this study guide is to help you get to the heart of what I have written and challenge you to apply what you learn to your own life. The questions have been designed for use by individuals or by small groups of Christians meeting, perhaps for an hour or two each week, to study, discuss and pray together.

The guide provides material for each of the sections of the book. When used by a group with limited time, the leader should decide beforehand which questions are most appropriate for the group to discuss during the meeting and which should perhaps be left for group members to work through by themselves or in smaller groups during the week.

In order to be able to contribute fully and learn from the group meetings, each member of the group needs to read through the section or sections under discussion, together with the Bible passages to which they refer.

It's important not to let these studies become merely academic exercises. Guard against this by making time to think through and discuss how what you discover *works out in practice for you*. Make sure you begin and end each study by focusing on God in praise and prayer. Ask the Holy Spirit to speak to you through your discussion together.

PART 1. EVIL AND SUFFERING – AND GOD

Revelation 15:3–4
1. The end of the story (pp. 15–24)

1 'Both the Old Testament and the New Testament, in essence, look forward' (p. 15). Can you think of other illustrations of this truth? To what extent have we Christians lost this forward-looking emphasis today? How might we regain it?

2 Do you agree that the 'four foundational facts' on pages 16–17 are a fair summary of the Bible's teaching? What would you say to someone who seems to believe that we have a right to expect that life will be free of evil and suffering or that the world is able gradually to get rid of all evil and suffering?

3 Work through the 'six sure statements' (pp. 19–23), applying them, where appropriate, to your personal circumstances and to the situations in the world around you.

Genesis 6:5–8
2. The beginning of the story (pp. 25–30)

1 Think through the implications of the statement on page 28: 'God's first reaction to the sin and evil of the world is pain. A broken world means a broken-hearted God.'
2 Previous generations have used the story of the Flood to urge non-Christians to flee from the righteous judgment of God. While there is still be a place for using the story in this way, can you pick out other elements of the story that can be helpfully used in our witness and evangelism today?

Exodus 34:5–7
3. The God of love and punishment (pp. 31–42)

1 What answer would you give to someone who raises the objection outlined on page 31?
2 Several theologians have written recently of 'tensions' or even 'contradictions' within God. If we are to accept that these are only apparent, and that the problem lies in our understanding and not in God himself, it is important that we find ways of developing our understanding to help resolve the tension. Try listing some of the 'tensions' we see in the life and character of Jesus and think of ways in which we can help people to understand that these are not in fact contradictory.

Psalm 2
4. Chaos and the King (pp. 43–50)

1 The final paragraph on page 44 suggests that the question 'Why?' does not necessarily have to be answered with a logical explanation; sometimes an answer that deals with the pain that gave rise to the question is much more appropriate. Do you agree? How might this insight affect the way we seek to present the gospel?

2 What rebellious powers do you see in the world today? How do Christians usually react to them? Can we learn something from this psalm on how we should react to them?

3 What does 'Jesus is Lord' mean?

PART 2. EVIL AND SUFFERING – AND JESUS

Luke 4:14–30
5. The coming of God (pp. 53–62)

1 Many people seem to believe that God is either helpless or useless in the face of evil. What would you say to them?

2 Who do you think are 'the poor', and how do we 'preach good news' to them?

3 Evil and suffering impact people's lives in many different ways; we could probably add dozens of categories to the five listed on pages 57–59. What categories would be included in a list that covers the people around you or those for whom you feel concern? How might 'the coming of God' make a real difference to them?

1 John 2:28 – 3:15
6. The incarnate God (pp. 63–72)

1 'We have to be ready to let our concepts of what is right and wrong, or good and evil, be shaped by what we read and what we see in Christ, rather than trying to reshape reality by imposing our preconceived ideas' (p. 65). Can you think of other examples where we or others need to apply this principle?

2 Many early Christians believed that since Christ deliberately chose the path of suffering, we who seek to follow him should consciously choose it too, and rejoice when evil and suffering come our way. What do you think about this?

3 Consider a range of definitions of evil, and try to formulate one that is both true to the Bible revelation and meaningful in our twenty-first-century culture.

Revelation 5:6
7. The scarred God (pp. 73–82)

1 The older theologians who held to a concept of a God who is immutable (unchanging) and impassible (unaffected by pain or feelings) may have been more influenced by Greek ideas than by the Bible, but they did have some valuable insights; perhaps we should not let the pendulum swing so far to the opposite extreme that we lose these. What elements of the immutability and impassibility of God do you think we ought to retain? How might we combine these with the concept of a suffering God?

2 How do you react to the statement: 'It seems inconceivable that the cross, the most significant event of all history, should involve just one of the three persons of the Godhead' (p. 79)? How do you think we should view the involvement of the Father, the Son and the Holy Spirit in what happened at Calvary?

Ephesians 1:9–10, 19–23
8. The conquering God (pp. 83–94)

1 Tragically, far too many Christians find the kinds of truth Paul is expressing in Ephesians 1 dull. Why do you think this is? How can we help them to get as excited about them as Paul was?

2 The paragraph on pages 88–89 illustrates how difficult it is to translate the glories of Paul's teaching into just a few words of English. Be generous and give yourself a few hundred words and use them to put the truths of Ephesians 1:9–10 and 19–23 into words that someone who has no knowledge of the Bible's message would be able to grasp.

Mark 1:14–15; Luke 6:20–36; Matthew 12:24–37
9. The teaching of Jesus on evil and suffering (pp. 95–105)

1 In what ways is it true in the world of today that the coming of the kingdom of God is the answer to evil and suffering?

2 In the light of Luke 6:20–36, do you think that the teaching on evil and suffering in the church in the West is sufficiently radical? Where – and why – have we watered down the teaching of Jesus? What might we do to get back to teaching as radical as his?

3 Do you agree with the interpretation of Matthew 12:29 given on page 105? If so, how are we to we 'go on the offensive against evil'?

PART 3. WHAT ON EARTH? THE NATURE OF EVIL AND SUFFERING

Genesis 3:1–24
10. The paradigm evil (pp. 109–117)

1 Recall some of those discussions you have had with non-Christians over issues of good and evil. Do the comments in the first section of this chapter help explain why this kind of discussion so often seems to get into difficulties? What key principles do we need to follow to avoid this?

2 Sadly, the teaching of the early chapters of Genesis has often been obscured by controversy and issues of interpretation. But though there may still be many unanswered questions, their insights are profound and hugely relevant to our understanding of evil and suffering today. Whatever your attitude to the details, pick out two or three of the underlying truths chapter 3 teaches and try to state them in ways that would be readily understandable to your non-Christian friends.

3 What do you feel is the correct interpretation of the term 'the tree of the knowledge of good and evil'? How does your understanding of it fit the twenty-first-century scene?

Revelation 12 – 14
11. The cosmic battle (pp. 118–126)

1 List some of the ways the cosmic battle outlined in Revelation 12 – 14 is being fought out in our world today. What elements can you identify that are encouraging? What specific strategies are the powers of evil using? How can we counter them more effectively?

2 Do you feel that 'holy people in a tough place' (p. 120) and 'agony and ecstasy' are appropriate phrases to describe the people of God today? Some would suggest that much of our weakness and lack of holiness arises from the fact that most of us have things far too easy, and that a good dose of persecution would do us a world of good. Do you agree? How could we encourage one another to be more holy and more effective in the cosmic conflict?

12. Suffering evil (pp. 127–140)

1 List the problems and setbacks Joseph faced; you may well find one (or more) that resonates with your own experience. Think through the differences between what we might call a 'natural' reaction to each of these, and the reaction of someone who, despite appearances, believes that God is with her or him.

2 Have a go at analyzing why the fearless prophet of Mount Carmel turned into the scared near-suicide of 1 Kings 19. Then trace the steps by which God renewed and restored him.

3 Why does God allow wars?

4 What do you think of the 'Comment' at the foot of page 133? Could God fulfil his purposes in the world without pain or cost? In the last analysis, would you want your service for him to be costless?

5 How can the sections on John the Baptist and on Paul help to enrich our understanding of prayer?

PART 4. WHY ON EARTH? REASONS FOR EVIL AND SUFFERING

Genesis 32:22–32
13. Wrestling with God (pp. 145–154)

1 What struggles have you gone through? Were they primarily intellectual or emotional, or what? How did you come through them? What did you learn from them? How did you grow through them?

2 Which of the theodicies outlined in section 3 do you feel would be most effective in our defence of the gospel before those who choose to argue on a philosophical level? Perhaps you may be able to use insights from more than one of the approaches to theodicy to build your own approach.

3 If it is right sometimes to struggle with the issues and sometimes to 'accept the mystery' (section 4), how do we decide which to do in any particular situation?

Romans 8:17–27
14. From suffering to glory (pp. 155–164)

1 'Glory can come only by way of suffering' (p. 156). Is this true? If it is true, how should it affect our attitude to suffering?

2 How would you answer someone who argues that since the created order is 'destined for destruction' (p. 158), we need not be concerned about ecological issues?

3 'Sorrowful, yet always rejoicing' (p. 159 n. 24). How can get we a right balance between 'groaning' and 'rejoicing'? Should 'groaning' always be kept 'inward' or is there a place for sharing pain and burdens, and, say, including sorrow and lament as well as celebration in our times of worship?

4 How could we seek to help Christians who feel that their present suffering is so great that nothing in the future could ever compensate for it?

Philippians 1:29–30
15. The gift of suffering (pp. 165–171)

1 'The gift of suffering is no unwelcome imposition; it is as much an expression of God's love and goodness as any other of his gifts of grace' (p. 166). How might you try to present this truth to a Christian who has been taught that it is God's purpose that the lives of Christians should be problem-free and pain-free?

2 What do you think about the debate between Fee and Moo and Silva over 'suffering in general' (pp. 169–170 n. 22)?

Romans 8:28
16. Good out of evil (pp. 172–185)

1 In the light of the discussion in section 2 (p. 174), what could we be saying about God and his ways to those who are not Christians and are going through a time of suffering?

2 Select two or three 'good things out of evil' from the list in section 3 (p. 180) that are paralleled in your own experience, and reflect again on the wisdom and power of our God.

3 Try adding to the list of 'good things out of evil' further examples from the Bible and from the experiences you or others have gone through.

1 Peter 3:15–16
17. Giving reasons (pp. 186–197)

1 Was the issue of evil and suffering a barrier to your becoming a Christian? Or has it seriously challenged your faith since you became a Christian? If so, how was the barrier removed or the challenge dealt with?

2 In these verses Peter gives two wise pieces of advice about how we should witness (p. 186). Try listing other considerations we should bear in mind when we are seeking to 'give reasons' to those who challenge us over the issue of evil and suffering.

3 What other issues, besides those dealt with in the dialogue, have people raised with you in the area of evil and suffering? How did you deal with them? What further answers might you give in similar situations in the future?

PART 5. HOW ON EARTH? LIVING WITH EVIL AND SUFFERING

Matthew 10:16–39
18. The suffering people of a suffering God (pp. 201–210)

1 What is your answer to the questions on page 202 about our 'relatively persecution-free lives': 'Is this because we have lost our distinctiveness and are no longer a threat to those who belong to the world around us? Or is it because, for us in our culture, opposition to the life and witness of the people of God that underlies open persecution takes other, often more subtle forms?'

2 How should we 'prepare people for suffering' (p. 203)?

3 Are there ways we can provide extra encouragement and support to those in our churches who face pressure or opposition from close family members who are not Christians?

Job; 2 Corinthians 4:7 – 5:10
19. Living with suffering (pp. 211–225)

1 Is it true that we have a 'debased' concept of faith today (p. 212)? Look again at the two sections on 'trust' (pp. 212–213 and 223–224) and try to formulate a biblical definition of faith.

2 Psychologists tell us that it is therapeutic and necessary to give vent to our feelings, whether in the dramatic way Job did or in the more controlled way Paul did (pp. 213–214, 218–219). How can we ensure that those going through difficult times have adequate opportunity to off-load their feelings in a way that will be positive and helpful?

3 In a similar vein, if suffering presents us with the choice to respond negatively or positively to what God is doing in our lives (pp. 217, 220–221, 224), how can we seek to help people to choose to respond positively?

Titus 2:11–14; Matthew 5:13–16; John 20:21–22
20. Living with evil (pp. 226–238)

1 Titus 2:11 gives us a foundational reason for hope in our dark world (p. 227). What other grounds for hope does the Bible offer us as we face the evils of our world?

2 Page 228 highlights 'one of the most powerful expressions of *asebeia* in our culture today'. Can you trace others? How should we be confronting them?

3 What should we be doing to enable the people of God to be a more effective counter-culture (pp. 229–230) and saltier salt (p. 234) in today's evil world?

4 How would you summarize the task that God is sending us to do in the world today? Where do you feel we are doing it most effectively? And where are we particularly weak? What should be our priorities?

5 'Ecclesiastical structures and influence in high places are not our God's primary answer to an evil world' (p. 231). 'Jesus did not set up leprosaria, but, confronted with a leper, he healed him' (p. 237). 'He who converts his neighbour has performed the most practical Christian-political act of all' (p. 238). What do you think should be the balance between confronting evil on the macro scale and on the micro scale?

PART 6. FROM THE EVIL ONE TO OUR FATHER

Matthew 6:9–13
21. The Lord's Prayer (pp. 243–262)

1 'The real disaster is not to suffer evil, but to be overwhelmed by the evil one' (p. 244). To what extent do you feel the traditional translation of the phrase in the Lord's Prayer, 'Deliver us from evil', has contributed to an unbiblical attitude to evil and suffering?

2 God has the right to say 'No' to our prayer, 'Do not put us to the test.' Can you think of instances in your life or in the lives of others where God did say 'No' to this prayer and did something beautiful as a result?

3 'Our lives must be characterized by forgiveness' (p. 249). Why do we find it hard to forgive? Why are we so often seen as 'condemning and rejecting' (p. 250)? What could we do to change this?

4 There are many ways of tackling world poverty and hunger, and God calls different people to use different approaches. What is the most effective way for you?

5 'Your will be done.' What problems have you encountered with the will of God? How have you coped with them?

6 How would you define the kingdom of God and what it means for it to 'come'?

7 'To say *Our Father in heaven*' is to acknowledge God as God' (p. 261). The foundational call that God should be accepted as God is a theme that has run right through this study. What do you believe are the key steps that need to be taken in response to this call?